HERNDON, Marcia. **Music as culture,** by Marcia Herndon and Norma McLeod. Norwood Editions, 1979. 196p index 79-19209. 15.00
This is a totally original book, treating the various philosophical concerns of ethnomusicology in an imaginative and thought-provoking way. It is written at the professional to advanced undergraduate level but is highly readable. It is designed as a textbook for a seminar in ethnomusicology with emphasis placed on the concerns of anthropology. There are sections on field methods, techniques, professional ethics, and the like; but the authors also deal in depth with such universal themes as the nature of music, the role of context in performance, the learning process, cognition and value judgments, and the relationship of music to social institutions, thus making much of the discussion interesting to the general reader as well. There are no illustrations or musical examples, but all points are well made with examples drawn from the author's own fieldwork experiences. Both authors are well qualified; McLeod was formerly editor of *Ethnomusicology* and Herndon was her graduate student. A glossary, index, and bibliography are included. Paper is heavy stock, buff in color, printed with unjustified right margin; good layout. Highly recommended.

MUSIC AS CULTURE

MARCIA HERNDON
University of California at Berkley
and
NORMA McLEOD
University of Ottawa

NORWOOD EDITIONS
1980

Manufactured in the United States of America

NORWOOD EDITIONS, 842 Main Street, Darby, Pa. 19023

Music As Culture

This book is the direct result of extensive discussions, telephone calls and correspondence with many colleagues. At the annual meeting of the Society for Ethnomusicology in 1971, a number of people came together in a casual discussion of the needs of ethnomusicology. A number of areas were identified at that time, with agreement that the immediate need was for a comprehensive textbook for introductory courses in ethnomusicology. Although it was recognized that several good books are available, no one book had, to that point of time, attempted a synthesis of both the cultural and musical aspects of ethnomusicology.

Accordingly, we, the authors, set out to identify the areas which everyone agreed upon as necessary in a comprehensive introductory text of ethnomusicology. Having circulated a questionnaire and elicited responses both formally and informally from a wide range of colleagues, we created an outline. Our main area of concern was with the range of implications music has, both as a product of human behavior and as an integral part of human interaction.

The first questions which arise in preparing an introduction to ethnomusicology are: what is music and, what is ethnomusicology? In answering the first question, although agreement is reached that music is humanly structured sound, its particular aspects vary from culture to culture. The second question is even more difficult to address than the first, since it is necessary to consider approaches to music from anthropology, musicology, folklore, linguistics and, more recently, from a combined perspective of all the preceding.

The key to ethnomusicological investigations is field work in living societies. Field work is not simply a matter of knowing and acquiring equipment, taking recordings and photographs, keeping a journal and knowing procedures. Rather, one must have a firm ethical base and sound ethnographic background in order to prevent the recurrence of such atrocities as Densmore's teaching American Indians how to "sing properly" before she would record them (as mentioned in Sachs, The Wellsprings of Music). In addition, one must know how to formulate hypotheses and test them.

In the formulation of hypotheses, it is helpful to consider current theory concerning the musical occasion, the possible contexts for musical performance, and how context may affect musical form. Knowledge of the status and role of musicians and their inter-relationships with audiences is important background for the ethnomusicologist; as is knowledge of perception and the learning process (cognition, proxemics, myths, evaluation of performance, teaching methods, learning abilities). Music often plays a vital role in rituals, ceremonies, politics and social control. It may also be involved in many other aspects of human life. Since human groups are continually in a process of change, it is necessary to have some idea how music changes with time, and what factors may institute or prevent change from occurring.

Music may be removed from its context and considered as an isolated entity. In so doing, one traditionally transcribes recordings. This process initiates two major types of problems: the nature and goals of transcription and, the fallibility of Western notation. It therefore becomes necessary to discuss not only the problems, conventions and aims of transcription, but also, how the goals of the ethnomusicologist influence the choice of transcription philosophy. The best example of this to date is found in England's Symposium on Transcription in _Ethnomusicology_ (1964), in which several scholars transcribed the same piece, with markedly different strategies and results.

Since Western notation is incomplete -- not allowing for indication of such things as upglides to a pitch, rasp, or dozens of other performance devices -- conventional alterations of the traditional notation system must be considered. In addition, mechanical aids to transcription, such as Seeger's Melograph, should be evaluated. Finally, a methodology for transcription must be included.

Once the problems of transcription and notation have been considered, the real problem of analysis emerges. Approaching analysis in terms of its possible goals, each of the six current structural poses must be delineated (Tovey and post-Tovey, Kolinski, Merriam, Lomax, Hood, McLeod). Some of the problems one encounters are as follows: size of sample; determination of analytic elements; aesthetics and valuation systems; variation; definitive performances; analysis of a single song vs. analysis of a style, form, or genre; computer assistance.

Since much of the world's music is sung, it is only natural that attention be given to the relationship between music and language. What are the boundaries of speech and song and, how does one determine them? Does music constrain text or, does text constrain music? Are "nonsense" syllables really nonsense or, might they carry meaning? What are the possible levels at which meaning may reside in music? If music is a code or a multi-dimensional symbolic system, full clarification and decipherment of the code or symbol systems is vital.

In moving toward an ethnomusicological perspective, knowledge of what the analysis of sound reveals about culture is needed. Also, knowledge of what the analysis of culture reveals about sound is needed. Whatever its particular form may be, the inter-relationship of music and culture is real, integral, basic and approachable.

The limits, goals and prospects for ethnomusicology are similar to culture in that they are always changing. Through a view of past ideas and influences, it becomes possible to understand current trends: preoccupation with analysis, utilization of linguistic theories, search for objectivity and understanding.

Ideally, an introductory text should cover all aspects of human musical behavior. The ultimate objective has long been the fusion of the specifically musical and the specifically behavioral aspects of ethnomusicology.

There has been a continuing tendency toward separation between music studies and cultural studies. Unfortunately, Merriam's remarks about "...books, articles, and monographs...devoted to studies only of music, which is often treated as an object in itself without reference to the cultural matrix out of which it is produced" (1964:vii-viii) are still here. At the same time, there is an abundance of anthropological, linguistic and folkloristic studies which do not consider the musical parameters.

In short, the wholeness of an emergent discipline which gives equal consideration to the music, itself, and the behavior surrounding its origin, production and evaluation still eludes us.

The original intent of this book was to bridge the chasm separating these two camps. The authors, accordingly, planned, projected and produced a manuscript which would address itself to all aspects of the scholarly investigation of music. However, the anonymous readers who evaluated the manuscript in its totality eventually brought us to the realization that the ideal of a total discipline has not yet been achieved.

It was perfectly clear that two of the evaluators were musicologically inclined, because they indicated distrust and disdain of the behavioral portion of the book. Two other readers were anthropologically inclined, indicating disdain with the musicological portion of the book. One reader understood and applauded both segments equally.

After much discussion and, with a great deal of reluctance, it was finally decided that the manuscript would be divided into two parts. It should be made clear, however, that the authors do not feel that any introductory approach or any professional approach to the study of music should exclude any aspect of the investigation of music. We deplore any remaining feelings that a total study of music as culture or music as a fixed item of sound can be totally comprehensive without a full coverage of its so-called complementary aspects. We look forward to the day when such discussions are not only outmoded, but also unthinkable.

In preparing this book, we have drawn upon a wide range of examples from various areas of the world. We have not made any attempt to cover all of the geographic areas, or to arrive at a fair sampling of representative examples from the entire world. Rather, the strategy has been to use examples from our own field work, which covers everything from urban musics to peasant musics to hunting and gathering situations.

Primary emphasis throughout the book has been placed on ethnographic material from Malta. In so doing, we have made a conscious choice to provide the student with as much information as possible about a single musical culture. We have done so with the intent of providing a fairly comprehensive view of the various approaches one might take to musical behavior within a single culture. It is expected that the instructor using this book in an introductory course will add his or her own field experience within the lecture framework, thus providing the student with a contrast of information. The result, it is hoped, will be a depth of understanding which can be transferred to whatever situation in which the individual might find him/herself.

Another strategy in preparation of this book has been to maintain a thoroughly professional stance. Although our full expectation is that most students or other interested readers will never earn a livelihood by professionally studying musical cultures, nevertheless, we feel that the exposure to professionalism will provide a formal insight which will enrich one's appreciation of his/her own music.

Perhaps a more selfish stance is the hope that people who are not themselves musical specialists will have the courage to produce articles, monographs and books dealing with the information they find. Ethnomusicology is a field of study which has few practitioners and vast areas of study, geographically and culturally. Therefore, it becomes necessary for input from a multitude of sources in order to sufficiently understand the true nature of the diversity of music as human behavior.

In preparation of this manuscript, thanks are due to many, many people. All of those who befriended and helped us in our various field studies are the primary sources of inspiration. All the students who heard the ideas in the formative stages, and the colleagues who have provided various kinds of input are muchly

appreciated. In particular, Charlotte Frisbie, Barbara Krader
and Robert Garfias are greatly appreciated.

    Also, thanks are due to the various organizations which have
provided funding for portions of this study: the Wenner Gren
Foundation for Anthropology; Tulane University; the University of
Texas; the University of California at Berkeley; and the University of Ottawa. The tireless efforts of Linda Moran in typing the
first, second and third drafts of the manuscript are truly appreciated. Finally, thanks is due Billye Talmadge who valiently took
on the massive task of editing this material and preparing it in
its final form.

    In retrospect, the final appreciation should be for the op-
portunity afforded by the writing of this mansucript, because it
has given us a chance to review the field, its current situation,
and its future prospects.

                              Marcia Herndon

Berkeley, California
May, 1979

Table of Contents

Sound, Meaning, and Diversity

Ethnomusicologists study music in different cultural settings which creates two major questions: "What is music?" and, "What is ethnomusicology?"

The incredible diversity of music throughout the world makes it necessary to consider the first question because, if the term, music, is not clearly defined, then the same hesitancy applies to the sub-discipline or focus represented by the clumsy term, ethnomusicology. In this introductory section, only the broad implications of these two questions will be discussed.

THE NATURE OF MUSIC

Definitions of basic terms are elusive and, as might be expected, many variations exist in the definitions of music which are readily available.

The Harvard Dictionary of Music, a standard reference source, approaches the definition in a historical manner, citing Greek and Egyptian concepts, and mentioning the sub-categories for music in the Middle Ages (Apel, 1969:548-49). This classificatory approach is a common one, but the authors' information about music rests on its classification within any society. Definitional problems become apparent when a universal view is attempted.

Most definitions imply that music is a form of sound and that it is a human activity. Sometimes, music is defined by its subdivisions; sometimes, by its characteristics (pitch, rhythm, intensity, timbre). Occasionally, one finds the term "singing" loosely applied to other creatures, such as whales, or "dancing" applied to the courtship movements of birds. It is generally agreed, however, that music is sound (and sometimes movement); that it is created to be performed and listened to; and that those who participate in it and/or appreciate it are human beings.

Bird-cries are a case in point. Are these music or territorial signals? To be music, sound must be fairly lengthy in extent and have variance both within a performance and between performers. With the exception of the imitative birds, such as the Mockingbird, these criteria are not met.

Studies of the dolphin indicate that these intriguing sea mammals have a wide range of sounds, which may be something like language. They have been known to try to reproduce human sounds under laboratory conditions as well. Here is one of the elements which might be expected from music: a wide range of sounds, apparently recombined continuously. Until the evidence is complete, it is difficult to tell whether the dolphin is a singing mammal or a speaking mammal. In either case, the exclusiveness of man is being broken, but it is presently difficult to determine in which direction the dolphin approaches our sound-making patterns.

The work of Jane Goodall (and others) on chimpanzees in a natural environment also tends to make humanity less an exclusive club. Analyzing the sounds of chimpanzees is now underway -- sounds which include a wide range of coughs, grunts, whoops and pitched sequences. The sequences with pitch are of most interest to music students, of course; it is a great shock to hear chimpanzees "singing" major triads. Until the analysis is complete, it will not be known whether these sounds represent a language, a set of signals, or a very simple music.

The older literature on Africa contains occasional references to dancing among chimpanzees. Until physical anthropologists began a close investigation of primates in their natural habitats, all these accounts had to be disregarded. The dramatic image of chimpanzees flinging mud at a spot on the ground until a central platform was built up; the delightful idea of a group of chimpanzees circling the platform, arms waving, whooping, while one old male beat vigorously on the platform -- such stories were dismissed as fantasy -- until scientists actually saw it occur.

Chimpanzees are among the primates customarily brought to the Delta Primate Center near New Orleans, Louisiana, where they are used for medical and behavioral experiments. The first group imported, which came directly from their natural environments, were not well and were isolated from the other species for treatment and study. This is significant, in that zoo-bred animals are now thought to behave quite differently from free-ranging members of the same species.

At the time of the authors' observation, this group of chimpanzees was restless, sick and angry. They were caged separately in a large square area, with each cage open to the outside world.

One old male was aimlessly playing with a piece of tin which projected from the bottom of his cage. He struck it with his clenched fist and then sat back. A moment later, he struck it again, two or three times. Then he raised his head and gave a series of high barking sounds which were immediately repeated by all the chimpanzees in nearby cages. He returned to the piece of tin and began striking it rhythmically with alternate fists, barking all the while. The other chimpanzees rose in their cages, barked furiously (but not in unison), and, raising their arms above their heads, began to skitter about their cages. It was not

2

a regular dance, nor were the sounds co-ordinated in any way, but the old bull gave a steady, continuous beat on his piece of tin.

But was it a dance? Not quite. The restricted animals could not see one another and thus could not co-ordinate their movements. However, reports from Africa indicate that such activity does occur, mainly in the rainy season. When chimpanzees in a troupe are thoroughly wet from the continuous rains, tempers shorten, and eventually the animals will break into a sort of furious barking, accompanied by much arm-waving and skittering. Reports of the great mud-drum have not been verified, however.

Such examples will undoubtedly multiply as more is known about animal behavior. Since man is a primate, it is probable to expect behavior similar to music from other primates. Some biological base can be assumed for music-making, although at present the evidence is far too tentative to discuss. This does imply, however, that ethnomusicologists may be recording primates other than man in the not-too-distant future.

Until such time as the evidence is fuller, one can only speculate that man is probably not the exclusive music-maker. Much will depend, however, on how one chooses to define music. Are chimpanzees making music when they bark? Does a regular drumming beat constitute music? Will dance notations be able to record their skitterings and arm-wavings? Will their activity be formal enough to constitute dance and music?

MUSIC AS HUMAN ACTIVITY

Before one can begin to say what constitutes music in the broadest possible sense, one ought to be able to say what, of human activity, is music. This is not easy. As long as music students are dealing with their own music, they are fairly sure of the borders between music and non-music. Any music specialist will say that music should have certain general characteristics, such as pitch and rhythm, and will be able to distinguish between music and non-music, at least in his own area of concern.

The distinction between music and noise is never an absolute one; but rather, a matter of cultural conditioning, personal idiosyncracies, and group identity. What is accepted as music by one group or generation may be ignored or dismissed by another. As a human activity, then, music is culturally defined. For a good illustration of this, one has only to examine the statements quoted in The Lexicon of Musical Invective (1965).

In the study of musics outside one's own culture, even greater definitional problems are presented. The Maori haka or war-

3

dance is not sung, but shouted rhythmically. Yet, in spite of its lack of pitch, it must be regarded as music because the Maori so regard it. The Cuna Indians make fine distinctions among styles of vocal expression. Instead of separating speaking from singing (and, by implication, language from music), they have three "ways of speaking", at least one of which would be identified by an outsider as singing (Bauman and Sherzer 1974:263-282). The Koran cannot be sung, since music is not allowed in the Muslim religion. Therefore, reciting the Koran cannot be called music, even though it is pitched.

These few examples give some idea of the difficulty of defining music only in a human sense, without including the behavior of other animals. If a hard line is taken, defining music as a form of sound with certain characteristics, such definition will be forced to exclude numerous examples of sound from consideration. If, on the other hand, the cultural definition of music is followed in each case, some kinds of sound normally thought of as music may be omitted.

LIMITS ON MUSIC

There are certain biological aspects to the study of music, mainly pertaining to the outer limits of perception. The perfect human ear can hear sounds between approximately 20 and 20,000 cycles. The average person of 36 years of age or so can hear only to 8,000 cycles, because hearing loss of high pitches often occurs first. Sounds softer or louder than certain levels are also hard to discern. Ten to 100 decibels is a reasonable range for human hearing; below 10 decibels the sounds may be inaudible; while above 100, they may register as pain rather than sound.

Numerous mechanical devices can produce sounds which are inaudible. The most common is the Jew's harp, which uses overtones on a single fundamental to produce a melody. When the tuned prong is struck, it sounds a fundamental pitch plus a stressed overtone. The strength of various overtones is altered by changing the shape of the mouth cavity. One overtone is emphasized at the expense of others; these latter are not heard, and are not part of the music.

Electronic devices sometimes exceed the limits of human hearing, both in producing and recognizging pitch. The commonest is the signal generator, which can produce sounds into the microwave range. At the upper end, the sounds are inaudible. At the lower end, the sounds produced are so slow as to register as clicks rather than pitches. Thus, pitch is a function of the rate of vibration. Another such device is the Melograph, which registers pitch, loudness and timbre.

4

There are also limits on duration. When a sound is too short, it will not be heard; when too long, it will not be heard as music.

Information about other biological limits on music comes from studies of the brain, where it has been shown that some aspects of music are stored in the sub-dominant cerebral hemisphere, others in the dominant (Music and the Brain, 1977).

Although the brain is divided into two symmetrical halves, one side stores speech and is dominant over the other. With increased specialization in music, musical information passes over to the dominant side of the brain.

Persons with brain damage only on the speech side of the head may lose the power to speak, but may still be able to sing. Oddly enough, brain-damaged persons of this type frequently retain the words to songs in addition to the melody. From this, it can be assumed that songs with words are stored as a whole, a fact which explains the difficulty some people have in speaking the words of songs without singing them. EEG tracings made of musicogenic epilieptics show that attacks from listening to music occur in either the right or left hemisphere, which indicates that both hemispheres are involved in music-learning (op. cit:344-53).

While little is known about the mechanisms involved in the storage of musical information, all ethnomusicologists have encountered one or another of the physiological reactions which occur when listening to music other than one's own.

As children, certain kinds of musical information are firmly stored -- pitch is the primary example. The European scale system has severe limits placed on it by traditions. Children are taught to play "in tune" and pitch perception is high, storing information of an exact nature about pitch. In some cases, pitch learning is so firm that individuals develop "perfect pitch", the ability to name or reproduce pitches within very narrow limits. When a trained musician becomes an ethnomusicologist, he or she is forced by the nature of the work to listen to pitch spacings which may vary significantly from his/her own.

Persistent listening to non-Western music pitch sequences for a considerable length of time tends to cause the listener to either accommodate the pitches heard to his own system, or not. If accommodation is possible, the listener remains comfortable. If, however, the pitches in question are so different that accommodation is impossible, the listener may suffer some form of physiological discomfort. Migraine headache, diarrhea, stomach cramps, double vision, or extreme muscle tension is common. Once a musical system is well-learned by an individual, one conclusion is that it interferes with new information. This represents a significant contrast with language. Given time and training, almost anyone can learn a second language; to learn a second musical system may be painful, however.

5

The dominant cerebral hemisphere is involved in this process, as well. If one is given verbal information about pitches in a new music, the listening process is less likely to be physiologically disruptive. This implies that there is some form of transfer of information possible between the cerebral hemispheres, so that verbal information stored in the dominant hemisphere can allow new learning to take place in the sub-dominant. Unless this were so, no person trained in one culture could ever sufficiently learn the music of a foreign culture. As there are many successful examples of new music-learning, this is obviously not the case.

The biological limits on music recognition are perhaps not as significant as the cultural. As mentioned above, duration of sound, if too long, will not be heard as music. This is more prominent when patterns of sound are considered. While precise documentation for types of musical patterns which humans can perceive is not yet available, many cultural factors may be involved. Phrases in Western music generally do not exceed approximately seven seconds. Verses or strophes of phrases are usually fairly short, as well; four to six phrases within a strophe are normal. In Japanese music, however, one can listen to up to fifty sound segments before a sequence is repeated. Thus, human beings can be trained to expect sequences of sound of various lengths, with cultural considerations dictating the length.

This appears to also be true of longer sequences or patterns of music. Western opera usually ranges between fifty minutes for a short opera and five hours, perhaps, for a Wagnerian opera. Japanese or Italian music may continue for much longer periods of time without distress to the audience. Again, this is cultural, rather than biological. In the longer performances, Eastern audiences are allowed to move about which is impossible for a Western audience imprisoned in an opera house, waiting for the second act to end. Thus, the nature of music is definable at its boundaries both in terms of biological and cultural limits.

What sort of human activity is music, then? Music can be thought of as a series of characteristics, but some may be absent in certain types of music. Music can be described as a combination of pitch, duration, timbre, melody, patterning and improvisation. However, the pitchless Maori haka is still music -- at least to the Maori. The rhythmless funeral dirges of Tikopia are still music. Improvisation is hardly allowed in Western fine art music. What all musics share is the concept of patterned sound, even though the components of the pattern differ from one situation to another.

Music, then, has both biological and cultural limitations, but cannot be defined too tightly. Perception is limited by biological mechanisms and altered by culturally acceptable regularization of sound. As a culturally defined mechanism, music is perceived through cultural canalization and is defined by specif-

6

ic groups who participate in particular genres. It contains silence, interspersed with patterned sound, of which the characteristics vary. It is, and perhaps is not, a strictly human activity. Such a definition of music is puzzling in that, with the exception of the concept of articulation, this could be defining language. This is deliberate; for the authors believe that music and language represent parts of a continuum of patterned sound, particularly since songs may have texts. The fact is that human beings (and perhaps some other animals) pattern the sounds that disturb the air in others' ears. When this sound is highly regularized, it is frequently called music. Perhaps one day music may be defined more correctly through the tedious process of deciding what music is not.

THE NATURE OF ETHNOMUSICOLOGY

The term, ethnomusicology, has been ascribed to Jaap Kunst, who proposed it in his book of the same name (1955). Earlier scholars, whose interests lay in the strictly musicological areas, grouped themselves together loosely under the term, _Vergleichende Musikwissenschaft_, "Comparative Musicology". There seems to be no school of thinking connected with the term; the subject of study at first consisted mainly of the "exotic".

Almost all definitions of such earlier studies indicated an interest in the "other" kind of music. Most early definitions involved geographic concepts (Gilman, 1909; Bingham, 1914; Sachs, 1959; Kunst, 1955; Nettl, 1956; Rhodes, 1956; Schneider, 1957), and were rather selective. Bingham suggested that exotic music should include primitive, oriental, and the music of Dalmation peasants (1914). The assumption of all of these definitions is that ethnomusicology confines itself to the study of musics other than that of the fine art system which developed in Western Europe and spread throughout the industrial world.

While such an approach is certainly reasonable (in view of the present situation of musicology, where many scholars labor on the specific problems created by the written art music of Western cultures), the geographical approach to ethnomusicology is still an anomolous one. It implies that there is an "in" and "out", and that never the twain shall meet.

Some scholars have taken a different approach. Alan Merriam (1960, 1964) shows his anthropological bias by the definition of ethnomusicology as "the study of music in culture". Gilbert Chase views ethnomusicology from a more general principle:

> The present emphasis...is on the musical
> study of contemporary man, to whatever

society he may belong, whether primitive or
complex, Eastern or Western (1958:7).

He goes on by stating that "musicology" is now almost entirely an historical discipline, frequently calling itself "historical
musicology". The tendency of musicologists in the past few decades
has been to restrict their work to composers, artists and perform-
ance-oriented impresarios who are no longer living. Chase, then,
distinguishes between ethnomusicology as a study of present-day
phenomena and musicology as the study of the past. In this perspective, there is no necessary restriction on the geographics of
ethnomusicology. This may have influenced Kolinski's assertion
that ethnomusicology represents a difference in general approach
from musicology (1957).

That these distinctions between musicology and ethnomusicology are more a matter of practice than of theory is well presented
by Mantle Hood, who added "ethno-" to the American Musicological
Society definition of musicology:

> (Ethno)musicology is a field of knowledge,
> having as its object the investigation of the
> art of music as a physical, psychological,
> aesthetic, and cultural phenomenon. The
> (ethno)musicologist is a research scholar,
> and he aims primarily at knowledge about
> music (1957:2).

From this point of view, ethnomusicology is the study of music, wherever it may be found, and can be historical as well. In
addition, the concept of music in culture is embodied in the definition.

The authors' definition: ethnomusicology is the study of the
music either past or present, of all who participate in music as
creators, performers, or hearers of sound patterns; taking into
account all factors which lead to a better understanding of this
particular type of creative, human display.

MODERN CULTURAL TRENDS

The nineteenth century represents a vital era because new
approaches to learning and thinking developed almost simultaneously throughout the Christian world. The most prominent trend --
the full development of the Industrial Revolution -- led eventually to a firm position for the middle-class in the economics of
most industrialized countries. At the same time, the nineteenth
century saw the final break of the dogmatic hold which had been
squeezing scholarship to death for some four hundred years. The
Catholic hold on art, morality, ethics and the humanities crumbled

8

under the assault of Charles Darwin, as, indeed, did other Christian doctrines. The restricted content and context for music had already been breaking down; the Protestant movement began the process of secularizing musical forms; new trends in rhythm and harmony were allowed into some liturgies, and even the so-called "Devil's Interval" or tritone (e.g., F-B) began to appear in liturgical music.

The nineteenth century also saw an increase in transportation and communication around the world. Coming on the heels of an established colonialism, adventurers and missionaries grew in number as general wealth increased. This trend brought about a proliferation of material, however badly stated, about the music of people of many cultures.

It is to certain developments in linguistics, however, that ethnomusicology owes the major impetus toward the study of the music of other cultures. The discovery of Sanskrit and its relationship to modern European languages in the nineteenth century gave respectability to the study of non-European cultures as did no other discovery. With the unravelling of Sanskrit came the realization that India was a fully developed civilization as early as the fourteenth century B.C., a time when even Greece was thought to be barbaric. The linguistic unfolding of the world to study, in this dramatic way, cried for imitation in other human areas. If languages were related -- were arts, or musics, poetry, or myth? The stage was set for social Darwinism in all areas pertaining to humanity.

Later in the nineteenth century, linguistics as a study of formal integrity developed fully in the works of Ferdinand de Saussure, whose scholarship (1908, 1916) revolutionized ideas about all levels of language study. Linguistics also led to one of ethnomusicology's most significant tools, when the phonetician, A. J. Ellis, developed the Cent system for measuring pitch.

By the end of the nineteenth century, the outreach of the Western world was growing with one startling discovery after another. In archaeology, Ur of the Caldees, the pyramids of Gizeh, Schliemann's discoveries of Troy and Mycenae brought the glory of gods, graves and scholars into a new prominence. Franz Boas, a geographer, became enthralled with the Eskimo; the sailing ships of the world developed to their full potential, and adventurers and seekers after fortune blundered upon one new discovery after another.

The combination of the development of the social sciences and the discovery of art forms of great majesty and beauty led, naturally, to a new awareness of the world of the West. This was developed further in the twentieth century in such forms as a new humanism (symbolized by the League of Nations and the United Nations), the development of great museums and a subsequent interest in all aspects of the arts from all over the world.

9

As these events and trends came together, Western Europe stepped into a new role: more aware, less introspective, less monistic than before. This was not a sudden or extravagant move because Europe's isolation was broken first by the Crusades; later, by the Renaissance; and finally, by the gathering snowball of forces which led to a more expectant view of the world, which is still maintained today.

It is no longer surprising to find fine art composers, graphic and plastic artists of the Western tradition showing an interest in folk and primitive art and music. With the discovery of the African carving and metal-working traditions, the European fine arts were broken away from formalism and naturalism by the startling discoveries of arts which could be appreciated by Western eyes and ears. While this development had taken place previously in the more philosophical areas, its entry into the world of the fine arts was the final stamp of approval on "humanity".

Tinges of condescension were still to be heard. Early writers on music maintained that the music of the other people of the world was simple -- a hangover from the unilinear evolutionary view of anthropology in the nineteenth century -- and epithets of "crude" and "primitive" were regularly applied to the graphic and plastic arts of others until recently. It took the discovery that behavioral diversity is as great in economically simple cultures as in complex ones to explode the idea of an unbroken development of mankind displayed in the present day by "primitive" contemporaries.

The concept of "other" is still very real in the study of non-European music. While this is a general manifestation of scholarship in all disciplines in this century, it seems to be reinforced in the study of the fine arts. One reason may be that present art music has always been considered an isolatable element which does not depend on cultural trends, economic conditions, or history, but rather on the singular abilities of composers and artists.

Music is psychologically removed from personal lives and considered as a god, but one that is semi-divine. The great composers of the Classical and Romantic periods of Western fine art music are also frequently deemed either divine or semi-divine beings. For example, Charles Seeger quotes a conversation between himself and the eminent musicologist, Manfred Bukofzer, after hearing a session on jazz at a meeting of the American Musicological Society. In leaving the room, Bukofzer remarked, "Those people think jazz is sacred!" Seeger said, "Well, you think Bach is sacred, don't you?", to which Bukofzer replied, "Oh, but he is!"

This tendency to view great creators and performers as semi-divine ("the divine diva") may have led musicology to a certain shyness in dealing with living creators and performers, and may be

10

responsible for the modern trend to await someone's death before
beginning a study of his or her music. But the subject matter
is still "holy", and one may think of the musicologist as a person who is handling dangerous material and who must carry himself
like a priest. Thus, art music is used as a removal device by
those who have been trained to consider it in this manner. One
escapes from daily problems by listening to music; one is en-
lightened or uplifted by great music; or one is re-invigorated
and given strength by the thought that man can create such beauty.

If these assumptions are correct, the development of ethnomusicology lay partly, at least, in this tendency to avoid the
living composer in present-day society. The study of "others" is
safe; they are outside one's ken and thus beyond the range of one's
psychological devices. Musicologists, on the other hand, may view
ethnomusicologists as tradition-breakers; after all, they talk to
live people who also happen to be creative artists.

Thus, the concept of an "other out there", combined with
one's own internal restrictions on the study of the present-day
creative art, may have led inevitably to the development of something called "ethnomusicology". Are ethnomusicologists a safety
valve for aesthetic studies? And if so, what is their position?
Are they to be the breakers of tradition, and the makers of new
traditions? Having personally felt awe of an aesthetic nature in
the presence of a great performer in another culture, one can understand how difficult it must be for persons sensitive to the
beauty of music to work with living composers. The dedication to
the concept of music interferes with its study; one finds one's
self undone by beauty, caught unaware by it and whirled away. In
a sense, it is safe to study traditions not understood, for one
is less likely to be psychologically removed from reality by them.

This may be a venture completely new in the history of mankind: the subtle study of aesthetic traditions not one's own,
with the aim of understanding them and, thereby, better understanding one's self. This type of study is not exclusively Western; it is wise to remember that others have also studied aesthetic traditions beyond their own. According to the Chinese classic,
the Fze Chun, the Emperor Chow Wen Whang maintained a bureau for
collecting the texts of folk songs throughout China, in order to
determine public opinion of government: "Wen Whang gathers folk
songs in order to testify his failure or success" (Wang, 1965:
312).

Ahmad Faris reported on European music in the nineteenth century. His visits to Malta, England and France led to observations
on music which are no more naive than nineteenth century Western
comments on non-European music (Cachia, 1973).

In reporting on the musics of present-day cultures other than
the Western or Western-oriented, ethnomusicologists may take two
different approaches. First, they may wish to perform music. In

11

so doing, understanding is effected through the learning process, generally of an instrument demanded by a musical system. Students who do field work following this tradition are likely to learn to play instruments and thereby gain knowledge about the musical system with which they are working. Thus, practical music at the university level is generally followed by practical music in the field.

Another method revolves around the concept that music occurs within a cultural setting, and that a full understanding of music requires an understanding of the cultural setting. While the learning of musical instruments is not eschewed, it is not recommended. Thus, persons trained in this system tend to ignore the learning process (for an instrument or for singing) in favor of the more abstract and theoretical approaches characteristic of anthropology.

In both cases, the system of training is oriented toward the same goal: the understanding of music. While neither concentrates exclusively on any one area, there is a tendency for the theoretical premises to reflect the special emphases of each system of training. Thus, students from these two different schools of thought might find themselves reporting on the same society very differently. Neither reflects a complete study of music. In emphasizing the cultural context, much valuable information about the nature of music and the nuances of performances are lost. In emphasizing the learning process, many of the reasons for the performance of music remain unclear.

Not all scholars accept this as a schism. Information about music can come from any reasonable source and should be as wide in scope as possible. In many instances, an ethnomusicologist will be forced into the role of a performer whether this is useful or not. In others, an ethnomusicologist may never learn to perform even upon one instrument within a culture because of the complexity of the musical system being studied. A perfect study has probably never been done, nor has a perfect research design been constructed. What is required by each individual situation often determines the results; what is called for in a scholar is flexibility and diversity.

PRESENT SUCCESSES

The most significant aspect of ethnomusicology today is the beginning of a cross-cultural understanding of the nature of music. The realization that music is _not_ a universal language, but that it differs markedly from one society to another is a first step. The secondary understanding, that the meaning of music differs radically from one society to another, is not far behind. The statement that yet another human value is, in fact, provincial, local and culture-bound is not the most pleasant discovery.

12

In view of the vast accumulation of evidence that man is an exceedingly flexible creature, ordering his life in an infinite variety of ways within the framework of human survival, should not give too much pause. It is sad, perhaps, to discover that music is not a means by which man can bridge his cultural chasms with others; however, in view of the experiences of other scientists who have also reached out to the rest of the world, it is not unexpected. Music has no charms to soothe the savage breast, nor yet to instill in all men the same values, as Merriam has pointed out (1964).

A slow realization has developed that there must be a constant revision and re-ordering of the consideration of the nature of music. Music represents one of the most puzzling aspects of human behavior. While it changes through time, music retains fragments of information from the past; it also changes at various rates, depending on many factors. While its meanings and values shift from one society to another, the scholar's search for the nature of man in this most delicate of areas is enlivened and enriched by the depth of introspection displayed by musicians throughout the world and the dazzling variety of techniques and underlying aesthetic values displayed by its perpetrators. No scholar could ask for more. Music represents one of the most puzzling, varied and unknown qualities of human life.

Ethnomusicologists have made the usual mistakes, having tried to patronize music and the musicians of other cultures; having called some primitive, some boring, or limited. There has been a tendency to attempt to force the music of other people into a chronological mold. It is difficult to explain something which is different; without the benefit of terminology, one is lost. However, it is not possible to use a single terminology set for historical musicology of Europe.

As new concepts emerge in other areas of scholarship, there is an attempt to apply them to music. In the near future, undoubtedly, a host of post-Freudian analytical devices will develop for a full understanding of the nature of music, as presently seen in the influences of structuralism and semiotics.

All of these tendencies in ethnomusicology have one factor in common. They indicate that, as yet, this field has developed no dogma of its own and is not yet molded into a discipline so rigid, that persons interested in the study of music may no longer contribute anything new. This is an important period for these reasons. It is during such moments in the life of a discipline that its best thinking can be done for, when scholars work on the edge of an unknown, they frequently transcend themselves, producing work and ideas which would be impossible in a later, more stylized period.

This, then, is the Halcyon time for ethnomusicology. There is much to be learned in all areas of the world, through no matter what methodological frame.

CONCLUSION

Ethnomusicology as a discipline is, as yet, an undefined area of study. Its focus is music. Its scholars may have formal training in several different disciplines. There are no limitations on what may or may not be done and the problems thus far encountered still outnumber the scholars in the field.

As in any other field of study, ethnomusicology has its specialists in certain areas of the world, whose information is precious because of its depth; and its few generalists, whose contributions encompass aspects of the field as a whole. Thus, ethnomusicology is an area of study with a name with which no one is happy, and an aim of which no one is sure. The work is done in the roistering, rollicking atmosphere of goals too high to reach and problems too large to solve.

This is a situation which always arises when man first turns attention to something not previously considered. The breadth of possibilities of study are limited only by the imagination and ability of the scholar. The results are as unpredictable as one would expect creative art to be.

Context and Performance

Music, as implied before, is patterned sound limited by biology and culture. In this chapter, the more specific ramifications of the areas of context and performance will be discussed.

CONTEXT

A context is either that which precedes or follows an item and thus explains it, or the totality in which it is found. A context may be any referent point plus any locus. If two trains are moving near one another, one cannot tell which is moving unless there is a third point of reference. In terms of music, a single pitch is not music when heard in isolation, but becomes music through the accumulation of other points of reference.

"Context" may refer either to the actual time sequence in which an item of music is found (such as the ordering of a ceremony), or to the ideal time sequence in a category of events. Alternately, context may be any aspect of patterned relationships within which the pattern of music is considered apt. For music, then, contexts are of several orders. They may be geographic contexts such as African music, North American music, Baganda music or Sioux music. Contexts are also seasonal: those involving cyclical events, seasons of the year, or seasons within the human life cycle such as birth, marriage, childbirth, or death.

Time-space relationships may be regarded as a type of context, with the right time and place for the performance of certain kinds of music. The Indian raga determines the improvised pieces; the time of day determines the raga. In Western society, radio stations usually do not broadcast sopranos between 7 and 9 o'clock in the morning, although no one is quite sure why. It is traditional to avoid high-pitched sounds early in the morning while people are driving to work, listening to the radio.

Statements of 'who', 'where', 'when', 'what', 'why' and 'how' symbolize the types of metaphysical, existenial and actual environments (or circumstances) in which music occurs. There is no limit to the number of applications of the concept; context may be as broad or as narrow as the individual researcher desires to make it.

The concept of context is particularly helpful in the study of music, since the tendency, historically, is to emphasize only

15

certain aspects of context. Viewed in the larger sense of the interweaving of parts within a whole, out of which a researcher may
choose to investigate any sets of integumental relationships, the
concept of context proves exceedingly valuable. Past tendency was
to define parts of a culture's music in such terms as drunk songs,
gambling songs, war songs, funeral songs, et cetera. This approach, while somewhat useful, breaks down immediately if one begins to study the ways in which a particular society classifies
its own music.

Among the Kutenai of Northern Idaho, certain gambling songs
appear in ritual contexts, with appropriate changes in form. Are
they gambling songs, then? Are they ritual songs? In fact, they
are neither; they are songs to the nupika, who bestow good luck.
To call them gambling songs or ritual songs is a cover term which
may be useful in certain circumstances, but does not aid in the
understanding of what music is.

There is also the tendency to define the music of a culture
as what that culture does, which can be a tremendous problem. As
McAllester inquired, when a Japanese violinist plays Beethoven,
is he playing Japanese music? Music crosses cultural boundaries
and, in some cases, it is re-defined when it does so. In other
instances, it is not.

The relationship between two cultures is so sufficiently complex that entire books on the process of acculturation have graced
publishers' lists for years. The implication that a culture may
borrow the music of another culture completely destroys the statement that Cherokee music is what the Cherokee do. This emphasizes
the need of a variety of viewpoints which will destroy old para-
doxes. The concept of context helps to unravel such problems,
giving a framework of explanation which is extremely useful at all
levels of analysis.

One of the most interesting things about music is that it is
the most highly patterned form of human behavior. Music is not
only highly patterned, but also staged. This implies that the
pattern called music coincides with certain other aspects of behavior which, themselves, have become patterned as a result.

In some cases, this is called dance; in others, it is called
costuming. In yet others, it might be called stagecraft. The
fact remains that whenever music occurs, some kinds of behavioral
alterations which are patterned and formalized occur with it. Thus,
the context of music becomes an indicator of the quality not only
of performance, but also of the nature of the human behavior en-
acted.

The study of context raises a major question: why do people
do this? Like the ritualization of speech in religion or in certain types of expressive culture, music tends to formalize the be-

16

havior around it. The study of that formality is one of the most pertinent ways of understanding the music, itself. The authors have called this formalization of behavior "staging" in order to emphasize what is perhaps one of the most fascinating aspects of the study of music.

LEVELS OF CONTEXT

Merriam (1964) mentions that culture is a context. While this is certainly true and it may be wise to begin with the largest level of generalization, the concept of culture is far too diffuse to be of use in every situation. The authors' researches in Malta led to a guitarist nicknamed Il-Bozen, regarded as the natural heir to the great guitarist, Cardona, who was a solo guitarist in the older improvisionational style. When singers perform any of the various Maltese musical styles, guitarists interpose an improvised sequence (usually of four phrases in length) between each verse of singing. Il-Bozen, while a traditional guitarist, occasionally uses European melodies as the basis for his improvisations.

At the level of culture as context, then, Il-Bozen could be regarded as an atypical musician. Closer attention to the immediate context of situation in which Il-Bozen used foreign melodies in his improvisations gives another picture. If the singer mentions foreigners in the verse immediately preceding his improvisation, Il-Bozen uses a foreign melody as the basis of his improvisation. In no other context does he do this. Thus, the "meaning" of the use of foreign melodies implies that each of Il-Bozen's improvisations may be a coded comment on the verse sung just previously. In this light, Il-Bozen no longer need be considered an atypical musician, simply an individual musician's interpretation of a coded system needed to be deciphered.

As can be seen from the above, the immediate context in which a piece of music is performed may be highly significant in explaining what is happening in the music. Not only this, but it is to be expected that there will be levels of contexts for music, both within and without the form, itself. These are powerful explanatory devices for different levels of significance.

At the level of context of culture, the most important researcher to date is Alan Lomax (1968). Lomax maintains that there may be an intimate relationship between musical and primarily cultural features, so that a particular orchestration, musical form, voice type, or type of range will be found only in those cultures which exhibit certain cultural features.

For instance, sung music may be performed in different ways with respect to control of the throat and facial muscles. Sound

17

performance may be augmented by stiffening the muscles of the throat and jaw. Singing "on the diaphragm" produces a variety of sounds, depending upon the opening or closing of various resonators within the head. Singing "on the throat" produces a harsh, constricted tone, characteristic of parts of Italy, Malta, North Africa, Spain and many other parts of the world. Lomax maintains that there is a relationship between singing with the muscles of the throat tightened and the sexual restrictions on women in various cultures. Thus, a musical phenomenon is explained by a cultural one.

These are exciting ideas; it is patent that there is some relation between culture and the conceiving of music. It is obvious that there will be some relationship which can be postulated and proved by cross-cultural comparison between some aspects of music and some aspects of the culture in which that music is found.

Because of the diversity of culture, it is probably impossible to define the total range of contexts available in the entire world. Context, as has been mentioned before, can be thought of as all those elements which go together to make up a whole. Music has a series of contexts at various levels, each of which may cause shifts within the formal structure of the music, itself. Context, then, is a variety of limiting device.

By beginning with the concept of music and moving outward to the concept of context, undoubtedly it will be found that a particular music responds to more than one context. Features within the form itself will be found to be responsive to very different contextural, or limiting, levels.

For example, a given style may be based at least partly upon the historical context of the sounds already chosen as music. In addition, the instruments which are used will be those which are available and allowable. The persons who play the style will depend upon the nature of the status of musicians and cultural limitations -- such as who may or may not become a musician. Thus, there will be a series of tangential influences upon music, some on intersecting planes. The idea is to conceptualize an unknown in each case which is knowable, complex and flexible. To do this, one must have a starting point or points which will lead to an increasing perception of the whole.

PHYSICAL CONTEXTS

One of the most fascinating things about the study of music is the way in which performers stretch the concept of the physical limitations of the human body in the performance of music. Ordinarily it is assumed that women cannot sing bass, nor can men sing soprano unless castrated. Yet, in every society, there are voice types which require some members of the community to actually expand their physical limitations in order to achieve the style.

If a tenor voice for women is favored in a given society, as it certainly is in many parts of Eastern Europe, then a selective process will take place unless women's voices can be lowered. In portions of North Africa and in Malta, men preferably should sing in the soprano range, without resorting to falsetto. Some singers can achieve this; others cannot.

There are clearly some physical limitations on what can be done with the human hand, the human voice, and the embouchure of the human mouth. Depending upon the complexity and rigidity of a particular style, some degree of physical mutation will be necessary. String players must develop calluses on their fingers. Every violinist who works at his craft will have a scar on his left shoulder. Some musicians must grow long fingernails, while others must keep them short. To the practiced eye, there are often physical signs which accompany the context of instrument player.

This is a wide field of investigation which has hardly been touched by scholars. The extensions and accommodations which music requires of the human frame can potentially serve as potent indicators of limitations of music within the physical realm. In addition, knowledge of the bodily alterations caused by particular instruments can be a valuable aid to a scholar trying to locate musicians in the field.

SOCIAL CONTEXTS

In the broadest sense, separating the cultural from the social context is impossible. For the time being, the assumption will be used that all contexts which are social in nature have to do with the structure of social relations between individuals within a culture. These limitations seem to relate primarily to the question: Who may become a musician?

In Madagascar, there is great variance in the status of musicians. On the high plateau, the Merina and the Betsileo have developed singers who are highly regarded. For the Merina, this results in an upward movement of musicians in the stratified society; while among the Betsileo, musicians arise out of the class of classless men who do not fit into the social strata at all (c. f. McLeod, 1964). In the southern desert, musicians are identifiable by living beyond the garbage dumps of any settlement. They are of the lowest class and can display behavior which is unacceptable to all other members of the society.

Where musicians arise from lower classes of from the class-less strata in society, not all members of the culture may wish to participate in musical activity because of the pressures which will be placed upon them socially. Obviously, this restricts the number of persons who will enter into the musical craft, reducing innovation because fewer persons will engage in the trade. Similar pressures undoubtedly exist when a musical style is regarded as the province of upper class individuals.

In Malta, folk music is mainly the province of the lower class. This has not restricted certain members of the upper class from engaging in it, but family pressure is placed upon men who desire to sing to cease and desist. One sad example was that of a contractor who sang briefly in his youth, until his wife objected violently. After her death, he attempted to re-enter the musical community where he was welcomed. Unfortunately by this time, he was an old man and could no longer take the pressures of constant improvisation, and soon dropped out.

Where a style is difficult, as is the Maltese, the end result may be that fine minds, like the gentleman above, may not be able to add their genius to the repertoire through purely social factors. It is important to recognize the nature of social factors. In particular, those constraints which limit or define the population of musicians should be noted, as should any sanctions on the nature of music or its audiences.

LINGUISTIC CONTEXT

As Durbin has pointed out (1971), music and linguistic texts which accompany music interweave with one another in a special way. Shifts in grammar of major proportions occur regularly between conversational speech and poetic speech. Poetic speech is the very basis of musical texts; but even between poetic speech and song, certain shifts may be expected. Sometimes, burden syllables or other devices for allowing musical rhythms to take precedence over poetic meter are used. Thus, language changes in the context of music. In the same sense, music changes in the context of text.

In the song, "Zadoahy", quoted by McLeod (1966) and Herndon (1974), long duration, high tone and heavy accent occur in conjunction with dipthongs, or silent consonents. Thus, music is constrained by text as well as the other way around. This relationship, such an acute one for the study of music, deserves serious consideration. One of the most significant factors for the formation of style may lie in text rather than in tune. While this is not a one-to-one relationship, it is clear that in some cases, music takes precedence over text, while the reverse is true

20

in others. The unscrambling of this particular problem is perhaps one of the most interesting challenges available to ethnomusicologists.

THE OCCASION AS CONTEXT

Of all the explanatory devices used by the authors, the concept of the occasion has proved to be the most powerful. While
songs can be studied in any manner, one of the most revealing ways
is through the occasions upon which music occurs. This is not a
theoretical concept; rather, it is a methodological one.

The occasion may be defined as the point of focus encompassing the perception, performance or creation of music. The occasion includes what Westerners call performances, but is not restricted to formal events.

It is assumed that there will be something similar about all
occasions of a particular type upon which music occurs; one of the
similarities may be the kind of music which is performed. While
this idea is simple, it has extensive ramifications as far as the
concepts of repertoire, ceremony, ritual ordering and specialized
personnel are concerned.

The question, then, is "When is music?" In dealing with the
occasion as context, both the so-called "native" categories and
the scholar's viewpoint are involved. That is, not only those e-
vents in a culture's expression which are named or otherwise marked by it as points in time on which is to be expected, but also
those events which may be recognized by the scholar as having musical interest, whether the group concerned recognizes them as
such or not.

As a behavioral phenomenon, the occasion includes the full
range of human performances and includes not only such informal
events as a picnic, but also formalized events such as concerts
or coronations. It is to be expected that, in some instances, it
will be the informal events which provide insight into the more
formal occasions, since the latter are often complex and difficult to follow.

One of the best examples of the way in which the concept of
the occasion may be useful is to be found in the Hungarian Harvest
Festival in Louisiana. This event occurs at the end of the harvest season as a way of offering a thanksgiving. A hall is decorated with fruit, flowers and vegetagles; children come dressed in
their native costumes. A band is assembled, usually consisting of
a violin or two, clarinet, and czimbalom (the struck zither) and
such other instruments as may be available. The members of the
community come for two reasons: to see one another and to watch

21

the dancing of old Hungarian dances by the young people dressed in their special costumes. Chief among these dances is the <u>Czardas</u>.

Although many points of reference can be mentioned here, only one will be pointed out. Song texts, especially the <u>Czardas</u>, tend to emphasize beautiful young girls. For a Hungarian, the most desirable woman in the world is between twelve and fourteen years old; women are considered to have lost their beauty once the peach fuzz disappears from their cheeks.

In the Harvest Festival, the problems of Hungarian marriages are played out. Here, the beauty of youth is extolled in song, but the beautiful young girls are rebuffed by those whom they would like to meet, for men must avoid women of marriageable age. Bachelors are not masters of their own fates; the songs portray this in many ways.

Thus the poignancy of songs, the talk of ripening wheat, of brightness, of gaiety is combined with talk of great sadness. Fathers and brothers must, traditionally, avoid their daughters and sisters in public; potential husbands must do so as well, for no one is in control of this situation. Here can be seen one of the most important principles of the occasion; that of the presence within music of ideas which are too dangerous to handle. The extreme segregation to be found in the Hungarian Harvest Festival is probably the result of strain within the family, as well as rivalry among the matriarchs for pride and place. Seating is done strictly according to status within the community, especially among matriarchs.

Given the importance of sexuality, it is publicly stated in song and because of the fact that no one controls it well, it is stated muscially rather than verbally. The occasion for this music in this community, the Harvest Festival, brings out all aspects of the nature of womanly beauty and displays them in more or less rigid form for the community, itself.

The range of information which may be discerned from a concentration upon the musical occasion as the context for musical activity is wide and unpredictable. The scholar may be dealing with very small or extremely large numbers of people in attempting to study a single event. It cannot be predicted with any degree of certainty what kind of information will be gleaned from a particular study, but the nature of one's understanding about a particular music will undoubtedly be deepened through continued focus on musical events and occasions.

THE INDIVIDUAL AS CONTEXT

It has been previously mentioned that there is a distinction

to be made between performing music and simply hearing it. An individual may, at different times, have different degrees of involvement in music. This, like the occasion, is a simplistic
statement; however, it is an extremely important one.

The individual scholar can, through continued observation of
a number of contexts and on many occasions, provide himself an
area for better comprehension of the range of aesthetic experiences in a given culture. As anyone who has ever listened to music knows, one's reaction to music differs depending on where he
is and how he feels. One's reaction to music also depends on _who_
he is.

An individual is a context in any sense in which he finds
himself. If he is purely a listener, then it is through his mind
that the music must be appreciated and judged. Each culture teaches its members how best to judge music and the other arts, in more
or less well organized verbal statements.

Western society tends to isolate performers from audiences in
many ways calling our opera singers "divine" and staying away from
them. This is currently changing; but in the 1930's and 1940's,
it was common for great singers to be given favored tables in
restaurants; to be protected by special cars, drivers, clothing,
and male escorts; to be lauded with flowers; to be surrounded by
helpers of various kinds. Today's working opera star does not have
to endure this as much; however, even today the cult of awe does
surround these ladies and gentlemen to some extent. She is called
"diva" or "divine diva"; he is called "master" or "maestro". In
other societies, a listener may have a more casual approach to his
performers.

Just as music may be isolated, the performers of music may be
isolated. As a result, the audience is segregated from the performer in some situations, but in some societies this may not be the
case. In Malta, a fine performer may be the object of direct contact with his listeners in many ways. As one singer said, "If I
hear a fine man sing, I want to go up and shake his hand." When
this gentleman was given an explanation of the way in which American performers are treated, he thoughtfully said, "So that's why
they assassinated President Kennedy". He felt the same appreciation of a fine performer as anyone might, but his reaction was
completely different.

The varieties of involvement of an individual in performance
may differ radically from those found in Western society, with its
segregation of performer and audience. In Malta, the word, _dilet-_
tante, is used to describe both those who sing and those who love
to listen to music. It is easy to slide from one "status" to another; the ranks of performers are drawn more easily from the ranks
of listeners. There are many occasions when individuals from the
audience are asked if they wish to sing; young children are toler-
ated in singing situations or occasions. Singers are noted for

their permissiveness; even women may sometimes join in singing if they so desire.

The point of view of the actual performer is again different from that of the individual who stands outside. He is in better command of the rules and regulations by which he performs and has a better grasp of where he stands within his musical milieu. In another respect, the performer has a narrower point of view; he is often compelled by an inner desire to perform.

Each individual has as his context for music a different point of view. Those who would study this phenomenon can learn much from speaking with introspective persons who are listeners, as well as those who are performers, of good music.

Some persons are taken unaware by musical forms they have never heard before. McLeod (in Herndon and Brunyate, 1976) reports a case in point of a woman weeping uncontrollably. She had come to the movies early in the afternoon and was unable to leave the theatre. She had to keep returning to the theatre to hear the beautiful music, but was then so compelled to cry that she rushed into the ladies' room and burst into sobs, and had been so reacting for five hours. She had never heard an opera before and had come upon the great beauty of Italian opera suddenly without preparation. The woman was a member of the lower class and had not been taught that it was proper to cry in a theatre.

Music is a powerful tug at human emotions. It would be foolish to ignore the fact that almost all listeners and almost all performers are compelled to do what they do by inner feelings too strong to ignore. This is dealing with passions and when passions are the subject of study, it is to the passionate that one must turn for information.

KINESICS

Mention has been made above of the Hungarian community and the division of the community by status and sex within the hall; these are examples of "kinesics", the way in which people move in order to demonstrate their position within a community. In the same way that other people display their roles and status by the way in which they move and hold their bodies, musicians, too, have revealing kinesic indicators.

McLeod mentions for Madagascar (1964) that musicians are allowed more extreme behavior than other members of the community because of their association with ritual danger. It is uncommon to see a Malagsy normally using completely open arm gestures; musicians, however, do so. Bear hugs are even common among Malagasy musicians.

In every community, some kind of special behavior marks the musician as such. White jazz musicians frequently are "night people" and have little or nothing to do with normal society, demonstrated both verbally and in kinesics. Jazz musicians frequently form barriers between themselves and the audience; they often wear sunglasses and refuse to look directly at their patrons. The back of the piano is placed toward the audience and the musicians huddle behind it; huge music stands are placed on the stage. All these gestures and manipulations of space indicate aversion, a fact which can be verified by the speech patterns of musicians, who use in-group dialects and who refer to their listeners with contempt and condescension.

Musicians throughout the world have their own ways of expressing themselves. Much of what they say with their bodies is a direct result of the kind of music they perform. Jazz, for instance, was regarded as evil in the early part of the century (c.f. Merriam, 1964). This caused people interested in performing jazz to take on the characteristics they believed to be associated with it -- i.e., difference from the ordinary.

Musicians know that the performing of music is a passion. Most of them also know that the public display of passion must be handled carefully and kept firmly under control. The way in which they move in order to do this is frequently an indication of the basic values which the music represents for the community. If nothing whatsoever was known about Western classical music, it could be guessed that it is an historical phenomenon from the fact that musicians on the stage wear clothing styles which went out of fashion twenty to fifty years ago, depending on the community. The tendency to play music by persons who are dead and revering them especially, is another part of the cycle of values which surrounds Western music.

Musicians, then, act out their parts. The blues singer who looks only at his guitar is clearly indicating that nothing is there by his guitar. The jazz musician who hides behind a music stand is saying that he is going to play another way, in spite of what people think about his music. The violinist who glorifies dead composers does so in clothing and with gestures from the past.

In some cases, musicians act their parts so well that the whole central meaning of a musical system may be acted out before the eyes of the observer. In Malta, one of the more heavily populated areas of the world, it is normal for people to have very small space envelopes around them. The Maltese live close to one another by choice as well as necessity. Crowds are intense; but musicians demand and receive an exceptionally wide space around them. Two musicians who are singing to each other may be found at either end of a long room, or with the barrier of a table between them. People back away from their bodies; they never look at one another. They look at the ceiling or play with matches or gloves, look down at their hand, or generally avoid eye contact.

What are they saying with these gestures? If one looks at the music, one finds that the variety of music being sung is the song duel of Malta in which two men attempt to cleverly insult one another in public. The fact that these are insult songs helps to explain the very wide space envelope and the aversion gestures so common to individuals singing this variety of music (for an example of this form in English, see Herndon and Brunyate, 1976).

The kinesics of musicians are frequently helpful in understanding the nature of the music created and sung, particularly if their body movements and gestures are compared with those of the general public. So fascinating is this study with so little done about it, that the authors wish to stress it as a field of study well worth investigating.

PERFORMANCE

The concept of the occasion mentioned above involves the performance of music in a context. This is an obvious concept, but one which moves away from simply emphasizing music per se. This concept differs slightly from that of music as "song in culture", in that there is a focus upon the moment of performance. But what is performance? How may the concept of performance be integrated in ways that are useful? How might it be distinguished from the concept of the occasion?

The first mention of this usage is that of Milton Singer when he speaks of the "cultural performance":

>..."cultural performances"...include what we in
>the West usually call by that name -- for example,
>plays, music concerts and lectures. But they also
>include prayers, ritual readings and recitations,
>rites and ceremonies, festivals and all those things
>which we usually classify under religion and ritual
>rather than with the "cultural" or artistic (1955:23).

For Singer, a cultural performance has a specified time limit with a beginning and an end, an organized program of activity, a set of performers, an audience, a place, and a pre-specified occasion for performance. Still focusing on the context in which music is performed (by using Singer's approach), those occasions would be included which are fairly tightly organized. Many occasions for the performing of music, such as singing a child to sleep with a lullaby, game playing, singing to one's self, cannot be included in this approach. Singer chooses the more tightly organized aspects of musical occasion to be singled out because these are generally isolatable segments of activity, believing that they demonstrate cultural encapsulation of basic ideas.

26

This accords well with the very definition of the term "performance". When a cultural performance takes place, elements of culture are presented to the carriers of that culture in highly symbolized forms, supposedly to demonstrate basic ideals and principles upon which society operates. As Herndon stated, "...he views cultural performances as isolatable segments of activity considered by a group of people to be encapsulations of their culture which they exhibit to visitors and themselves" (1971:339).

Singer's view is important in that it implies that highly formalized human behavior is a cultural focus and that it is probably symbolic and meaningful on several levels. It is a commonplace that public presentations are usually symbolic re-statements of some kind. The repetitiveness of art form implies that something is being told, whether words are involved or not. By including the concepts of ritual, rites and ceremonies, Singer extends the concept of performance into a social statement about mankind which is probably valid. The distinction between play and ritual is slight: both have role-playing, constuming, an order of performance, proper words which must be said in the proper sequence, et cetera. Play and ritual, both, involve standardized speech, behavior and, frequently, standardized settings.

This view looks at the occasion for music from the structural point of view, as does the concept of occasion. Abrahams (1976) has discussed performance in terms of social interactions, which is a difficult task. He has distinguished between performance and normal behavior on grounds similar to Singer's, but focuses on quality, rather than on time or setting.

The concept of social interaction implies that for a performance to occur, there must be more than one person involved, either in terms of two or more performers, or one performer with an audience. According to this conceptualization, performances may occur only on approved and accepted occasions; only certain members of the community will have license to perform; a framing device will be present to indicate that this is a different type of behavior; a repertoire of actual performance items must be slotted in which the requirement of the generic expectations involved will be fulfilled. Thus, for a performance to occur, there must be a coming-together of acknowledged performers, marked times, places, occasions and a repertoire. This is what Abrahams calls "pure" performance.

Like Singer, Abrahams' definition implies that for an activity to be a performance, there are strict patterns of expectations: more than one person, and a high level of stereotypic behavior on the part of performers and listeners alike. The stress is laid upon the "something special" about times and places when performances occur and the heavy formalization involved. Singer focuses on the facts of culture; Abrahams on the behavior of interacting individuals. Each of these concepts is complementary to the other, and, each has its place in the study of music.

27

Richard Bauman holds a similar view, stressing the more formalized aspects of behavior. "...the act of performance as situated behavior, situated within and rendered meaningful with reference to relevant contexts. Context is another way that performance is patterned in communities." Contexts, says Bauman, may be identified as a variety of levels. Religion, education and politics may be viewed from the perspective in which they do or do not represent contexts for performance within communities (1976:35).

Bauman goes on to clarify the concept of performance through a behavior term, "event" -- "a culturally-defined, bounded segment of the flow of behavior and experience that constitutes a meaningful context for action" (loc. cit.). He assumes that Singer's cultural performances are obligatory performances, whether organized for entertainment or some other purpose. He mentions other situations in which events are non-obligatory or optional, but not unexpected as the telling of jokes at a party. He also discusses ranges of events where performance is not a relevant variable -- not fully categorized within a culture.

This latter view is very helpful in that it distinguishes between types of performance. The authors would tend to accept this concept as similar to the concept of occasion in that whenever something musical happens, the investigator will observe it.

In the definitions of both Singer and Abrahams, the concept is too tight to include all the times and places when music can occur. More importantly, Abrahams' defintion omits all occasions in which there is only a single individual performing music. It would be impossible under his definition to discuss the famous American Indian example, the Vision Quest of the Plains Indians. Here, young boys isolate themselves for a number of days -- fasting and praying -- in order to receive power from the Guardian Spirits in the form of songs.

Abrahams would question whether the Vision Quest is a musical performance since no human audience is present, and no social interaction takes place. Singer might include the Vision Quest in the concept of cultural performance, even though the time and place are not well organized and the order of events may not be very clear. Baumann would undoubtedly include this as a performance of music. It would certainly be an occasion for music under the somewhat simplistic definition the authors present here.

For the authors, performance should not be tightly defined. Rather, it should include full consideration of all those moments in time in which music occurs. This is considered a necessary preliminary step to the understanding of the context of music. If one does not discuss all the contexts in which music occurs, one can hardly to a reasonable study of music in context.

How can performance be helpful in the study of ethnomusicology? Probably the major usefulness of this concept is to point out that music is highly patterned and is frequently found in contexts which are highly patterned. Thus, the concept of performance may be one of the focuses of the field. Since this emphasis is synchronic, the concept of performance is both a theoretical and descriptive device -- not of the broadest possible application -- but still useful. It stands in contrast to the concept of performance practice which implies only the study of music.

The study of performance includes both performance practice and its contexts. Performance is the most obvious of the synchronic, syntagmatic views of context. While students of the fine arts may content themselves with the study of manuscripts, ethnomusicologists must study performance of music, since that may be all there is in a community.

If one wishes to study the way in which music is used in a given society, the first test under this approach would be to determine the names of various types of occasions. Every society has not only names and genres for styles, but also named occasions for the performance of music.

Every musician can describe a normalized version of the setting in which music takes place, including the kinds of people who attend to listen, the kinds of people who will sing in different settings, the kinds of settings themselves, the limitations on those settings, et cetera. The presence of named occasions indicates that at least some degree of cultural formalization has already taken place. Once this is known, one may be asked to be taken to a named occasion and to observe that particular idiosyncratic set of events.

Subsequent study of similar examples of named occasions will produce a normalized statement which can be checked against particular occasions. One may consider the rigidity of repertoire, of personnel, of audience and of general behavior in a setting which is already formalized. This is the easiest way to approach the kind of music which only disturbs the air and other people's ears, but which has never been set down on paper.

Once these more highly formalized contexts have been understood, one may then move to the study of the less formal occasions on which music occurs. These will be more difficult to acquire since they usually occur intermittently and frequently in private. With some kind of approach already instilled into the music of a given culture, it is not difficult to find and to record those occasions on which music is less formal.

The authors' own experience in the study of these less formal occasions is that it is frequently necessary to make recordings of the music out of context, and while they have some reasonable record-

29

ings of children's songs for instance, the vast majority of their recordings are taken out of context. The same is true of nursery rhymes and lullabies.

The significance of the distinction between the highly organized and the less well organized, the public and the private performance, can be discovered in any society provided that a framework includes all the types available. This is the only reasonable view of an entire community of music. In the less formalized occasions for the performance of music will be included rehearsals, lessons or training sessions and practice. Each of these moments when music is performed has its own validity and will teach something new about the way in which music is created, presented, or conceptualized.

Thus, in the authors' view, the concept of occasion and its sub-set, that of performance, is a powerful organizing principle by which the vast majority of information about the nature of music, as such, can be gathered. It is a methodological frame into which music may be placed or from which music can be withdrawn for analysis. The interplay between the situation in which music occurs and the musical event itself, or, in Abraham's terms, between performance and performance items, is the study of form in performance.

As mentioned above in the case of Il-Bozen, the context (in this case, musical and textual) in which guitar improvisations take place in the song duel, dictates some of the melodic content of the improvisation. While this is on another level from the concept of performance, it is apparent how this approach illustrates the concept of "contexts within contexts".

CONCLUSION

This chapter has attempted to discuss music as a focus of study and context as a referent and locus of music. The concept of context has been emphasized as an interweaving of factors, one of which is music. The concept of context has led to an understanding of limitations as a way of viewing musical performances. Certain limitations has been mentioned, such as the physical, social, linguistic and cultural. The more specific situational limitations, such as the occasion and performance have been discussed. All of these approaches move away from the simple emphasis on music, per se, which, it is felt, has only minimal usefulness in the study of music.

It was popular some years ago to assume that the only meaning which music has lies in its form. This emphasis, clearly a result of the view of music as an isolated element, has proven to be less valid than was hoped. The contextual view may also prove to have its limitations; currently, however, the ideas presented here seem to have the most explanatory power of any which the authors have investigated.

All the ethnomusicologist has to work with is the moment in which a piece of music is performed. This is so because there usually is no score from which to work or no manuscript. All that exists for an ethnomusicologist is the performance. The more one knows about it, the better one will understand music.

THE LEARNING PROCESS, MYTH, AND KINESICS

This chapter deals with those aspects of culture which shape and surround the music itself. As a cultural expression and arbitrary pattern of sound, music must be learned by a human group. Learning occurs at many levels, taking a variety of forms. In the process of learning, performing, hearing music, much surrounding myth is created. Additionally, the playing of music, as mentioned before, requires movement which is frequently a sort of dance. This chaper will be concerned with some of the mental processes and aspects of context which relate to the learning process, myth and kinesics.

THE LEARNING PROCESS

The learning process is not a simple matter for it involves not only how performers and creators learn their respective crafts, but also how hearers learn. It is not restricted to the training of the young, but is a continual process which continues throughout an individual's lifetime. It is possible to consider learning as a process within the context of human awareness.

The learning process may be formal or informal, obligatory or voluntary, aural or non-aural. Whatever may be involved in the learning process in a particularistic sense, all learning at a given point in time is a consequence of the tonal preferences and the history of a particular group who is teaching the music. The learning process involves what anthropologists have called "enculturation". Enculturation, briefly, is a term which means the development, through the influence of members of a society, of patterns of behavior in children or outsiders that conform to the standards deemed appropriate by the culture. Enculturation or "socialization", as it is often called, incorporates all means of learning of behavioral patterns.

For the purposes of music, the term enculturation includes all forms of learning; all forms of acquisition of increasing awareness of musical behavior, musical appreciation and comprehension. Within this concept, one may point to more formalized methods of learning, such as schooling, which include all forms of intentional instruction, and education which includes instruction given by individuals recognized as specialists -- removed usually some distance from the student's home and located in a specifically named place. While all music learning involves enculturation, only some may involve schooling or education.

In acquiring competence in dealing with music, it is again necessary to distinguish between those who actively participate and those who do not. In both cases, the designations cited above apply. In some societies, musicians learn to play an instrument, dance, sing, or listen to a style of music through formal lessons; in others, the entire process is informal.

In Western society, it is common for an aspiring composer or performer to spend a number of years in formal student/teacher relationships. Western audiences are not always exposed to the formality of music appreciation classes and tend to acquire their taste informally. Some styles of Western music are performed by persons who have not received formal lessons, but it is probably safe to say that all Western musicians who perform in the so-called high art traditions (such as opera, symphony and ballet) have encountered formal lessons.

The music learning process may be obligatory or voluntary. If the acquisition of musical competence is obligatory, it is much more likely that the requisite aspect of the process will be directed toward the performers or composers than toward audiences. In Tikopia, it is necessary for chiefs to compose songs at certain periods of their life cycles, whether they are musically inclined or not. It is a matter of rank, birth, and status which dictates the obligatory assumption of musical competence to the point of being able to compose a song. It should be pointed out that if the chief is an inadequate composer, he will hire a "ghost writer" to perform the task for him.

Another type of obligatory learning process is involved with aspects of status alone, and may be best illustrated by the common practice of certain American middle class families who felt their children should be forced to learn to play the piano, despite protest from the children (and sometimes from their instructors). Some children learn to play a particular instrument, to dance, or to sing, as a voluntary act rather than an obligatory one.

There are probably as many ways to learn a musical style, instrument, or genre as there are people to learn them. It has been demonstrated by Suzuki and Alvin for the violin and the 'cello, respectively, that the enculturation of young children in music behavior is best done aurally. Both teachers train children of four or five years of age to play stringed instruments through a combination of carefully designed encouragements to "make a beautiful sound". Through a well-designed series of steps, emphasis is placed on the enjoyable achievement involved in making a tone sound good. Children begin immediately to play Western classical pieces, although difficulties are omitted at first. Students develop a consciousness of tone and pitch as well as an enjoyment of the process of making music. It might be said that, at least for young children, the aural method of instruction produces more rapid results.

33

Teaching by methods which are not aural, but usually written, can take place either with or without the presence of a teacher. It has long been the practice of aspiring Country and Western musicians to send for an instrument and instruction book. In the 1920's and 1930's, the Sears Roebuck catalogue was responsible for the fostering of much interest and learning throughout the United States.

It is necessary to distinguish between aural and oral means of learning. With many teachers throughout the world, some degree of verbalization of concepts or desired effects will be made to the student. These verbalizations are, of course, oral. In contrast, aural statements may include performances by a teacher, record, radio broadcasts, films, other mediums, or live performances. The aural experience may or may not have verbal cues or instruction accompanying it.

It would seem logical that the initial acquisition of musical competence by both hearers and performers should have received some scholarly attention, although this has not been the case. Until recently, little attention was placed upon children's acquisition of verbal or musical skill, and almost no attention was given to the development of children's motor abilities in order to know what areas of physical exertion might be helpful and which might be harmful at a given state of maturity. There has recently been an increase of scholarly interest in this area; but for music, such studies are so new as to be in process at the time of this writing.

In Malta, children learn their musical competence in an informal, voluntary, aural manner. Although there is some encouragement of male children whose fathers or uncles are well-known singers, children are not pressed to become musicians. Infants and young boys, as well as the occasional young girl, often accompany their older male relatives to the bars where singing takes place. The entire family hears traditional Maltese music on many occasions and is generally exposed to the Maltese song duel on an average of one to two hours a week. On their way to school, children often sing verses at one another which are sometimes insulting, and which approach the style of adults to a certain degree.

At other times, a mother may instruct her son to go to the roof of her house to sing an insulting verse or two at an offensive neighbor. Older children are encouraged, if they so desire, to sing with the adult males on certain occasions. If they prove to be good, they are given encouragement and advice regarding singing strategy and may take their place with the men as soon as they are capable. Guitarists, in contrast, often apprentice themselves during adolescence to a master guitarist in a more formal student/teacher relationship.

Children's songs, games and dances have received some attention, particularly in the literature of folklore. These genres have not been treated thoroughly with regard to aspects of the learning process. It is hoped that further work will be undertaken in this area.

HOW AUDIENCES LEARN

A distinction can be made between the learning process necessitated by being a member of the audience, or a hearer of music, and the acquisition of competence in the performance of music. Since the hearing of music is common to both performers and audience, if a layman were asked, "What is an audience?" the response would probably be one of incredulity. Yet, the nature of music as a process taking place through time and aiming at an audience, would seem to indicate that at least as much emphasis should be placed on the audience as is placed on the performer or the composer. An audience is the person or persons who hear the process through time of those aspects of patterned sound which is called music.

There are many types of audience; however, the basic distinction to be made involves the question of whether or not the audience is separate from the performers. Audience responses involve a range of obligatory and possible behaviors, whether the audience is isolated from the performers or not. In urban situations, it is necessary to consider the unique set of problems posed by the distant audience; for when sophisticated recording devices and broadcasting media make possible the hearing or viewing of performances separated in time and place from the actual origin of the sound, the audience is enlarged and diversified. It is an audience, nevertheless, and must be dealt with.

It is also necessary to consider the range of both actual and potential reactions of audiences to various genres of music. Some societies have music designed more as background than as actual sound events to be listened to carefully. A prime example of background music is to be found in Western society in the incessant droning of sound from "Muzak" and other commercial background music systems which inundate America. Background music is also a frequent accompaniment of dining or courtship. The idea of background music is certainly not a new one, nor is it confined to Western society.

Audiences tend to take their cues from particular contexts; their reactions are defined, delimited, and constrained by the nature of the occasion. Those who stray from approved audience behavior in a given context soon learn what behavior is appropriate.

This is particularly true of more formalized situations. The acute embarrassment of a neophyte concert-goer, applauding vigorously after the first movement of a string quartet and greeted by icy stares from all around the audience, is an intense and immediate learning experience. Anyone with the audacity or the lack of foresight to arrive improperly dressed or to behave improperly, will soon receive the negative sanction of other members of the audience and, in some instances, may find himself forcibly ejected from the premises of a musical event if his behavior is too improper. On a simply formalistic level, audience behavior is not usually formally learned, but is the product of the process of enculturation which takes place at the experiential level.

Audience reaction is based, in part, upon the degree of audience sophistication with regard to the particular type of performance which is taking place. With a large audience, it is to be expected that there will be a range of sophistication from untutored, disinterested individuals to a set of devoted admirers. These devotees may or may not possess a formal sophistication regarding the structure of music, or they may be so transported by their own expectations that they are unable to hear the actual sound. These factors must be taken into consideration in any evaluation of audience behavior, reaction, or conceptual relationships within a formal design framework.

HOW PERFORMERS AND CREATORS LEARN

As soon as the question of how performers and creators learn is considered, the concept of talent arises. Very little is known of talent outside the fine art traditions of Western Europe, India, Southeast Asia, China and Japan. Part of the lack of knowledge about the question of talent has probably arisen from the assumption that in those areas of the world lacking a fine art or high art music, "group performance" is the rule rather than the exception. A perusal of ethnomusicological studies will disprove this assumption at once; music requires certain special capabilities in every society, even the smallest.

The problem of the definition of talent is immense. This can best be brought home by a discussion of the "naturally talented" children in Western society. Many children learn music with an immediacy which is almost uncanny. Taken to church on a Sunday morning, they will listen to the hymns, return home and play them on the piano. For these children, there is an immediate relationship between hearing and reproducing sound. They learn so quickly that they do not have the patience to learn to play well; they simply learn to play.

The immediacy of transfer from hearing to performing is not only the imitation of a particular piece, but also the imitation of styles. Some youngsters can be asked to "play like Beethoven", "play like Wagner", or "play like Sweet Emma the Bell Girl", and they will be able to reproduce a style without necessarily reproducing a piece. The noted concert pianist, Sylvia Zaremba, adds another facet to this information. At about age thirteen, she had to re-learn her entire repertoire because she found she could no longer memorize in the same way as in the past. Her new method of memorization involved visually learning bits of music, rather than simply hearing it and reproducing it.

Two points of reference arise here. First, it may be that there is a dysfunctional relationship between certain types of musical "talent" and normal teaching procedures. Second, there may be a shift in learning method at some point in adolescence; it could be postulated that our society loses many of its talented youngsters through one or another of these experiences. This would imply that each culture chooses from its pool of talented youngsters those who can learn within its precepts and ignores those who cannot.

Western society offers two choices regarding musical expression. The fine art tradition stresses the written musical score and a highly involved teaching method which is progressive in nature. In the popular music field, however, those who have more aural than visual perception listen to recordings hour after hour until they have caught the style they choose to play. They then build upon their knowledge through performance, either alone or in small groups. If this is the case, then, the visually-oriented would tend more toward the fine arts, while the aurally-oriented individual would tend more toward popular music.

All of this makes the assumption that there is such a thing as talent. The question of talent, however, must remain moot. Each culture expresses certain qualities which it prefers its musicians to have. Those within the society who live up to those qualities or who possess them may be called "talented". Those who do not, do not become musicians. Cultural ideals are interposed between the individual and the music.

An example from Malta will illustrate this well. In order to become a singer of the style called spirtu pront, or song duel, an individual must have the following qualities, according to the singers: cunning, genius, drive, courage and self-discipline. Of these, the most important is genius for without it, none of the others matter. The genius in question is the ability to improvise verses within the space of 20 seconds, which will follow the complex maze of rules proscribed upon linguistic texts. It is convenient if the man who chooses to sing spirtu pront can sing soprano, the primary criterion for a beautiful voice. If he cannot, but yet has the mind to create beautifully shaped verses within the rules and regulations of the style, he is still regarded as a good singer.

One of the major criteria for musical talent in Malta is poetic ability of a highly refined and complex sort. In this way, the culture interposes itself between musical "talent" and the fi-

37

nal product by shaping the music in the fashion it desires.

HOW PERFORMERS LEARN

There are several methods of learning presently in use throughout the world. The validity of each method depends partly upon the musical style being learned, its complexity and the amount of improvisation involved within it. The commonest type is teaching by example. Here, beginning performers learn by listening to a teacher playing at full speed. This is the method of teaching the valiha or tube zither of Madagascar. The implication of such a method is that an individual has already learned something about the music and its instrumentation before he begins.

Among the Merina, musicians frequently make instruments; young persons wishing to learn will often sit with them in the marketplace, playing one valiha after another. When business grows slack, the teacher will pick up an instrument and play, saying little or nothing; the student imitating whatever has been played for him. Young men can spend several hours a day at this engaging trade and, after some time, they become quite proficient, branching out on their own and trying new songs. This teaching method is more frequently found with the study of instruments and in areas where set pieces are the norm.

Another variety of learning procedure is that which might be called teaching by metaphor. Certain movements which are necessary to the creation of the proper sound seemingly cannot be taught directly. Verbalizing them will cause the individual student to tighten the very muscles he is supposed to loosen, and loosen those he is supposed to tighten. For this reason, some singing teachers in the United States instruct a student to imagine a hole between his eyes and to conceive of the sound of his voice as a fountain of water flowing out of the hole. A young singer might be told to hold his mouth as if he had a pear in it.

One 'cellist in the United States teaches entirely by metaphor. He asks the student to imagine that he is riding a motorcycle instead of playing a 'cello, or chopping wood, or sawing logs, or that he is a piston engine. Singers who are told to imagine that the sound is actually coming not from their mouths, but from a space approximately one foot directly above their heads are dealing with a concept which is half myth and half metaphor. Many metaphorical statements merge into mythical ones.

There are two ways in which one may use such statements. Either the teacher has found through experience that directing a student's attention to the musculature involved will cause him to do the wrong thing or, a decision has been taken that teaching is

38

a mystical statement. This implies that it is impossible to teach anyone directly because the learning process involves such qualities as "talent" and the approach to divinity. This more mystical attitude, while useful in the understanding of great talent, probably has its roots in the culture.

Another common method throughout the world is teaching by rote. In this method, with or without the use of a notational system, students are asked to play something which might be called non-music, such as the Dastgah exercises of Persia or the scale patterns taught to classical music students in the European tradition. Here, what is learned and memorized is pre-music -- a series of study devices -- meaningless, musically, but they produce flexibility. Once learned, they are frequently used to warm the hands or voice before performing. The method of learning by rote is often exceedingly boring to the student, and seems to work better with older students than with younger ones. Older students can understand why they must go through these physical exercises such as lying on the floor and allowing someone to stand on one's stomach, lifting weights, jogging, or doing some other physical exercises which seem totally un-musical.

An extremely common teaching method throughout the world is what Europeans and Americans call "coaching". In this style of teaching, an assumption is made that the individual already knows a piece of music fairly well. The business of the teacher is to comment on nuances, rather than basic design.

Hours of discussion are spent over nuances in Maltese singing. The proper way of approaching a subject is hashed over afterwards and, if the singer is an apprentice, his teacher usually talks about the lofty ideals of singing, the responsibilities of genius and the beauty of proper expression. In this way, young men learn not only what is an acceptable verse, but what is an exceptional one. Famous verses of other singers are remembered for many years and often quoted as examples of the fine turning of a phrase. In American society, coaching is reserved for that period in time when a piece has been thoroughly learned but requires finishing touches.

Many styles involve learning without a teacher. Many individuals do their learning through listening to live music, radio, records of film music. The desire to learn may be so great that the individual who is isolated from established learning by one situation or another will turn to this method. Jazz musicians frequently learn their styles from intensive listening as teenagers. Shamans among the Kutenai have a body of liturgical songs which they must learn to perform properly. As there are no teachers, they must simply go from one shaman to another, learning their trade. The authors recently watched a young banjo player teach himself. He sold flowers on the same street corner all day, every day, performing on the banjo as he waited for customers. As the year progressed, he grew more and more accomplished.

Finally, mention must be made of learning with a supernatural teacher. This is, of course, a metaphor of some kind. Among the Central and Southern Sakalava and Vezo of Madagascar, the salegy or case zither is believed to be the instrument of the dead. Dead persons, especially nobility, are said to desire to hear or to play the salegy. An individual may find himself seized with the desire to learn to play and is thought to be possessed by the spirit of a dead nobleman who wishes to perform. All salegy players agree that their teacher was the dead individual who possessed them and made their fingers move upon the strings. The burden of this type of performance is that the individual may be asked to play at any time, for anyone who is seized with the desire to hear salegy playing is also possessed by the spirit of the dead.

The most prominent example of learning from a supernatural teacher is the Vision Quest of the Plains Indians of North America. Young men who venture on the Vision Quest expect to see the manitou of a particular animal who will give them special powers, including songs. Isolated from the rest of their culture, hungry, often thirsty, frequently tired, these young men experience visions in which animals come to them and teach them songs said to have specific powers. They are taught more than the songs; they are given the meanings behind the songs and taught how to apply them to specific situations. Deer, for example, is the spirit of the great hunters. Special songs are believed to have the power to draw game, if sung in the proper context and performed in the right manner.

Another slightly more complex form of learning from the supernatural is the situation found among the Cherokee, where music has a special power. Life situations are countered among the Cherokee by the use of ritual formulae; any formulae can be thought, whispered, spoken, or sung. Singing is the most powerful use. Those who perform ritual formulae say that there is a particular kind of singing which is correct or proper, called the "straight voice". A song sung with the "straight voice" is one in which the quality of the voice carries directly to the spirit for whom it is intended. This is obviously a metaphor and not a comment on voice type; but "correct" singing is verified at least partly by the results, for if the correct results occur, then through time, the specialist learns which performance technique is regarded as correct by the spirits.

As can be seen above, music is learned by a number of different methods. It should also be apparent that the statements about learning are, in fact, cultural statements about music and not statements about learning. The method a culture chooses to pass on its musical traditions is predicated as much on cultural beliefs as upon musical exigency. This is undoubtedly one of the most difficult aspects for the understanding of the acquisition of musical techniques, since two levels of understanding are dealt with within the same conceptual package.

What does a Cherokee diviner mean when he says he has a "straight voice"? Do the Sakalava really learn to play the sa-legy from the spirits of the dead or do they learn the style from listening to other salegy players? Are we cheating certain of our talented young people through our teaching method and its visual implications?

All of these aspects of the questions of both teaching and learning move to the heart of the problem of ethnomusicology: the variety of human experience. Without multiple examples of learning procedures, understanding of the process will not soon be a-chieved. Each example, however, is rife with cultural implications and the ultimate necessity will be to extract from all these learning procedures the principles which will apply to the process itself, if that is possible. As yet, the study of learning techniques is in its infancy. This is an area which is well worth stressing for future students in the field.

HOW COMPOSERS LEARN

In many societies, the composer is not different from the performer. This is particularly true in those societies where im-provised music is more frequently found. There are numerous cases, however, where the composer is not always his own performer or where not all performers are composers.

In Tikopia, the composer is known as the purotu, or "expert". This is an individual who has been creating new songs of his own volition and whose songs have been judged to be good. Such indi-viduals are frequently called upon to create new songs for speci-al occasions, such as a district or clan feasinga, or anga feast for a privilege ceremonial. After consideration of the song to be created, the individual will ask for a rehearsal and will teach the singers the new song by the agonizing process of slowly re-peating each syllable, with the singers following after him until they have caught both words and music. These practice sessions last for several hours; at the end of which time, the song is up to speed and the dancers are beginning to move to it. Thus, even in the simplest community, specialized composers are to be found.

This is an important point. Once again, the myth that "prim-itive" peoples have simpler music and simpler forms of composi-tion, performance and audience response than our own, is open to question. Throughout the world, composers exist at all levels. In some societies, they are named and their talents proclaimed. In others, each individual is a composer if he is a performer and no one repeats what he has done. In yet others, composers are in-novators of new styles rather than of set pieces. This is true of guitar music in Malta where each piece is an improvised entity, but where three styles of guitar playing have developed in the present century, each due to a different man who is known as the father of the style. His innovations have been accepted; he cannot be personally imitated since the music is improvised; but his style can be copied.

The subject of composers is much more complex on a certain level than that of performers since it implies something which may or not be true, elsewhere. The concept of the creator of music is one of the most difficult to handle well. Again, cultural impositions make it difficult to discuss composers as a whole. In some societies, such as the Hopi, no new compositions have been produced for some time. The liturgical repertoire is set (Black, personal communication). In others, the dead, or spirits of the gods themselves, are the composers.

In societies where improvised music is the norm, creativity is the realm of the performer. As Herzog has put it: "For us, it is an obvious matter to think of a piece of music apart from its performance; for a traditional singer, it is just as obvious that there is little, if any, existence to a song apart from its performance." He states that the creative process precedes in time the performance which "merely reproduces" what has been fixed into a form. There is room for individual creation in traditional music, he says, but that the creative process consists mostly of re-creating and re-molding the music as it is being performed (Herzog, 1965:174).

This re-molding process is an example of what folklorists regard as versions. There is no actual tale or narrative; rather, there are versions from which an ideal can be drawn.

This is also true of music. Who, then, is the composer? While one person may have created a particular piece of music initially, each performer or set of performers frequently changes it in process. In these terms, they are adding to or subtracting from the initial plan. Thus, it is not the isolated composer who, like the Tikopia purotu (a specialist), creates his music beforehand, but rather that whole range of persons who have to do with the process called "creativity" and who, whether called composers or performers, are part of the creative process in music.

This view immediately creates a composite model of the nature of creativity which is very different from the usual Eruo-American view. The question is: What is creativity in man?

It is to be distinguished from discovery in that a discovery is the verbalization or revelation of something which is already there, such as gravity. The term, creativity, is usually reserved for those instances where man has taken upon himself the task of bringing something entirely new into the world. In these terms, the harnessing of fire by early man was not a creative act, but the cutting of certain stones to form tools was. The use of the principles of cross-breeding to produce different coat colors in

42

horses is a discovery. Taken in this meaning, there have been few truly creative acts.

In these terms, is the "creation" of music a "creative" act? It occurs frequently and does not involve bringing something new into the world, so it is not "creative"; neither has it yet been demonstrated that music involves a discovery of natural principles. Another term, innovation, is reserved for this. The distinction between creation and innovation is that, while a creative act produces or manifests something totally new, an innovative one works within a set model to produce a variant of something already in existence. Thus, anyone who writes within the sonata form is producing or innovating another sonata within the same style.

In the same way, a person who makes a pot of soup, writes a sonnet, or composes a political speech is putting together items or ideas within a context of traditional form to produce a variant example of that form. The techniques in a particular form are probably similar; the individual item was created within a cultural style.

In music, this is most easily seen in improvised music; it must be extended cognitively to include other styles. Whether there are set pieces or improvisation, there are limits as to what new material is acceptable or expected. Items which fall outside the limits of style do not generally tend to be repeated; through loss of currency within a musical tradition, they are lost entirely.

Once again, the authors are maintaining that culture is the basic limiting context for music. Culture sets the following limitations upon music. First, basic trends represent types of music which are found to be acceptable within the framework of culture. Those items of performance which do not conform sufficiently to the basic trends usually are not repeated, and thus do not influence future events.

Second, the culture determines who may be a creator or innovator of music, whether tightly or loosely fashioned. At one point in history, it was acceptable for members of the Western upper class to indulge in the writing of music. In more recent times, however, very few upper class Europeans find this an acceptable mode of existence. In more traditional societies, the performance of music and the creation or the innovation of new elements within the style, have been tightly controlled by such devices as the restriction of music to particular lineages, clans, political groups or particular economic strata.

Third, cultural limitations are placed upon those creations which will survive. Ritualized music tends to last longer than secular; partly because certain pieces of music or styles of performance are designated as proper to given, highly structured moments of time and place. More secularized items may fall into complete disuse in the same time period by being replaced by either other examples of the same style or, other styles.

Fourth and finally, one who creates music will probably never be completely free, for his position in society is usually determined. His status forces him into certain poses which cannot be avoided without the danger of rejection from within the musical performing group. For example, when the improvisations of Indri Brincat, the foremost Maltese guitarist, became too abstruse and complex for his musical participants, he noted less participation on his part in musical performances at a time when guitarists were at a premium. Complaints about his playing being non-traditional finally led him to the decision that he must revert to less daring improvisations as long as he continued to play in groups.

Thus, composers, too, learn their place within society and the limitations within which they may innovate; the styles within which they will be allowed to produce acceptable versions. Pressures are placed on all of the aspects of music -- listening, performing and composing. Because of the overwhelming influence of culture as context, almost no musical items can be said to be completely new or different.

FICTIVE STATEMENTS ABOUT MUSIC

Since music operates within the context of culture, a number of statements must be made which are presumptive of conformity to cultural ideals. In the broadest sense, it is these presumptive statements and their patterned results which are studied by ethnomusicogists. Many of these statements may be regarded as pure fiction; others, as superstition. Still others take the form of pure myths, being long narrative tales in which support for present action is placed into supernatural realms.

This collection of information is called fictive statements in order to include a number of different kinds of material, which, on the surface, may seem to have little or nothing to do with one another. They all represent accepted ways of governing the process of musical expression within standard lines. Such items may be of several orders, depending upon the type of music and upon the nature of a particular cultural set of beliefs about music. In essence, these are beliefs which may or may not be acted upon, but which will have wide influence on performers, composers and listeners.

Most types of statements are negative validations of some kind and represent limiting factors; thus, they are the statement of context, ranging from simple terms of conversation to full stories. Primarily, they are statements involved in the learning of roles and then, of re-creating an ascribed status or achieving a new status called musician. They are reflective of other contexts, the primary one being culture, itself.

The type of myth involved depends entirely upon the context of the music. For example, the Vision Quest seeks to acquire music as power. For the Cherokee, the singing of ritual chants adds special power to them; the context in which music is performed is that of spiritual or supernatural power. The purpose is to call spirits to the aid of man in the performance of certain duties which places a real proscription upon both those who sing and those who hear. The status invovled is not so much that of musician, as of holder of spiritual power.

The role of musician involves several concomitants. The broadest is that of relationship of the musician to the society in which he lives. This is frequently explained in semi-musical statements; i.e., it is still common in New Orleans for jazz musicians to believe that the performance of any variety of secular music, and particularly jazz, invites eternal damnation. Jazz musicians are frequently shunned by good church-going people outside the context of musical performances; preachers denounce jazz from the pulpit, calling it the work of the Devil.

The Devil is unusually active in this syndrome because of the general association of Satan with stringed instruments and, particularly, with the guitar. Jazz performers still declare that it is the Devil which tempts them to play the guitar. This old European myth, taken from the older assumption that it is the Devil who teaches the violin, has marked jazz musicians in New Orleans as "different" from the average individual.

In a related semi-musical statement, both authors were told that musically talented young Southern ladies should not be trained to become professional musicians; their training should allow them to play the piano or sing only for company on Sunday afternoons or at teas. While many adventuresome and forthright young Southern ladies have calmly ignored this cultural proscription, it is, nevertheless, an old one.

There has long been an association in the minds of Eruopeans between the need to acquire knowledge of the fine arts and something called sophistication or "culture". The educated young man or woman should be able to recognize Beethoven or Reubens, converse intelligently about the books of Meredith, know a smattering of philosophy; but it is not their place in life to write music, paint pictures, or write books. Any member of the upper class must take the fine arts lightly, and young Southern ladies are no exception. Musical accomplishment is perfectly correct; musical professionalism is not.

The relative status of a professional musician within the profession, especially that of a soloist, is predicated on other fictive statements. For Americans before World War II, there was the fictive statement of "arrival". The opera singer or concert artist of American descent who did not go to Europe on a tour was not considered to have "arrived", although this phenomenon seems to have broken down somewhat. Grace Brumbry, however, was ignored until she had visited European opera theatres. After this, her invitation to sing at the Kennedy White House assured her American career.

Similarly, to some Americans, an opera singer is not regarded as having "arrived" until he or she has sung at the Metropolitan Opera House. The best example of recent years is Beverly Sills who was not invited to sing at the Metropolitan until late in her career and only came into national prominence with the publicity surrounding her late Metropolitan "debut".

Role and status are supported and controlled by fictive statements about the nature of "proper" behavior, "professional" achievement and general life condition. Musicians throughout the world are forced into roles which relate to their status as musicians.

In Malta, in order to be a musician, one must not only be a genius, but also must bear the stigma of a fighter. It is assumed by those who do not sing that all singers, regardless of their singing style, are irascible fighting men. So firmly is this believed that bars must get a license from the police for singing performances, must stop all singing at 11 o'clock in the evening and are patrolled by the police for that time period.

This is undoubtedly the reflection of the spirtu pront, (mentioned before) in which two men attempt to insult one another so cleverly that each is not offended by the insults. The proverbial and metaphorical statements used in such singing are of such value that it is a literary exercise rather than a pugilistic one. Nevertheless, singers are regarded as having bad tempers and he who would sing must bear the stigma.

The fictive statements concerning music may involve the questions of ownership or rights to music. This is an area where a clear-headed examination of the facts is necessary, since one believes so firmly in the fictive statements concerning music. Music is essentially ephemeral. It is performed; it disturbs the air and dies away. Attempts to put it into notation give only a partial imitation of what actually happens within a performance.

So, the question of the ownership of a song or of right to sing, specified under law or custom, becomes difficult to enforce. According to American ASCAP rules, anyone performing a song copyrighted by a particular composer must pay him or her a fee for the privilege. In fact, it is impossible to completely monitor the

46

singing of music in American society or any other.

In some societies, ownership is regarded as absolute and supported by supernatural sanctions. Among certain Plains Indian tribes, only one man may sing a particular song and is generally the person who has received it during his Vision Quest from a spirit. In some cases, however, such songs may be transferred to others through inheritance; but supernatural sanctions occur when a song is sung by someone to whom it does not belong. This contrasts with the situation among the Merina of Madagascar, who have songs which are in the public domain. Anyone may sing them at any time. In Tikopia, music is recognized by special titles, but once a song is launched, anyone may change it.

In Malta, songs called _fatt_ are individually created by singers of that style. Such songs are usually long, running sixty verses or more and requiring about half an hour to perform. The words are sometimes published in broadside sheets and sold on the streets although theoretically, only the composer, himself, should sing the song. If it is popular, however, others may choose to sing it as well.

During their first field investigation in Malta, the authors heard a somewhat changed version of a well-known song by the _fatt_ composer, Joseph Fenech. Upon query about what should have been done, he said he did not know his song had been revised by a younger singer; that such action was all right, but that the young man should have acknowledged him as the original author and asked his permission as a matter of courtesy.

Here are a number of examples of different ideas about ownership of music -- all supported either by supernatural sanctions or simple recognition. Some societies mention the name of the composer; some do not. In each case, there are statements about what should have been done concerning ownership.

Rights are similarly differentiated from one society to another and the right to perform a piece of music varies widely. Among the Plains Indians and among the Kwakiutl of the Northwest Coast, no one has the right to perform a song except the owner or inheritor. The Kwakiutl owner has absolute right to perform the song, although he may choose to give it away in a potlatch. The right to perform songs is similarly controlled in our own society, through the fiction of copyright; as mentioned above, a fee should be paid if a song is to be performed.

In some cases, the right to perform a particular piece of music is controled by religious sanctions wherein certain religious music is only performable by priests or shamans. The revolt of Martin Luther was a shocking shift in cultural emphasis, with one of its most potent revelations the thought that lay persons might have free access to the Bible and sing hymns. Catholics were similarly outraged by the idea of the Black Mass, in which the Mass is performed backwards. The right to perform may be controlled by fictive statements as well and, in the Inquisition, such statements were backed up by negative sanctions.

The use of time and place as limiting factors upon the performance of music might also be included in the concept of fictive statements. Certain types of song are performed only in seasonal feasts, festivals in their proper position or at piacular moments. The concept of proper time and place for the performance of particular pieces of music is frequently backed by true myth, as in the case of religious ritual.

In the Work of the Gods of Tikopia, ownership, privilege of performance and proper time of performance are all tightly controlled. Many songs have accompanying myths indicating why they are sung in their present position in rites. At the other end of the scale, secular music in Tikopia is similarly controlled as to time and place, but by more prosaic means. In the evening mako, or dance, when young people get together for a pleasant evening of entertainment and recreation, songs called tauangutu and feuku are sung only after all married people have left the grounds. As these songs are of a derisive sexual nature, it is felt improper to sing them before one's mother's family or in-laws. As this includes only married people in this instance, the implication is that the young wait until authoritarian figures have left the field before using dirty words.

There are a great number of fictive statements concerning performance. These are usually taught either by a specific teacher or, in ritual circumstances, by fictive statements which support the assumption of rightness or properness for particular styles. For Western cultures, the minor mode is usually regarded as proper to sad music; for Arabic cultures, the reverse is the case. Therefore, certain associations grow up between musical style or type of mode and type of feelings. This is the broadest possible context for such fictive statements.

Others which will seem familiar are, "You cannot play the Bach Unaccompanied Suites in public until you have practiced them for at least six years". These Unaccompanied Suites for 'cello are not, for the most part, sufficiently difficult to require six years of practice, yet young 'cellists are frequently told that these simple pieces are difficult, so that as a result, they have great trouble interpreting them properly. Here is a case in which a fictive statement has been introduced to change behavior in that what was easy has become difficult.

In certain popular music circles, it is felt appropriate to say that one cannot play particular kinds of music well "unless one is stoned". As a result, aspiring musicians frequently feel that they must smoke marijuana or take stronger drugs for musical inspiration; however, the source for this fictive statement may well be that particularly able musical innovators have so many de-

mands for performance that they have had to resort to drugs in order to continue to meet continual concert or recording pressures.
Whatever the source of this statement, this approach clearly
changes behavior.

Although the locus and intensity of fictive statements vary
widely, depending on the society or sub-group being investigated,
it is of considerable value to the researcher. Proscriptive
statements of this variety tend to indicate more clearly than do
instructional procedures how one is to approach a particular style.

Perhaps the most interesting area in which fictive statements
are used has to do with instruments. As King has mentioned (1976),
musical instruments are not only objects, but also cultural objects, which live a life of their own. For example, European
stringed instruments have many of the characteristics of human beings: they have necks, heads, bellies, backs and ribs. They are
said to live and die and to have the need to breathe in humid wea-
ther. They are believed to be able to catch cold -- probably a
reference to a shift in tone color. Older instruments are described as getting tired. Certain instruments made by the Amati
family, for instance, are now regarded as "too tired" to be played
in public.

The French violin maker, Villaume, attempted to improve the
tone of his instruments by carving out a thinner space inside the
belly (some storytellers say that he carved the thinner portion on
the cheeks of the instruments, i.e., that portion above the f-holes
on the front) in order to make them more responsive. All of these
instruments are said to sound beautifully, but to tire quickly so
that after half an hour, the sound is gone.

Fictive statements of this kind concerning musical instruments occur in almost all societies, whether the instruments are
used for sacred or secular purposes. The individuality of sound
of particular instruments, the peculiarities of the wood or metal
used excite comment. Such comments tend to fall into categories,
although they will vary from culture to culture. While Europeans
seem to believe that their instruments are partially alive and
partially human, other societies may have a different concept.
These are metaphorical statements, but the fact that they fall into
a pattern indicates an underlying basic belief system. These are
more than simply metaphors; they represent an attempt to make an
object into a cultural object with qualities ascribed to it according to whatever principle is at work in the society in question.

Ownership of instruments is often an easy way to understand
the fictive statements about them. In Western society, rare
stringed instruments are not regarded as owned; they are historical
objects, on loan for the lifetime of the performer. This concept
places some distance between the performer and the instrument upon
which he performs and gives him a certain level of respect for it.
Musicians would tend to agree that it is difficult to own an in-

49

strument created before they were born, which will undoubtedly be in use after they are dead. The sense of continuity is given reality by the fictive statement.

In spite of the fact that they are bought and paid for, some instruments can never be truly owned. The sacred drums of the Buganda are the property of the king, or, more properly, of kingship, for the drum-makers and their performers are employed by the king. The drums, themselves, are regarded as sacred and have their own house in which to live. Among the Betsileo, tube zithers are highly personalized objects. In order to make them perform better, they are covered with amulets of various kinds to insure that he who plays upon them will be adept. Such instruments do not pass from hand to hand. They are not for sale; each musician must make his own. Old instruments belonging to someone now dead are regarded as having lost interest in the world, themselves. They, too, are semi-human after the death of the owner.

In some societies, the right to own and play an instrument is determined by desire, as in Western society and among the Central Sakalava. In others, musical instruments are a mark of the distinction between one style and another in the sense that only those who have the right to perform a particular style may own the requisite instrument and play it. Instruments frequently partake of the basic ethos that lies behind the style.

Among the Bara of Madagascar, the musical bow is an instrument devoted to magic, used to accompany songs by which the singer tries to force new patterns of activity on the world about him. When a man is drafted into the Army against his wishes, for instance, he visits the desert with a musical bow, playing and singing the same song repeatedly. The words of the song are designed to stop him from being drafted. Or, a Bara being forced into marriage may sneak off into the desert with his musical bow, trying to forestall the marriage. The bow is believed to bear the message to friendly spirits who will hear one's plea and correct the situation. While musical bows are easy enough to make, their association with magic precludes their being used for anything else.

The viol, on the other hand, is the primary instrument associated with bilo, that variety of possession in which an individual is either made sick by evil spirits or is forced to dance by them. Once the condition has been diagnosed, viol players are called and asked to play for the sick person until the spirit has been driven out of the body, either by recovery or through exaggerated dancing. The music of the viol and its association with bilo means that the instrument, itself, is a restricted object and cannot be used for the singing of love songs, minor magic or sagas.

The pattern of relationship between musical instruments and cultural ethos is also found in the concept of "breaking in". New instruments in Western society are believed to be inadequate to their task. It is said, for instance, that it requires fifteen years of playing to "break in" a Steinway grand piano. Stringed instruments are regarded as similarly unresponsive; during the first ten to twelve years of their effective life, their tone quality is considered faulty. This is the motive which lay behind Villaume's attempt to create an instrument with thinner cheeks, for he was attempting to reduce the breaking-in time. This concept fits in well with the idea that no individual owns an instrument. Fifteen years is a long time in the life of a professional performer; to waste it on a new instrument is regarded as criminal.

It is interesting to note that only expensive instruments of our culture are regarded in this way -- a new flute, costing less than $1,000, is regarded as playable at once. The idea that extremely expensive instruments, such as grand pianos and stringed instruments, must be broken in and are therefore not worth making, is parallel to the present trend in Euro-America where the manufacture of fine instruments is declining. Given the present conditions in which a fine Stradivarius 'cello would now cost upwards of a quarter of a million dollars, one would think that players would be glad to have modern instruments. Whether this is the final playing out of the myth that no one owns an instrument or a simple rationalization for the end of an era is not known.

These few examples of the nature of fictive statements about music-learning, ownership, performance and instruments are exceedingly tentative, partly because this material is not well investigated throughout the world. However, there is enough information available to indicate that a wide range of statements about the nature of music and the proscriptions placed upon both instruments and performers exist.

What is significant about these statements is that they seem to be patterned in some way. It can be estimated that such statements represent some kind of basic ethos about music which is culturally defined and maintained. To know more about music, the recovery of such statements and their organization into the basic patterns is an area of investigation which might prove extremely fruitful. At this point in time, this is no more than a suggestion; but like all aspects of music study, it will take on a life of its own if those interested in studying music care to pursue it.

KINESICS

In previous sections, items of learning have been discussed which are perhaps more basic to correct performance than is kinesics, the study of physical movement. Some physical movements are clearly related to the task of the performing of music, taught in fairly prosaic ways, having no undue verbal or metaphorical implications. Others are not; they seem mainly to be the end result of what might be called virtuostic embellishment.

Whatever the case may be, musicians generally move differently than other human beings, thus producing a visible impression
for the observer. Musicians kinetically mark their social difference by physical movements, some of which is explicable by the requirements of the instrument they play; some are not.

This impression of virtuoso embellishment has been noted before by ethnographers working in other areas, particularly religion. In speaking of Polynesian religion, Lowie notes:

> ...We must not be hypnotized by the high-sounding
> concoctions of the native priests. These were
> specialists, and like all specialists, tended to
> become virtuosos, who ostentatiously exhibited
> their skill in handling and amplifying traditional
> lore. A favorite device of theirs was to picture
> the gradual unfolding of the world in successive
> generations marked by distinct entities...Whether
> we regard this as profound wisdom or pretentious
> and meaningless verbiage, will depend on our
> metaphysical taste. But no one can seriously
> believe that anyone, the priesthood included,
> turned to such phraseology for a solution of life's
> problems (1947:304-305).

While some Polynesian specialists may cavil at Lowie's implication here, he has stated fairly well a major characteristic of
all specialists: one of their tasks is to embroider upon basic
designs.

While the playing of music obviously requires movement, there
is no real need for that movement to be as stylized as it is; nor
does playing the role of musician need be as stylized. The fact
that embellishments of behavior of this kind exist are interesting
and sometimes useful.

What a musician does with his body might be described as a
kind of dance. In the context of highly formalized behavior called music, musicians also formalize other aspects of their behavior.
There is a wide range of possibility here; for example, brass sections in orchestras frequently use mutes which come in two varieties, wooden or metal. One way of formalizing non-musical behavi-
or is for the section leader or conductor to insist that all mutes
in the section be made of the same material, be it wood or aluminum. As King has put it:

> ...When you formalize, what you are in effect saying
> for the audience, or the participation of the
> audience, is "this is our specialty, this is something
> that we do, and we are showing you this." In other
> words, "these are things that you do not find time to
> learn, or you do not have the circumstances to learn
> in our culture, so we will formalize this and show it

52

to you"...I think that when you get to the point
of performance there is formalization because the
specialist -- who is the musical performer or the
group of performers -- is signaling the whole
audience that this is the way we communicate to
you what we do and what you don't do (1976:231-232).

King is indicating a spillover from the formalization of music to the formalization of the behavior surrounding music. Herndon calls this dancing:

...I've dispassionately watched a pianist dancing
over a piano, or a 'cellist dancing over a 'cello
with a special kind of ferocity which is totally
unnecessary to technically performing a piece of
music. It is stagecraft (op. cit.:232-233).

Some varieties of stagecraft of this kind are stylized and conscious. When violinists bow together in ensembles, when brass sections all use the same kind of mute, when performers must all dress in the same kind of costume, one is dealing with conscious stagecraft.

Among the Betsileo all players of rija (a variety of minstrelsy) wear sunglasses and berets. They consciously attempt to undermine class behavior by placing audiences in the position where persons of higher class must lower their heads below those of lower class in order to listen carefully to their music. They do this, generally, by scooting up to a wall of a bandstand instead of playing in an open space so that persons in the first row, usually of higher class, must therefore lean down if they wish to see them. The rija player thus deliberately attempts to produce negative behavior on the part of the audience.

Jazz musicians may well be conscious of their aversion to contact with the audience, as mentioned earlier. In New Orleans at The Famous Door, the stage is actually inside the bartender's area; the bar is U-shaped with the musicians' raised stage behind the bar. The performers, all white, wear sunglasses or look at the ceiling in order to avoid eye contact with the audience.

A vast contrast is available just a half-block away at Preservation Hall, the major arena for old-time jazz in New Orleans, where the vast majority of the performers are black and over 60 years of age. In this hall there is no stage; performers are on the same floor level as the audience without a protective rail or any other device. When the chairs have been filled, the audience members sit on cushions directly in front of the musicians. Under normal performance circumstances, jazz is played here without any barrier between audience and performer, with the audience so close that those in the first rows can smell the breath and body sweat of the performers. During performance breaks, performers and audience mingle with no physical barriers exhibited by performers, who look directly at the people, allow themselves to be touched and converse freely.

This marked contrast between black and white jazz performers in New Orleans is an indication of the kinesic and stagecraft styles of two different cultures approaching the same music. It is a startling contrast, particularly in view of the fact that the same persons may be in both audiences on any given evening.

In Bali, performers are taught correct facial expressions as well as correct performance styles. Thus, cultures demonstrate in many kinesic ways that an individual is doing a performance and, since music is a performing art, it partakes of this quality.

The significance of kinesics has yet to be properly investigated. Such stagecraft and formalization of behavior is patterned and highly so. It is practically axiomatic in anthropology that wherever general behavior is so patterned, the culture is expressing something specific. In view of the fact that these formalized behaviors are associated directly with public performances where such symbolic cues are usually presented, it is practically incumbent on ethnomusicology to further investigate this little-known area.

The question of why a particular behavioral pattern occurs is difficult, if not impossible, to assess at the present time. It is easy enough for the authors to say for Malta that the reason performers keep such a wide space between them when singing is that they are performing an argument in public. Their gestures, lack of eye contact and physical distance are a play upon the normal conditions of two persons who are having a serious argument. Of course, the musicians are not really arguing; they are acting out an argument.

This becomes even more significant when one realizes that, in Malta, the greatest fear is of vendetta, that condition in which an argument leads to total lack of social contact except for violence. Vendetta can go on for generation after generation; the arguments of the fathers are visited upon the children. Property is destroyed; lives are lost or twisted by association with one or other sides of such a quarrel. Yet, it is this most feared element of culture which is acted out by singers of spirtu pront, the most popular of the singing and performing styles of Malta. Why?

One explanation lies in the old adage that people sing what they cannot say. People cannot talk about vendetta easily; their fears are suppressed. Maltese talk around the concept by various means, but it is only musicians who can freely discuss it. These are the knights errant of Maltese culture, men strong enough and courageous enough to face the culture's greatest fear in public, by performing insults. Is this a general function of music? Is music the area in which a culture allays its anxiety? From the Maltese example, this seems to be an adequate explanation.

54

CONCLUSION

This chapter has been concerned with what is learned about music as well as how music is learned. An attempt has been made to indicate the way in which music is framed within a culture. Stress has been laid upon the ability of a culture to encapsulate experience, formalize it and control it through tradition.

Some of the means are the instruments chosen; how the performers are taught to play them; the styles which are obligatory; the way in which performers are taught; the way in which audiences react to music; the kind of talented individual which any given culture will accentuate or emphasize; and the variety of fictive statements which surround teaching. In addition, the fact that kinesic behavior, itself, falls into patterns which may be culturally relevant has been discussed.

The major emphasis has been on the traditional aspects of a supposedly creative art. Music does not occur within a vacuum; it lives within a set of values which shape and control it almost totally. So traditional are the attitudes toward music that its formalized nature is not surprising; what is surprising is that new pieces of music are continually being put forward.

It is within the context of high formalization and heavy cultural pattern that innovation in music occurs. Although there have been a multitude of writings on the importance of the innovative quality of music, the question must be asked whether the emphasis on music as a "creative act" may be the result of subliminal recognition that music is hardly a free good. If music is compared with language, for instance, it is found that any human being who can speak correct grammatical sentences is forever creating new ones. Yet, language is never thought of as a creative medium, unless it is written.

Viewed in this light, language is a highly creative art, but a very common one. Music, on the other hand, usually occurs in repeated set pieces. What a musical performer does, essentially, is to repeat over and over the same musical sound. Consider the fine art tradition where the works of a Beethoven or a Bartok will be heard innumerable times within a single year. A new composition -- a new re-assembling of familiar sounds -- is an uncommon occurence in music; yet it is called a creative art. Why?

It would appear from this that music has been mis-labeled. Music is not nearly so creative as language; in fact, it is highly redundant and formalized. Yet, it is frequently to this medium that one turns when one speaks of the highest goals or the finest hour of human beings. To emphasize once more the creative aspects of music would be only to reinforce our culture's view of it.

For the Hopi, where no new pieces have been added to the repertoire of late, music is not a creative act at all. The learning procedures -- both formal and informal, musical and non-musical -- are highly stylized, even to the point of producing kinesics for performers when they are off-stage or not playing.

It would appear that this study is dealing with a variety of human behavior which is one of the most traditional and culture-bound in existence. Given the total range of human attitudes toward music, one would be tempted, at first, to say that there are traditional societies on the one hand and "fine art" societies on the other. These would be distinguished by a higher level of creativity in the "fine art" tradition, such as our own. Yet even here, major emphasis is not on the creation of the new, but on the reproduction of the traditional.

The only area in our musical repertoire where this is not true is in interpretive and improvisatory styles, such as jazz. In the area of popular songs which ordinarily would be called a mark of the traditional society, our own tradition is the most creatively active. It is here that new pieces are continually being added to the repertoire, not in the area of the fine arts.

Taken all together, the musical "creativity" of our culture is minimal in comparison with the ordinary conversation of a six year old child, when looked at as a creative art. There are probably an infinite number of sentences in English. Are there an infinite number of pieces in our musical tradition? This discussion of one of the fine arts has stressed the non-creative and sterotyped aspects of it. Many will balk at this view; but after due consideration, some will ask the most significant question which this text attempts to put forward: What is music?

COGNITION AND VALUE JUDGEMENTS

This chapter deals with the general mental processes and decisions made about musical systems and music, concerning cognition and value judgments. This is the area of categorization about the musical context which is sometimes highly specific and sometimes diffuse.

COGNITION

Cognition is a term which is used in its most general sense for all modes of being conscious or aware of an object, whether that object is material or intellectual. It is an ultimate mode of consciousness: strictly the presentation of an item to consciousness, whether through sensation or otherwise. It also involves judgment; the distinction of one object or idea from others.

Generally speaking, the concept of cognition takes for granted that there is a distinction between the mind that knows and the object or idea which is known. It takes no account of the metaphysical and ontological problem concerning the possibility of a relation between the ego and the non-ego, but assumes that such a relation does exist. Cognition, then, is a term used to refer to modes of awareness and perception. It includes rules, maps, strategies and routes of perception.

In order to understand the nature of perception, it is first necessary to know what knowledge is; but in order to know the nature of knowledge, one must first recognize that all knowledge is cultural knowledge. To understand cultural knowledge, one must first have an awareness of the nature of culture which is tighter than that previously presented in this text.

The concept of culture, while central to the study of anthropology, is not defined in a unitary manner. It is a much cherished concept, but one which is often misunderstood or loosely used. There is no "true" meaning of the term; rather, culture has a large number of overlapping and occasionally contradictory meanings. Perhaps the most general and most widely used meaning of the term is the omnibus definition of culture -- culture is the ways of man. Such a definition includes the thoughts, behaviors, beliefs, institutions and artifacts of human beings. While this definition is useful as a rationale for many diverse studies, it is not particularly helpful in the present consideration.

Two definitions of culture which may of use in a consideration of cognition and value judgments are more behavioral and specific in nature. Harris has remarked that "the culture concept
comes down to the behavior patterns associated with particular
groups of people, that is to 'customs', or to a people's way of
life" (1951:16). A second definition, more clearly related to
cognition, excludes behavior and restricts the concept of culture to mental constructs such as ideas, beliefs and knowledge.
Such a consideration of culture has emerged primarily from linguistics.

Ward Goodenough suggests that "A society's culture consists
of whatever it is one has to know or believe in in order to operate in a manner acceptable to its members and to do so in any role
they accept for themselves." He says that culture is not a material phenomenon; consisting of things, people, behavior, or emotions, but rather, an organization of these things. "It is the
forms of things that people have in mind, their models for per-
ceiving, relating, and otherwise interpreting them" (1956:167).

Although there has been some movement toward a total divorce
between behavior and mental constructs, the question involved is
merely one of emphasis. Following the practice of Werner and Fenton (1971), the authors will speak of cultural behavior and cultural knowledge, or behavior and knowledge, implying that both are
cultural. For this purpose, the concern is with the nature of cultural knowledge as well as its potential shaping of cultural behavior.

Cultural knowledge is not to be equated with an ultimate reality, nor should it be taken for granted that reality is perceived similarly by all people. Some items of knowledge may appear to be perfectly obvious. The sounds made by a bird, the o-
dor of gasoline, the brightness of a star, may all be perceived,
for such events are encountered directly by the senses. However,
even at the empirical level of knowledge, all people do not perceive things in the same way or with the same degree of intensity.
Nor does the same individual always perceive the same stimulus in
an identical manner. In the non-empirical realms of the mind,
knowledge becomes even more diffuse and difficult to discuss, investigate or explain.

Cross-cultural studies have shown that the way people conceive of their environment and the universe differs radically
from one society to another, and that what people take for reality
is socially constructed (Berger and Luckmann, 1966). Within a
given culture, information is patterned ways. These patterns are
part of the arbitrary universe of human cultural behavior. They
result from percepts and the formulation of concepts within a cultural setting and it is in this manner, that human beings are able
to communicate with one another, creating conceptual roles which
are vastly removed from sensory experiences.

Knowledge is received, stored and processed by the mind. What is known is not simply a Xerox copy of material objects and signs in our environment. Rather, information is channeled through a physical receptor and converted in the human neurological system to a percept. For example, if a man is playing a flute, this may have various meanings to those who hear him; but before they can make use of those meanings, they must first perceive that "sound" is "happening". The percept of this event is not the flute, the man, or the music. When the vibrations of air reach the ear, the information changes form so that it may be transmitted to the brain where it is then stored as a percept. Other sensory stimuli are transformed and stored in a similar way.

The universe of incoming information confronts an individual with an infinitely varying, complex set of percepts. Without some means of sorting information, an individual would soon be lost in the uniqueness of each event, object or perception. The chaos of incoming information is reduced to manageable form through the formulation of concepts.

In this process, human knowledge is transformed from a large number of percepts to a limited and manageable number of concepts. Human beings learn to give attention to some features or events and to ignore others; but in most cases, concepts arise out of several sensory inputs. At this point, some of the "sounds" of flute-playing are ignored and others emphasized.

In order to cope successfully with the flood of incoming sensory stimuli, one must have some means of sorting and classifying them. The categories of concepts and the inter-relationship of concepts which result, are arbitrary and are generally agreed upon by most of the members of an individual's group. The final concept of "flute-playing" is the result of such categories.

The study of cognition is concerned with cultural knowledge as it has been received, transformed into percepts, sorted into concepts and sets of concepts and communicated to others. Musical cognition is the portion of knowledge which deals not only with the learning of music, but also how that learning is structured; how an individual conceives of and classifies various points of focus within music; how groups evaluate performance, instruments, styles, events and all other points of focus within that which they designate as music.

The idea of cognition is not a new one. It has been a topic of interest to scholars in many disciplines: anthropology, economics, linguistics, psychology, sociology. It should also be mentioned that during the last two decades, a number of anthropologists have been working toward achieving more rigor in their ethnograpic method. Their work has been referred to as the new ethnography or ethnoscience (Sturtevant, 1964), or as ethnographic semantics or ethnosemantics (Kay, 1970). Ethnoscience is, for purposes of this book, essentially the same as studies in cognition.

59

Whatever terms they choose to use, the study of the nature of cultural knowledge about music will provide us with a key to deepening the understanding of the nature of this phenomenon. Music is an arbitrary structuring of sound into pattern. Since this pattern is culturally conceived, culturally produced, culturally perceived, it is clear that an understanding of the mental process and categories of any given group may lead, ultimately, to the establishment of a basis for understanding the central question of ethnomusicology: What is the nature of music?

KINDS OF COGNITION

It has been repeatedly asserted that music alters awareness; some scholars speak of music as heightening the awareness. As with discussions of altered states of consciousness, however, it is meaningless to assert that something is altered or heightened without knowing what an unaltered or unheightened state might be. A search for a pragmatic approach to ascertaining the kinds of effects, generally speaking, of music on the perceiver as well as the performer of music leads to a meager inventory of clues at this point of time. Much work will have to be understaken before it can be said with any degree of certainty what music does to human perception.

Not unexpectedly, it is Charles Seeger who has pointed out a basic distinction within the musical experience. He has suggested that one should distinguish between two modes of discourse -- speech, or _talking_ about music; and music, or _making_ music:

> The relationship of the (intrinsic) music-rationale known by the musician to any of the (extrinsic) speech-rationales of music or to the whole collection of them constitutes one of the fundamental problems of musicology (Seeger, 1960:225).

This is an opposition which Herndon (1974:244) termed "Seeger's Dilemma". Although Seeger was not referring directly to kinds of cognition, he was pointing to the difference in cultural knowledge between the performing of music and the knowing _about_ music. Similarly, a distinction might be made at a very basic level between performing music and hearing music, with a third distinction between either hearing or performing music and simply talking _about_ it.

These are very basic, broad, and as yet unproved distinctions or categories; nevertheless, they are useful assumptions to keep in mind in the study of cognitive differences within musical systems. In a particularistic sense, there are several areas which may now be investigated by the scholar; these include rules, maps, strategies, routes and events.

60

RULES

Human knowledge, as stated earlier, is shaped by what is selected and how that selection of experience is transformed by the
learning process. The sensory input is never everything which
can be perceived or even an objective sampling of it because one
selects the stimuli which will reach the brain. This may be particularly true of visual and auditory stimuli. At a concert, one
is not usually aware of the sound of the air conditioning or heat-
ing system, paying little attention to coughs, rattlings of pro-
grams, squeaking of seat backs or scuffling of feet unless these
become fairly intense. Thus, knowledge is selective and awareness is, in many cases, culturally determined.

There are rules governing the selection of important or marked behavior and cognition. For cognition, rules may be stated in
varying degrees of specificity. This specificity does not imply
that rules should be equated with laws, however. In the realm of
the mind, things become extremely arbitrary.

Although there are potentially thousands of combinations of
ways to identify, use and classify aspects of experience, they
will not all be used in any one culture. Cultural behavior is customary behavior -- which means that human thought and action does
not occur randomly, but is put together in a patterned manner.
Each society selects only a small portion of the actions and
thoughts which are humanly possible. For example, each language
involves the selection of fewer than 60 of the indefinite number
of vocal sounds which human beings are capable of producing. In
a similar manner, each human group utilizes only a restricted number of pitches, selected out of the universe of pitch variation
through the traditions of the group in question.

There are conditions which restrict not only the range, but
also the patterning, of human behavior. One kind of restriction
involves the rules which are learned by members of a society. This
is certainly not the only kind of restriction on behavior and it
is an important area of consideration.

It is fairly clear that a distinction should be made between
the "real" and the "ideal". That is, some rules refer only to i-
deal behavior while others refer to actual behavior taking place.
This can create severe difficulties. Some ideal rules are only
statements of historical practice and have very little to do with
current action.

It is said, for instance, that a Cherokee ceremony requires
four different kinds of singing specialists. While this may have
been true in the past, it is no longer the practice. This would
have to be interpreted as an historic ideal, rather than a reflection of ritual practice at the present time. It is necessary

to distinguish carefully between those statements which are i-
deals never realized, or not currently realized, and those statements and rules which are actually followed.

Another area of possible confusion arises in the distinction
to be made between rules and concepts which an individual can
formulate with clarity and those rules which are only vaguely
stated. It is probable that a specialist may be able to formulate rules which the majority of a population would never consider. Therefore, it is probably necessary to delineate a level of
expertise before rules are discussed.

It is also necessary to remember that rules, as aspects of
human knowledge, have their locus in the mind. Like the program
stored in a computer, human rules are made up of bits of information stored in the brain which are used to process other information as well as to organize and direct behavior. Like a number
of other mental phenomena, rules can be represented by symbols
outside the mind. While rules are known by an individual, he may
not be able to state them explicitly or clearly; nor will an individual necessarily be able to replicate the totality of rules
stated by any other individual. Like the grammar of the language,
many rules are difficult to verbalize, although they may be understood in practice and tacit in knowledge.

Each person actually knows more than he/she can relate, verbally. Recognizing a person's walk, stance, head movements, features of face or uniqueness of voice is a matter of intuitive recall -- one that is extremely difficult, if not impossible -- to
describe in words. This type of knowledge, such as rules of human behavior within a culture, is known, understood, but often
simply cannot be placed within the limitations of vocabulary.

Certainly, not all kinds of human knowledge about music are
impossible to verbalize; in fact, one might find one's informants
verbalizing more than once can deal with. However, it remains a
task for the researcher to formulate the tacit rules which members of a group are using in order to create their music, as well
as those rules which are stated by members of a given society.

It should be remembered that rules are learned at different
levels, also. This in turn determines the effect of those rules
on behavior. In Malta, it was discovered that there were several
singers who were unaware that a good singer rarely mentions the
central subject of the duel directly more than once in a song, in
most contexts. These singers would simply repeat the subject of
the duel continually, providing a source of amusement for those
singers who did understand the rules, and who encouraged the unaware singers to continue their practice.

62

There are probably an infinite number of gradations of learning involved in the internalization of a musical system. A child who says "me done it" has not quite learned some grammatical rules; similarly, when a child is learning to play an instrument, mistakes will be made. The levels of learning begin with an individual who has just heard about a new rule. He may not understand it or even recognize it as a rule if it is not presented as such. At the other end of the spectrum is the individual who has learned the rules so well and internalized them so thoroughly, that he may not be able to speak of them except in the most metaphysical terms.

In Malta, a master singer stated that "the bormliza is the stringing together of pearls" and was fully satisfied that he had clearly stated the boundaries of that particular musical form. It was only when lesser singers began to talk about that form that more explicit rules were stated; that it involved singing soprano and "moving the voice around a lot".

While there are probably an infinite number of degrees to which a rule or a set of rules can be learned, it may be of help to consider the five levels proposed by Spiro in connection with learning the concepts of an ideology:

(a) The actors have learned about the ideological concept, i.e., they have been exposed to it in some manner, ranging from formal instruction to informal gossip.

(b) The actors have not only learned about the concept, but they also understand the meaning that a text or a key informant attributes to it.

(c) Understanding its meaning, the actors believe the concept to be right or true or valid.

(d) Constituting a salient element in their cognitive systems, the concept serves to inform the actors' behavioral environment (as Hallowell calls it) and to structure their world.

(e) In addition to its cognitive salience, the concept has been internalized as an important element in the actors' motivational system, so that it serves not only to guide, but also to instigate, behavior (1966:1163).

It becomes clear that the reseacher must make every effort to determine an approximate level to which concepts or rules have been apprehended by his informants.

Perhaps one of the best means for arriving at an understanding of the rules of cognition is to be found in their negative

63

applications. For example, marriage is a rather amorphous concept in most of its definitions and it is only by a careful examination of the way in which divorce and property settlements are handled that some of the basic aspects of marriage in a given society can be discovered.

Generally, if a society customarily requires that the former husband return his wife's dowry upon divorce, it may be assumed that the dowry has an important symbolism in marriage. For musical investigations, two approaches are possible in the use of negative aspects to discover the meaning of rules. First, one may investigate the manner in which rules are broken by individuals who are still learning a style or who are not achieving an extremely high level of competence in it. Second, one may investigate the manner in which rules are bent and finally broken by those individuals whose innovative powers cause them to exceed the bounds of prescribed custom and to create new forms and, thus, create new rules of musical behavior.

In Malta, the authors were privileged to witness the formation of a new approach to guitar playing. Maltese guitar playing has changed over the past 60 years, but basically requires the musician to improvise. Each key contains certain traditional melodic "bits" which are combined differently each time the guitarist plays in that particular key. Innovation occurs in very minute detail for the most part. In the eyes of the guitarist, a new compostion does not need to be a totally new piece; all that is required is a new interplay of existing material. At the beginning of this century, the guitar part was almost entirely chordal. Today, true melodies appear as the result of past innovations of several fine guitarists, and the present forms involve an interplay of melody-types against one another.

In the beginning of the average Maltese guitarist, innovation takes the form of instantaneous, impromptu re-ordering of a limited repertoire of melody-types. Most soloists have a stock of 20 to 30 melody-types which may occur in any order or at any range. Within the space of three or four phrases, a guitarist may use only one or as many as six melody-types. The final phrase, or _teghla_ (fall), is more stable. About 10 to 12 patterns of falling 16th and 32nd notes are used as cadential patterns with each pattern one phrase in length. This places the guitarists' innovation within the same category as the improvisation of early 20th century New Orleans Jazz players, where the instrumental "breaks" usually involved such a re-ordering of basic material, plus a cadential pattern. The step from germinal idea to final song takes place at once, without the intervention of time for consideration or the working out of new patterns.

In spite of the fact that the Maltese state an ideal need for constant creativity in which a performer never repeats himself within an entire lifetime of playing, forms must remain stable in order to allow for the type of innovation Maltese playing requires.

In such a situation, stability of form is a prerequisite to performance, and one should not expect new forms to arise easily.

However, a new form has arisen. It is called kitteri bis,
(guitars only). It may be the invention of one man, Indri Brincat,
a guitarist who is undoubtedly the best of the Maltese performers.
In kitteri bis, there are no singers and any style of music can be
played. The only means of identification is by the name of the
key. Changes are occuring which may eventually lead Brincat completely out of the realm of Maltese folk music as it is now known.
As kitteri bis is presently played, two layers of development may
be seen. At first, Mr. Brincat was imitating the local style faith-
fully. The guitar soloist merely "sang" the singer's parts and
then supplied an intervening interlude. In time, Brincat began to
elaborate his playing; several singer melodies could be heard in a
given guitar performance, making Brincat's playing a catalogue of
recent musical history in Malta.

In the intervening interlude, the four-phrase structure so
carefully presented by most guitarists, began to disappear. It was
replaced by phrase structures of any length, up and including the
total interlude. Melody-types, as a concept, were still present in
Mr. Brincat's playing but they were rapidly merging into other,
more complex statements involving diminution, inversion, recapitu-
lation and other variation forms.

During the second layer of development, the statement of the
singer's melody came to have less importance. The strophe became
less clear, melodic content became almost skeletal and traditional
chord lines began to be questioned. Mr. Brincat began teaching his
accompanying guitarist new chordal combinations, all of which were
practiced with ferocity. Shifts from major to minor occurred within a single performance, triple meters appeared and exaggerated ac-
celerandos developed. Thus, one man had so thoroughly broken with
tradition as to create a totally new form. He developed it out of
traditional material, slowly shifting his emphasis until improvisation broke the bonds that held the form stable.

This did not occur without repercussions, for Malta is not a
society which allows change to override tradition easily. The composer, the creator, the innovator in any sphere of customary action
is literally taking his chances. Mr. Brincat, recognized as the
greatest of the living Maltese guitarists, was chastised indirectly
and later ostracized because the other musicians felt that he was
no longer playing traditional Maltese material. In their criti-
cisms of his playing, the other musicians revealed quite clearly
the boundaries of traditional Maltese folk music. By following the
ideal statement rather than the practice, Brincat had broken another set of rules and, in changing the musical form, had encountered
a high degree of resistance.

This example indicates that, although they may not be verbalized directly, there will be rules for performance in all styles.

These may be stated clearly or indistinctly, but they will be known to the performers, however. It is vital for the scholar to attempt to discover, through whatever means may be available, as many levels and forms of rules as possible.

There are at least two caveats to the study of rules for musical behavior, as there are for any kind of cognitive study. It has been mentioned that there is a distinction to be made between real and ideal behavior. In many ways, this dichotomy represents an over-simplification. There is usually an ideal pattern in most cultures -- that behavior which the society members feel is appropriate or "proper" and/or "normal" -- and that behavior which is the real behavior or what members of the society actually do. There is also that behavior which is presumed or assumed which is action(s) that members of a group assume its members perform.

Clearly, there is no guarantee that the rules inferred by an observer of behavior are the same as the rules employed by the person or persons performing the observed activity. Nor can whatever devices an observer may construct in order to account for behavior ever be a full representation of the mental phenomenon which generated the behavior.

That is, cognitive descriptions and models do not replicate on paper the actual perceptual processes of the persons studied. Cognitive explication of rules is a means of explanation of behavior which, while it may approach an actual process or reasoning, does not and should not claim to replicate it.

MAPS

One aspect of human sensory input rarely investigated is that dealing with human mapping procedures. This is the area dealing with the concepts formed by humans regarding where in space events are found, as well as those mental domains which might be called semantic space.

Consider the following English words: city, county, state, courtyard, neighborhood, exit. This list includes several different kinds of space. Everyone has a set of spatial categories, only some of which are shared. Events take place in space; objects occupy it, are separated by it and move through it. There has been much attention in various disciplines to physical space, but little scholarly notice has been taken of the symbolic and expressive aspects of space. These subjective aspects are less easily measurable than physical space and it may be that such investigation, of necessity, has had to await the discovery and development of cognitive methodologies.

66

In investigating the symbolic and expressive aspects of space, one might include the ways people experience space, how they make use of it and, how they are influenced by it. Some space (such as the internal structuring of buildings, cities or towns) is fixed in nature and not readily changeable. Other aspects of space such as furniture, screens, curtains, or other items are moveable. At the smallest level there is what might be called individual space or microspace, which includes human use of the space around them.

In the consideration of cognition, the discussion of mapping will be limited to what is generally called "social space". That is, the concern with the question: "Where are you?" Social space is multi-dimensional.

In order to describe an individual or a group location, choices must be made as to frame of reference. For example, the question "Where is the Micmac Indian Reservation?" might be answered in a number of ways: (1) 48 degrees North, 67 degrees West, in North America, the province of Quebec, Bonaventure County; (2) About 350 miles north of Boston; (3) Up North; (4) Down South. Each description would be appropriate in some context. In each case, however, there are culturally derived categories which indicate and delimit spatial dimensions.

Areas of social space are generally associated with particular social groups in most instances. The territory of a tribe or nation is given a geographic locus. Thus, one can speak of the Tikopia occupying a certain island, as opposed to those islands occupied by the Maltese. Or one can speak about the Eastern Band of Cherokee who live in North Carolina, as opposed to the Western Cherokee who live in Oklahoma. Within a generalistic geographical territory, there are boundaries which may be a matter of dispute, but are always forms of cultural conventions. The links between groups and their territory are likely to be quite strong.

One has only to consider the historical removal of Indian tribes from the East to the area West of the Mississippi River in order to begin to understand this concept. Territories are often defended, particularly those which have some form of "no trespassing" sign on them. Boundaries are thus strongly linked to human groups.

Access to certain areas of social space are often used to mark status. This marking may be used to distinguish between high and low status as well as sacred and profane status. For example, in New Guinea, boys may not enter the men's house until initiated and women may never enter it. Similarly, in Madagascar, the noble's head has to be higher than anyone else's for various ceremonial and religious reasons.

In matters of protocol and rank, space is used in motion to play out status; most obviously demonstrated by processions and banquets. In some societies, one's place in a procession is a clear mark of rank in that society; the highest rank is sometimes last; sometimes first. At banquets, there may be a clear illustration of rank based on where one sits. These boundaries are arbitrary in nature because what indicates high status territorially in one society may indicate low status in the next. It is the general use of concrete spatial relations in the statement of relative status which is the justification for the more abstract notion of social space.

People live where they do in part because they "know their place". There is generally some equivalent in almost every society of the American notion of "living on the right or wrong side of the tracks". In some instances, musicians are placed high up in the ranks within a society and their dwelling place in a town or village indicates this; in other instances where musicians are not well regarded, they may be placed on the other side of the garbage dump.

All of this kind of space discussion may be thought of as "horizontal space", as opposed to the "vertical space" of class distinction and the personal space of kinesics.

Social space is recognized in the individual and can be investigated, cognitively, through the formulation of cognitive maps. A cognitive map is a spatial representation of the mental concept of locus. For music, this is of several orders. It may include not only where music is found, but also such things as the locus of an individual musician within the hierarchy of musicians of a particular kind or, the restrictions on musical performance by the environment.

One important kind of cognitive map which may be collected is that of musical forms. It should be obvious that a person adept at a particular genre of music, while he or she may be cognizant of the others, will be partial to his own kind. The answer to the question, "What kinds of music are there in X?" will be weighted, depending upon the perspective of the person being asked the question. By collecting a number of these maps of musical forms, some idea can be attained as to a more generalized ranking of importance of various forms and styles.

A similar mapping can be obtained of musical instruments. It was only through persistent inquiry as to the kinds of instruments available in Malta that knowledge was gained of the stone whistle (which is now used by children) and of the one man on the islands who is still capable of making Maltese bagpipes.

It is possible that some instruments, not in general use, may be discovered through the process of collecting a number of mental maps of musical instruments. It is likely that much information will be gathered regarding the nature of instruments, the ranking of their importance to each individual and, perhaps by extension, such information as fictive statements regarding the place of each instrument in the general hierarchy of sound.

Perhaps the most important and productive of the mental maps to investigate are those regarding the occasion. As an illustration, a brief sketch will be given of the main musical occasions in Malta.

THE XALATA

There is a strong tradition in Malta of singing folk songs while riding in a cart, a type of activity called the xalata. Private hire buses have replaced the frequency of carts, but prior to World War II, at least two singers and one guitarist would spend the entire night riding about the island in a cart, singing and playing. Many romanticized stories are told of the cart and donkey plodding through the narrow streets of a rival village, its occupants well fortified with wine, singing the praises of their own village and denigrating the rival.

Today, the xalata is confined almost exclusively to warm, summer weekends when groups of people hire a bus for this purpose. Such groups fall into three categories: (1) families, mostly women and children with an occasional man; (2) prostitutes; and (3) men. Each xalata participant pays a small fee to secure his place on the bus; large baskets overflowing with wine, beer, melon, rabbit, chicken, bread and fruit are prepared. On the appointed afternoon, the merrymakers gather and pack into the bus.

When the xalata is a family gathering, there is a predominance of older women and children, with perhaps a man to lead the singing and provide rudimentary guitar accompaniment. Everyone sings, including the bus driver, who often pays more attention to the singing than his driving.

When the xalata is composed primarily of men and small children, the agenda is much the same. The men do not sing isolated verses or those made famous by others, however, but prefer to compose their own, creating dialogues with other singers. No attempt is made, here, to oranize a formal song duel, but any number of singers can and do carry on informal discussion in song.

The outings organized by prostitutes are much the same as those of men and family groups, according to all available information. Secondary sources had to be used and, according to some of the young, unmarried male singers reportedly invited to join these trips, the prostitutes are fully capable of constructing their own verses in the proper style, as the men do. The subject matter of their songs is rather bawdy for the most part.

In addition to the weekend xalata, it is traditional for villagers to celebrate on the day following the feast of their village patron saint. Since the feast day is usually on a Sunday,
these events are usually held on Monday. The people form a line
of cars, trucks, motorcycles and buses, having decorated their ve-
hicles beforehand with paper streamers, palm branches, religious
pictures or printed signs. Singing, eating and merrymaking is
much the same as on any other xalata; however, a special verse or
verses is written each year particularly for the occasion. These
special verses may be written by anyone and are quickly passed a-
long to the entire group; but they must be different from those of
previous years.

THE PROGRAMM

The musical occasion which involves taping or live broadcast
of a program for the Maltese Rediffusion, or television, is distinguished by the term, programm. The programm is a specific
length, usually much shorter than the normal time span of a song
and is taped for later broadcast, since officials have learned
that they must censor the singers. The programm is a paid performance, with a six-month or one-year contract between the Musicians Unions and Maltese Rediffusion; the television programm is
made under specific contract with the individual and is for one to
six broadcasts. The radio programm is recorded by members of one
Union on Saturday evening and by members of the other Union on
Thursday.

The programm on Maltese television is usually done in connection with a folklore series. In such cases, the music involved
is minimal. One to four singers and three guitarists will be asked
to play and sing for perhaps five minutes to illustrate the comments of a local folklorist; the songs taking various forms, depending upon the perceptive abilities of the folklorist conducting
the programm.

THE SERATA

The serata is any paid performance which is not for broadcast purposes and is, with the exception of informal non-paid music, the most common musical occasion. A serata may be held any-
where, but must be in a public place with an audience and with
paid performers. Bars, football clubs, band clubs, cinemas, ho-
tels, restaurants, political rallies or private parties are the

most usual locations. Payment may either be prearranged with a sum for each performer, a large meal at the end of the evening, or both.

The singing is more careful and more rigidly structured than when singers gather casually. Timing is less precise than for a programm; however, if there are tape recorders present, every effort will be made to have the end of a song duel coincide with the end of a tape. The serata usually lasts for a defined length of time which is agreed upon beforehand. At a serata, music will continue for slightly more than an hour per song; afterwards, the singers and guitarists pause for refreshment, resuming their activity after 10 minutes or so. A song duel will usually be the first offering and during the course of the evening, there will be a predominance of this style. This may be followed by a fatt or a kitteri bis section, or a bormliza.

The audience is usually quiet during the singing, particularly if a tape recording is being made. They drink and smoke but confine conversation to whispered exchanges; gossip erupting in the breaks between pieces.

THE FESTA

Certain feast days, or festas, are considered to be feasts of singing. These include the feasts of Victoria at Melliha in the first part of September; Santa Marija at Gozo in late August; San Gregor at Marsaxalokk on the first Wednesday after Easter; Lapsi (Ascension) at Xghajra; and Imnarja (the feast of St. Peter and St. Paul) at Boskett, in the end of June. All feast days (with the exception of the Imnarja) are much the same. Musicians gather, people appear in large numbers, picnic lunches are brought and singing is relatively informal.

Where there are musicians, the crowd is silent and attentive and it is on these occasions that the fatt singer is at his best. He may sing for 45 minutes to an hour of a gory murder while everyone listens intently, some members of the audience mouthing every word of this extremely long song. When the fatt ends, no one applauds or thanks the singer; it is as if he did not exist and he quietly disappears into the crowd. There is also the singing of song duels, which may be accompanied by the aggressive tape recording of duels by supporters.

The Imnarja, in reality, marks a different kind of occasion which includes two separate activities at the same time. The main portion of this festa is centered in Buskett Gardens where there are produce and livestock exhibits with prizes and a competition for singers. The general activity of this feast spans a three-day period rather than the usual one-day event for villages.

At the singing competition (which is arranged by folk-lorists), the rules are quite different from the usual competition. Wooden platforms are erected and spotlights set up. Three or four judges, prominent professional people from the city who know nothing about the musical style, sit behind the musicians seemingly paying no attention to them. Musicians must register for the competition. A singer is hired by the folklorist to reply to the contestants as a foil in the song duel competition. Subjects are assigned usually by picking them out of a hat, and it is expected by the judges that the subject of the song duel will be repeated in every verse. At other occasions, this would be regarded as a serious breach of the rules.

Although it was once the highlight of the festa, the singing competition is now entered only by mediocre singers and guitarists. This is due to the rumor that the judges can be bribed as well as the fact that the judges know nothing of the intracacies of folk music.

Elsewhere on the grounds, a song competition will take place lasting from early afternoon through the following morning. Songs on these occasions are extremely long, with song duels running more to the level of endurance contests than on other occasions.

THE COMPETITION

The competition is an event in which a private individual, usually a bar owner, offers a silver cup or other trophy as prize. He secures the services of one or more respected singers as judges and asks two to four contestants to pit their wits against one another until one of them makes a mistake and is eliminated. The actual form taken by song duels in a competition may vary; rules are set up for each event. The audience includes only musicians and avid supporters, mostly by invitation.

Everyone present considers himself a judge and lively arguments ensue as to which singer is the best. Nor is the decision of the judges considered to be final. Each person has his own opinion, which he will transmit to the general public at the outcome of the competition, whether or not the cup is awarded to his favorite.

THE SFIDA

The sfida, or challenge, is also between two singers or two guitarists. Although it resembles the competition, it is initiated by the musicians themselves rather than by a bar owner seeking publicity. The _sfida_ is a challenge of not only the individual's musical ability, but also of his entire personality. There are often rumors of a _sfida_ but few actually occur. In these, there is no judge, for it is merely a match of destruction in which no one can emerge a victor.

CHRISTMAS EVE

On Christmas Eve, it is traditional for musicians to gather in the village of Zejtun in one of two bars. Despite the fact that it is customary for Maltese families to spend this evening together at home and then attend Midnight Mass, these men leave their homes to spend the night in music and drinking. Singing is informal, the bar is crowded but relatively quiet, and people spill out of it into the narrow alleyway in front. As many as eight or ten men are involved in the song duel, but on this night there are no insults. This is an evening for philosophy, light joking and Christmas verses. At some point in the evening, most of the musicians order a round of drinks for the house. Soon everyone is drunk -- a breach of etiquette on other occasions. There is an air of permissiveness toward younger, inexperienced singers, who are allowed to try their wings.

Established singers, particularly the better ones, strive to maintain their self-control and perform with their usual expertise, so that their reputations will not suffer. A double tempo style known as the "Tra La Li La Tra La Le" is undertaken. This song has a chorus, unlike all other Maltese styles, and the extemporaneous leader part is taken in turn by almost everyone. There is no continuity except sentiment. Singing continues until dawn when everyone goes home for a few hours sleep before attending Morning Mass with their families.

INFORMAL OCCASIONS

In a very real sense, Maltese singers perform almost any time or place. Maltese women, washing clothes in their own courtyard, may sing to a neighbor. Serious folk music is more dependent upon the accidental meeting of singers and guitarists in any one of the thirty-some bars scattered over the islands. It is here that new singers practice, socialize and establish themselves; that new guitarists try their skill, and established musicians enjoy themselves. During the summer, musicians usually gather by the sea on weekends to enjoy the sun, water and singing with each other.

THE TRIUMPHAL TOUR

Yet another occasion for music in Malta is the triumphal
tour, another version of serata. This phenomenon developed as the
result of the record industry, and involves a special invitation
by a popular dance band manager, bar owner, or group of villagers
issued to a singer or guitarist who has produced a successful record. Musicians will travel to the appointed place and sing for
several hours, being provided with food and lodging if they have
to leave the main island. The audience pays to enter, is more formal and less informed than many other audiences. Performance is on
a stage; thus isolating the audience. In this context, some individuals may even ask musicians for their autographs. The musicians
take these to be festive occasions, often staying out all night to
have bull sessions, pillow fights, or to drink and socialize.

The musical occasion in Malta can be mapped. The examples
given here represent a composite (made from many descriptions and
personal observations) from which it is possible to arrive at either a simple listing, as above, or a more formal ranking.

ROUTES AND STRATEGIES

Far more attention has been given in the literature to rules
and to a lesser extent to maps, than to routes and strategies.
While it is true that routes and strategies may be seen as extensions of maps and rules, there is a distinct advantage to focusing
upon those aspects of cognition. This is primarily true because
cultural rules are simply instructions for constructing, combining,
interpreting and manipulating symbols.

There are many choices to be made among rules, for rules are
sometimes contradictory. It is in the superimposition of strategies and routes upon rules and, to a lesser extent upon maps, that
leads to the clear realization of behavioral patterns within a human group.

There is a distinction to be made between strategies and
routes, although the two areas are highly inter-related. Strategies can be seen as having to do with planning or managing activity, often through the use of consciously created, sometimes individualistic devices. In contrast, routes have to do with planning
or managing in a more generalistic sense; that is, as a highway
route is a course to be traveled, so in other areas of behavior a
cognitive route is a frequently used, known course of action. A
route is likely to be a cultural device, known to many, while a
strategy may be highly individualistic.

74

Routes, as a course of action to be traveled, refer to strategies employed by individuals in past circumstances in a successful manner which have become generally accepted. Until recently, the route to success in American opera was to be found in the process of hard study, diligent work and successful appearances in Europe prior to working in America. The situation is now changing, but success in European theatres or opera houses is still a recognized means of acquiring a position in American opera companies.

As expressions of tradition, routes are not firmly bound into one specific course of action, nor is there any clear distinction to be made at this level between routes which are generally acceptable to society and those which are not. Some routes may be more acceptable than others, but even a route which is unacceptable to the vast majority of society is nevertheless potential and known; it is these two factors which will test and disclose the availability of a route.

In Malta, any woman who sings in public is regarded as a prostitute, whether she is or not. Therefore, any woman desiring to be a singer has a potential set of routes open to her: she may be a prostitute, she may become a prostitute, or she may not be a prostitute, although in any case she will be regarded as one if she sings in public. The association is traditional.

It has been mentioned before that Indri Brincat, the Maltese guitarist, so thoroughly broke the tradition that he created a totally new form. He developed it out of traditional material and slowly shifted his emphasis until improvisation broke the bonds that held the musical form stable. He then had to take the cultural consequences of his action.

It is claimed generally that Malta is a highly egalitarian society. In some cases, this is true. Each person feels himself to be inherently equal to any other, in spite of the presence of a status hierarchy. This is particularly true of musicians where policemen, grave-diggers, business men, electricians and lavatory attendants forget their distinctions while singing together.

Although it is obvious that some musicians are better than others, the musicians, themselves, refuse to verbalize this directly. Musicians are by nature permissive; fine performers allow small children to sing or play with them. The best singer will sing with the worst, and Mr. Brincat willingly plays with visiting ethnomusicologists. Anyone may learn to sing; anyone may try; anyone may assess his own abilities as he wishes. The attitude is well conveyed by the Maltese proverb, "Whoever has a mouth to talk with, can say anything he likes."

In this egalitarian context, it would seem that innovation would be impossible, with high pressure to conform. This is generally true. If a person excels in any field, he immediately becomes the object of highly complex attacks and must run a gauntlet of envy and jealousy. If someone excels, their children may be scorned or slapped, and economically successful families suffer continuous thefts or high degrees of gossip. There is some belief that God takes vengeance upon the successful, and is expressed in the proverb, "If God gives you money, what else is He going to give you?"

This chilling Maltese atmosphere would seem to require tremendous ego-strength if one is innovative. In music, which is totally innovative by definition, a good musician needs genius, cunning, superiority and courage. To be a musician at all, one must possess an intense, burning passion for music. This quality is essential because of the pressure under which the creator is placed. Slander against good musicians is the norm, rather than the exception.

There are two sides to this problem. If one person is better at something than another, the reaction to this discovery is called ghajjur (envy, or jealousy). A jealous person feels a lack in himself when he sees the superiority of another, and it is believed that jealous people are not happy and die in misery. The true test of the presence of jealousy comes after death. The corpse excretes, but since this is a general characteristic of human corpses, the pervasiveness of the belief is apparent.

Jealousy, whether of musical superiority or another aspect of behavior, can take three cultural routes: witchcraft, rumor, or vengeance. With witchcraft, this is probably dealing with mythical statement, for no witches are known to exist on the island, yet all informants characterize their activities in the same terms. The witch hides his or her feelings from the person evoking jealousy and compliments him extravagantly, while secretly making curses. These curses can be countered by the burning of olive leaves, the blessing of the house, or attaching pairs of bull horns in prominent places.

The second route, that of rumor, is more complex. Lies are told about persons of ability. The vast majority of the authors' information about Maltese musicians took this form: this singer left his wife after three days (he has two sons by her, about six years difference in age); that singer doesn't write his own ballads (yet books of his songs exist); another singer betrayed his friends, and so forth.

The slander must occur outside the musical context to be the result of jealousy. There is always an accuser and an accused and the assumption is that the accuser feels himself to be of lesser ability than the accused. For this reason, scorn and slander are accepted with equanimity by most musicians; in effect, they are being complimented. Remembering that the compliment of the witch is regarded with grave suspicion, one can perceive a cultural model which is a reverse pecking order. The person best at his trade receives the most slander and enjoys the most honor, thereby. Thus, an insult is a form of compliment and a compliment is an insult.

The first two routes, witchcraft and rumor, involved internal action and are called "things of the heart". Both forms rebound on the jealous person and cause him great unhappiness. The third route, vengeance, is externalized and in this pattern, one individual physically injures another. He may scratch his car, steal his guitar, or slap his child. Apparently, musicians chose this route for some time; fisticuffs were once common. Police action has put an end to this route and this may account for the present proliferation of rumors.

All three reactions to expertise apply only so long as one remains within reasonable bounds. In musical terms, this means that musicians who create within the normal forms will be subject to jealousy reactions. Mr. Brincat enjoys any passing rumor that comes his way as a mark of his adaptability into "correct" behavior.

There is yet another cultural route, designed to define the limits of conformity. This is the challenge, the sfida. It is rarely used, although everyone knows about it and there is much gossip about it. This is not, as in Western terms, a call to competition. It is a blow at the entire personality of an individual who has gone beyond acceptable limits. In the case of a musician, this could mean that not only his musicianship was in question, but his very existence, also. Only one challenge was issued during the authors' work in Malta, and that was to Indri Brincat. By the time it was issued, Mr. Brincat had moved so far out of the musical system that a reaction was to be expected. It came in the most agonizing of ways.

Mr. Brincat was extremely careful to maintain a distinction between folk and popular music. Although other musicians, wanting "fame" or a little extra money, would create a typical Maltese verse form which could be sung to a popular melody and recorded, Brincat flatly refused. He considers himself to be a traditional Maltese folk musician. However, Il-Fanfru, an older singer who had started late in life and was in a hurry to establish himself, arranged for someone else to write verses for him, then asked Brincat to accompany him on a record. Brincat agreed; contract arrangements were far advanced when it was learned that the melodies were not traditional. Brincat was greatly upset and asked to be released from the contract. Without a word, Il-Fanfru contracted another guitarist and Brincat cut off relations with Il-Fanfru.

There are two versions of this story. The one above is that of Brincat. The version of Il-Fanfru stresses his innocence in placing Brincat in this quandary, and the care he took to let him

77

out of the contract before getting another guitarist. The challenge is clear. Here is a man who has progressed in innovation exclusively through the Maltese idiom until he began to burst its bounds. His music led him to alter the forms. But he is a folk guitarist; abhoring the idea of having his own traditions, in spite of the fact that he is the agent for change by virtue of his innovative genius.

It is also clear that Brincat imagined the challenge. This means that he knew he had gone beyond the limits of his tradition and was caught. If he was no longer a folk musician, what was he? Caught in the grip of his own progress, Brincat reacted. He began to berate his friends and cease to speak to them. He forced his opinions on his accompanist; one left him. He turned to outsiders for the comfort he needed so desperately. Arriving at the authors' house, knowing no English, he came just to play. Prevented by the ethic of non-interference in helping him across his barriers, the authors were in agony for the man. He ceased playing in public, pretending to repair his guitar and for weeks appeared only to play for contract arrangements.

In the meantime, he practiced; trying to move out of Maltese music to play popular music. He copied Spanish, Italian and other types of music while he poured out information to the authors on the nature of the traditional Maltese style. His performances vascillated between highly traditional music, mediocre imitations of popular music and truly inspired progressions beyond his own systems. He no longer knew who he was.

In this condition, he misinterpreted many signals from his fellow musicians. He had exceeded known cultural routes and had no strategy to protect himself. He finally faced himself and decided that of the options available to him, the only logical route for him to follow was to return to the general system. In order to remain within his tradition, he joined his worst enemies and began to play for Il-Fanfru and his friends.

Thus, the pressure of the tradition, in conflict with the requirement for constant innovation within it, was resolved in this case by total capitulation. Yet Brincat's captiulation was only apparently complete. He continued to display the appropriate public behavior and playing of many Maltese guitarists, but continued to innovate in private.

Brincat's action and choices in this matter represent strategies more than routes. In deciding to play publicly in a more accepted manner, while continuing his innovative activities at home, he created a plan and a device for managing his own public image and meshing it happily with his private goals and desires.

Strategies are not limited to reactions to given situations. They may represent plans created in an attempt to reach a future goal. In the highly innovative environment of Maltese singing, one must certainly have a personal strategy for creating a perfect four-line verse during the 30 to 40 seconds he has between his opponent's response to his latest comment and his own next verse. In order to respond quickly and well, one excellent musician stated that he always thought of the last two lines of a four-line verse first; in these lines, he placed the main message of his response to his opponent. The first two lines could then be filled in with introductory or padding material in order to create a perfect rhyme if necessary. Such a device was only one of many for managing a situation.

Both strategies and routes have great potential in revealing valuable information to the ethnomusicologist. Neither, unfortunately, has received a great deal of attention in the past. It is hoped that the investigation of not only routes and strategies, but also maps and rules will lead to an ever-deepening understanding of the nature of that complex phenomenon known as music.

Absolutely essential to any informed investigation of cognitive domains is care in elicitation of data. It is extremely easy in the formulation of questions to indicate to the informant what kind of a response might be desired. All too often the informant, particularly if he is being paid, will provide answers which are calculated to be pleasing to the ethnomusicologist, whether they are true or not.

Another pitfall in elicitation is to assume either that the informants are ignorant or that they cannot talk about something; it would be better advice to assume that the researcher has formulated the wrong questions.

In terms of interpretation or explanation of information elicited, it is very tempting to simply assume that the interpretation of a cognitive system is identical to that of the informants when actually, there is no evidence to indicate that maps or rules have anything to do with the way others conceive of them.

VALUE JUDGMENTS

If music is regarded as a human process, arbitrarily defined and delimited by human beings, the idea of evaluation or qualification of experience is obviously central to any understanding of the nature of the production of music. As Merriam has pointed out: "...despite the enormous literature devoted to aesthetics, it is extremely difficult to discover precisely what an aesthetic is" (1964:259).

In speaking of value judgments, this includes that ill-defined area commonly called aesthetics; however, the use of the

79

term "audience" conjures up sets of preconceived ideas which tend to lead Western scholars into dangerous depths of miscalculations in attempting to identify cross-cultural perception of emotional and intellectual experience.

In Western terms, aesthetics is often defined as the study of the beautiful or the perception of that which is good or beautiful. Apel suggests that "musical aesthetics is the study of the relationship of music to the human senses and intellect" (1969:14). Others feel that the aesthetic concerns sensuous more than conceptual data. The common definition regards aesthetics as the study of the beautiful.

According to Merriam, there are six factors which comprise the concept of the aesthetic in Western society: (1) psychic or psychical distance (Bullough, 1912); (2) manipulation of form for its own sake; (3) attribution of emotion-producing qualities to music conceived strictly as sound; (4) attribution of beauty to the art product or process; (5) purposeful intent to create something aesthetic; (6) presence of a philosophy of an aesthetic.

It is considered highly dangerous to follow Merriam's suggestion that "the problem is to attempt to ascertain whether this specific Western concept is re-duplicated in any societies other than our own" (1964:261). Rather, it is suggested that not only is the term "aesthetic" potentially misleading, but that it represents an alteration of a direction of focus which might well prove unacceptable in the investigation of the music of the world.

McAllester uses the phrase "functional esthetic" in discussing the Western Apache:

> There is little esthetic discussion in our sense. Appreciation of a song is nearly always phrased in terms of understanding it -- of knowing what it is for. One or two informants did speak of preferring songs with long choruses and short verses, since these are easier to learn, but the usual preference was for the important healing songs or the sacred songs in the puberty ceremony. This 'functional esthetic' is found very widely among pre-literate peoples (1960:471-72).

This begins to approach what is means by "value judgments", but presents a problem in that the material is simply left alone after the statement that the aesthetic is a functional one, which tends to dismiss the idea of any judgmental capability beyond the most rudimentary sort.

Kaeppler has arrived at what is perhaps the most useful definition of value judgments:

> ...art is defined as cultural forms that result from creative processes which manipulate movement,

sound, or materials. Aesthetics is defined as
ways of thinking about such forms (1971:175).

The aesthetic, viewed as ways of thinking, allows an approach
to an area of consideration which is no longer confined to the
good, the true and the beautiful. Rather, in discussing the ways
of thinking about musical forms or other contexts, one is lead into a more open and potentially exciting area of investigation.

Looked at from Kaeppler's point of view, aesthetics can be
viewed as value judgments and value field. This raises a wider
set of questions which, unlike the more restrictive concept of
aesthetics, allows a definite approach to these aspects of music.
Value judgments, being a general quality of human life, are made
at each level of cognition. Some of these levels are musical;
some are related to musical performance, but are only peripheral
to the music performed.

The most profound value judgments about the nature of music
are those general limitations on choice which each culture possesses. What an individual is allowed to hear may be profoundly
influenced by basic cultural values which either circumsribe him
or direct him. Choices may be made for the entirety of a culture.

For example, the Catholic Church made a strenuous effort to
restrict the performance of secular music in the Middle Ages.
Whether this had any real influence on the performance of secular
music is questionable; however, the attempt was made, representing
a general view of music for that time which undoubtedly had some
repercussions. Within the context of Catholicism, certain pieces
of music and certain intervals in music were similarly restricted.
The tritone was called the Devil's Interval and the mode containing it was banned in church music.

Equally restrictive attempts were made in the 1950's and early 1960's to restrict what was heard on radio and juke boxes to
those recordings controlled by certain criminal elements within
the United States. Some prominent recording artists were suddenly
not heard. Through bribes, certain disc jockeys were persuaded to
play only those recordings which would bring a profit to those
involved.

Cultural factors of a less pervasive type also influence what
music is heard and accepted by the people of a culture. A particular type of music may be culturally valued because of nationalistic
tendencies. It is commonplace in those societies which are changing rapidly that a point is eventually reached where the culture-
bearers realize they are losing their traditions. In this context,
what is left of a previous tradition will be over-valued in their
eyes, whether the musical type is itself of equal value to others
or not.

81

Wachsmann has pointed out for Uganda that performance types or genres which are being superceded are frequently highly-valued:

> This kind of idealization of an older style or styles fulfills the national aspiration, in a musical sense...I failed completely to find any-one who said "Oh, this is old stuff", although everyone knew it was old stuff, and on the way out. And this is an interesting situation, be-cause one would have to investigate carefully and clearly what was actually superceding what (1976:195-96).

The opposite may also happen, particularly in societies where the superceded form is still frequent. Among the Merina, for in-stance, there are two versions of stage presentation for folk mu-sic: the hira-gasy theatre, and that which is simply called "theatre". Hira-gasy is a staged presentation of long moral sto-ries sung by eight singers and accompanied by a small orchestra. This form carries basic culture values through their exposition in song. Theatre, on the other hand, is fully Europeanized; the usual version is similar to Vaudeville. Musicians take "turns" on the stage; other tribes are degraded in song through charicatures of their music; comics and straight-men make their appearance on stage.

These two forms are both available as theatre in large cities. The hira-gasy audience is mainly older men and women interested in the moral questions propounded by the singers, while theatre is the venue of the young. Here, the performance is toward the more modern stage presentations and the older style is devalued.

Value judgments of a non-musical nature may reflect class per-formance as well. Among the Maltese, members of the upper class rarely listen to Maltese folk music, preferring imported Italian forms instead. Their rationale for this is the myth that folk singers are always fighting. They raise horrid images of guitar-ists breaking guitars over singers' heads in scruffy bars, repeat-ing mythical stories about recent incidents of extreme violence. In truth, singers fight with words, not fists.

Here, the upper class is reacting, at least partly, to the close association among musicians, homosexuals, prostitutes and racetrack touts. Folk musicians are an out-group for the upper class. What they are avoiding is not the music, but the setting of the music.

The introduction of Christianity has generally meant the death knell of many older forms associated with religion. Christianized members of a community frequently avoid musical performances of a ritual nature on the principle that their presence there would be-lie their Christian faith. As a result, musical types die out for lack of an audience; frequently expressed by indirection.

Physical factors may also limit the public's participation in a particular place for, or type of, music. The Albert Hall in London is one of the major concert halls of the city. Many devotees of classical music refuse to go there, however, because the hall is a whispering gallery and performances are often ruined if one is seated in the wrong place. Thus, performance there may relegate a particular performer to a special kind of oblivion in London.

Many persons also suffer from the inability to physically listen to certain kinds of music. Men are particularly prone to difficulty with high sounds, and it is common for men to say they prefer not to listen to opera because sopranos hurt their ears.

Aside from those value judgments based on factors which are totally non-musical, there are a number of cases where value judgments are only partially musical. This is particularly noticeable when one tries to deal with the concept of the "best man". It was once axiomatic in the study of folk music that the first task of the scholar was to seek out the "best man" and make recordings of him in preference to other musicians. Unfortunately, many cultures have value judgments about musicians which relate not so much to their being the best performer, but rather the "proper" performer. "Best man" is a value judgment about the nature of the musician as well as the music. The "best man" is a consequence of Western tradition; however, a full understanding of the music of any society requires a study of the range of competence of various musicians within a style or genre.

This becomes particularly crucial in those areas where the "proper man" in a specific performace is not necessarily the "best man" to perform, in musical terms. Mention has been made above that in Tikopia the concept of "expert" (purotu) implies that some performers of music and dance are better than others. At the same time, noblemen frequently function as "experts" not by reason of their musical ability, but because they are the only "proper persons" to sing or dance in certain ceremonial circumstances. An element of Tikopian politeness also enters into the situation. When a nobleman attends a dance, his social position brings attention as it would in any other situation. As experts are normally found to the fore in dancing and singing, chiefs who attend dances are usually given the position of expert, whether they are expert or not.

Behague points out that in Candomble drumming, the master drummer is regarded as the "best man". This is the result not of quality of his performance so much as his knowledge of repertoire. Master drummers are confirmed and thereby socially recognized as having reached a certain level of competence which is only partially musical (1976:200).

Draper has pointed out that social recognition may not coincide with experiences:

Last summer, I went back to the Choctaw Indian
Reservation to get all the variants that I could
of a particular genre. When I had been there previously, there was a 'best man' for the Choctaws,
but when I got back last summer, he was too old.
He had forgotten the variants of a number of varieties of song. But he had maintained the social
role as best singer (1976:203).

While it is clear that cultural and physical tendencies may
intermesh with musical value judgments, there are yet some areas
in which music is judged by itself. The problem here is methodological: In what way may the investigator get at value judgments
about music? The authors agree with Merriam who states that not
all societies express their judgments concerning music in the same
way. The concepts of "good" and "bad" do not always apply. In
what ways, then, do societies express themselves in this area?

One common factor seems to be the use of native cognitive
categories about other things. In Madagascar, singers who are regarded as having truly great voices are described as having "blue"
voices. "Blueness" is the quality of sacredness, as seen in such
combinations of hazomanga (blue tree) which is the sacred tree of
the circumcision ceremony of the Sakalava; or Ambohimanga (Blue
Mountain), the name for the sacred fortified village of the Merina
where the remains of the great king Andrianampoinimerina are burie
The quality of "blueness" relates to excellence in singing because
of the association between Heaven and the sky, which is blue.

The same is true of the Cherokee "straight" voice. The quali
ty which makes a voice good is the ability to reach the spirits in
a straight line. This value judgment slides over into value judgments about the quality of a voice.

Among the Maltese, the situation is somewhat different. The
aim of the Maltese singer is to sing above his range and the most
valued voice type is a high tenor. Thus, the description of a
fine voice is usually phrased, "He sings like a woman", which
comes as close to expressing the ideal as their language allows.

Another way of expressing a fine Maltese performance is gestu
ral, rather than verbal. When a singer or guitarist has done a
fine job, members of the listening audience will either raise the
thumb of the right hand and jerk the hand straight up in the air,
or, holding all fingers extended, slash straight down through the
air. This gesture is closely related to the concept sewwa (truth)
That which is true in Maltese is also right or correct; the gestur
indicates the "rightness" of a performance. Also in the same cognitive set is the concept ezatt, (exact). Truth, correctness and
exactness are all qualities of a fine performance. While the verbalizations can be elicited out of context, in context the vertical gesture is used.

One of the reasons for the lack of verbalizations about ex-
pertness in Malta lies in the necessity not to compliment anyone
to his face. As mentioned before, a compliment is an insult in
Malta, since witches are said to compliment those of whom they
are jealous. Thus, verbal comments about performance which are
phrased in direct language could easily be misinterpreted.

It is possible, however, to compliment a performer by insulting him. After a particularly fine recording session, in playback for a group of musicians, the authors' interpreter became en-
thusiastic about the recording and said, "That was a lousy recording!" Cultural values made it impossible to comment on competence
in a direct manner; indirection, therefore, must be the rule.

In spite of the difficulties involved, the Maltese have a
complex, flexible means of defining the relative competence of a
performer. This system is based on naming devices. In Malta,
there are very few surnames and, as a result, many persons have
the same name. In the village of Marsaxlokk, for instance, there
were six men named Carmenu Bugeja. In a small alley in the village of Zabbar, there were two men named John Scicluna among ten
households. In order to avoid confusion, it is necessary to use
nicknames as another naming device.

Naming devices take several forms. One may be known by first
name plus surname; by nickname alone; by first name plus nickname;
by first name plus name of village; by surname only; or in cases
of dire necessity, by first name plus surname, plus nickname. Each
individual may be named differentially for clarity in different
situations. The musicians use these naming devices as a means of
indicating the relative competence of performers.

In order to clarify the naming system, here is the same name
of a single individual with all its variants: Anthony Borg (not
a real singer), is nicknamed in-Nahhu (the sparrow); lives in the
village of Zejtun. Depending upon his current situation, he could
be called Anthony, Borg, Anthony Borg, in-Nahhu, Tony in-Nahhu, or
Tony taz-Zejtun.

Fine singers are few. There are two ways in which one may
recognize the category of highest excellence. One may say that he
is a singer (ghannej) rather than an amateur or listener (dillet-
tante). This separates the few great singers and guitarists from
all others. One may also identify a truly great musician by using
the formula of first name plus nickname (Tony in-Nahhu). The entire evaluation system is listed in the following chart:

Master singer, leader	
Master guitarists	Tony in-Nahuu
Fine singer or guitarist	In-Nahuu
Fair singer	Tony, Anthony
Barely acceptable singer, or accompanying guitarist	Borg
Bad musician	Anthony Borg, Tony Borg
Returned emigrants who are not yet in the system	Tony taz-Zejtun

This system of evaluation of competence has two main values for the Maltese. First, the use of the naming device instead of a qualifying statement allows them to indicate their feelings about one another within the hearing of the individuals being spoken of. Thus, each singer may know his place in the system in the mind of every other. In addition, the system is flexible. If the singer has done a poor job on a given evening, he may find himself referred to by a nickname one or two categories down the list from normal.

A singer's status in any one of these categories is momentary and depends entirely on the relative evaluation of the speaker. As a young singer gets better, he may well move up in the system. Older singers may move down as they become less able to sustain the frantic pace.

A striking example is that of il-Bies, a blind singer who was once considered to be one of the greatest musicians on the islands. In 1969, he was always referred to as Pawlu il-Bies if past action was discussed; but simply as il-Bies if present action was discussed. One singer said of him, "Now he's getting very old and his mind is going. He is not the man he once was". His fortunes changed, however. In 1972, he had recovered status; clearer thinking was indicated in his performance and he was once more referred to as Pawlu il-Bies.

The last category, that of outsider, refers to those persons who are an unknown quantity. As an example, Zarenu Ellul went to Australia for a number of years. Upon his return, he settled in the village of Tarxien and attempted to enter a musicians' group. When he was an unknown quantity, he was referred to as "Zarenu from Tarxien". Two years later, he had moved in status and was then known as "Zorru", a short form of Zarenu.

The elicitation of evaluative judgments concerning the relative competence of musicians in the system is as yet very little advanced. This may lie in one of two factors. Given the examples above, ethnomusicologists may not have realized that each culture has its own way of verbalizing evaluative judgments, some of which may be exceedingly indirect and complex. The second and more insidious possibility is the disbelief that systems of folk music have an aesthetic component and have never looked for evaluative statements. This may also lie in the fact that value judgments concerning music are so frequently stated negatively. The negative statement of values so common in our own society can easily be used as a means of determining the grounds upon which a value system rests. Negative statements about performances or types of music will be found at all cognitive levels.

It is common in our own society to be told, "I don"t like Country and Western music; but I think Earl Scruggs is just great." Such comments indicate that while the class "Country and Western music" is not appreciated by the listener, one individual within the class does have qualities which are favored. In such situations, many persons may say that their favorite singer isn't really a Country and Western singer at all. This tendency may be viewed as the statement that a particular musician transcends the type of music in which he is normally placed.

Similarly, an individual may express a lack of tolerance for an entire category of music, such as "I don't like the modern American interpretation of Beethoven". Many musicians trained during the time of Toscanini find the modern interpretation of Beethoven somewhat unsettling. Wachsmann mentions a similar reaction:

> ...I went through this experience when I first heard Schubert Lieder sung in English by English singers. I felt like emigrating straight away again. But I did realize, as time went on, that I had a tradition that I valued very highly...I began to accept that there is an English way of singing Schubert Leider in English (1976:221-2).

The underlying canons or rules for making music may also be stated as value judgments concerning particular performances. This usually takes the form, "he made a mistake". The breaking of musical rules is often verbalized. It is common to hear someone say they will not attend the local symphony because the violins don't play in tune. This is the expression of a rule of competence, because, for performers to be competent in Western society, they must play in tune.

Other societies express themselves in a similar way. In the spirtu pront style in Malta, the improvised verse of four lines must rhyme with the end of lines two and four. Furthermore, the rhyming must not force the grammar; this is a primary rule. When an individual makes a mistake, the gossip is immediate and his

87

relative position in the evaluation system goes down. Other
rules are less strict. For instance, the best verse is in Latin
syllable structure: 8, 7, 8, 7. While this is the ideal, singers who include more or fewer syllables in their lines are not regarded as bad singers; but they will never be regarded as great
singers unless they learn how to create verses of perfect syllable structure.

In Malta, there are 37 "mistakes" in singing and guitar playing which are fundamental to the system. Yet other, more complex,
rules are known only to fine singers and guitarists. All but one
of these rules can be checked out in performance. The ineffable
rule known only to singers is, "If you think up a verse and then
forget it in the instant before you are to sing and are forced to
make up another verse to replace it, it is a mistake".

Using the basic rules or canons of music-making in Malta,
singers assess one another's individual performances in terms of
correctness. What is being discussed here is competence. A truly great singer or guitarist is one who is able to go beyond competence to that transcendent quality which, in the Euro-American
tradition, is labeled the aesthetic. However, consistent adher-
ence to the rules is the mark of a very fine singer.

Preferences between opposing items in the same realm may indicate style changes as well as preferences. In Madagascar,
there are two types of tube zither. The tube zither is made of a
large bamboo with an internode at least two feet long. In one
style of valiha, the strings are fashioned by slitting the outer
bark of the bamboo from the one node to another in two parallel
lines, then carefully cutting the outer bark away from the inner.
Bridges are placed beneath the now free string to tune it, and
the ends are kept from splitting past the nodes by tying them
with cord.

In the other type, metal strings made from telephone cable
are attached to the bamboo with nails, with splitting prevented
by wrapping the node with a slice of tin can appropriately nailed
down. These two types of strings have very different qualities;
the first is the older type, but the carrying power of the metal
strings is deemed much greater. In addition, the tone is clearer
since the slight irregularities in the bark of the bamboo can
cause the string to be untrue.

Similarly, change has taken place in Tikopia in respect to
a number of the less common dance types. This becomes particularly apparent at the feasinga, the larger daytime dance festivals
given by chiefs. Support for the chiefs at the feasinga is apparently not so strong as it was formerly. This seems to be related to the type of dances performed there and the preferences
of the young people. In one case in 1952, young people absented
themselves from the dancing of a tusoko, saying that they did not
care for it:

88

They say it's a lazy dance; they like their bodies
to sway in the dance. Their desire is for <u>matavaka</u>
(canoe-bow dance). They hold that they are not
skilled -- that they are skilled in <u>matavaka</u>. That
is their desire (Firth, field notes, 1952:xiv, 15).

On another occasion in 1952, all four chiefs came to a <u>fea-
singa</u>, but only about 15 dancers appeared and it was finally a-
bandoned. One of the men gave Firth a lecture on the younger
generation about how they no longer supported their chiefs. Here
is a case in which both personal preferences and changes in the
system are involved in the value judgment. The <u>matavaka</u> is the
most popular dance among the young people. Other, more formal,
dances are usually found at the daytime festivals and do not ap-
peal to the young people. In Tikopia, the right to absent one's
self is a form of protest; but it is difficult to decide what the
young people were protesting. Did they object to the dances, or
to the <u>feasinga</u>, itself?

Negative statements also occur in cases when a person has
committed himself to a particular category of music, but finds
fault with a performance within that category. This is perhaps
the most interesting area for study. This negative evaluation of
particular performances is one of the most valuable tools in the
determining of those qualities of the performance which give it
value for the listeners.

While it may seem negative statements concerning music have
been dwelt on, it is obvious that positive statements occur. In
Malta, fine singers have avid supporters who follow them from performance to performance, often armed with tape recorders to cap-
ture the moment of their latest triumph. One such man has a tape
library covering eleven years of recording.

The enthusiasm of listeners and singers alike is described
by the same term, <u>dilettant</u>. These are the lovers of the art who
follow it either as singers or as listeners. To be a <u>dilettant</u>
is not as good as being an <u>ghannej</u>, but it is a status within the
system. The passion for music in Malta is expressed by the word,
<u>namur</u>, which translates best into English as "intense love".

This concept of following given performers as well as styles
is present in Western society as well. While statements of this
kind are not aesthetic in the normal sense of the word, they do
indicate that a value judgment has been made and that certain expectations have been set up which the individual wishes to repeat.

The question of expectation has not been well investigated
in the study of music; though it is clear that each person who
responds to music develops certain expectations. If one performer or a group of performers fulfills those expectations better

89

than others, one frequently expresses that preference in terms of individuals or styles or genres rather than in more general terms.

Styles of music within the same society may differ widely from one another in terms of value opinion. In Malta, one element of music is valued over another in each of the two styles, the _spirtu_ _pront_ and the _bormliza_. In the _spirtu_ _pront_, it is the poetry and wit of the singer which is important; voice type is secondary. In the _bormliza_, voice type is most highly valued, for if a singer cannot create his or her own verses, someone will "feed" them lines. Each style has its own rationale within the system.

Such varied judgments are fairly typical of musical systems where different styles or genres exist. While a general statement could be made for music, differential emphases usually occur at the level of style. This may be why it is so difficult to define music in any given society. While the qualities of value in music may be stated in any particular instance, emphasis of one quality over another may be common.

Up to this point, those aspects of value judgments about music which relate to the concepts of competence and expectations within styles have been discussed. Attention is now turned to that area of musical performance in which verbalizations no longer serve a reasonable purpose. Until now, it has been possible to describe value judgments about music as "fit". The performers lived up to the expectations of the style; they were competent. This concept of "fit" (competence, or correctness) will suffice only so far. There are yet other cases where, when the expectations of the individual come together with the real performance, something beyond mere acceptance of competence occurs. Expectations can be either achieved or transcended; and if transcended, they become exceedingly difficult to verbalize.

What is the nature of the expectation of an audience or other performers when dealing with this area of judgment? There are two possibilities. Either the culture has taught individuals that they may at some time meet an unexpectedly beautiful performance with which they cannot cope in normal terms; or performers may be viewed as individuals walking a special kind of tightrope, in which disaster is always a possibility. The first concept is familiar. The second may explain why performances have such a quality of excitement about them. As Fernea has put it:

> ...in a sense, every performance is like the
> daring young man on the flying trapeze. There
> has to be that element of possibility that the
> violin will hit a wrong note, that the baller-
> ina will fall off her toe-shoe...It's the feel-
> ing that suddenly the person is transformed
> from prima ballerina, from Gisele, dancing her
> heart out, to a human being who's suddenly

90

twisted her ankle. It's that sudden loss of
illusion, that sudden recognition that the
man is just like me, he's forgotten his line,
that's what I'd do if I were standing up there.
It seems to me that this is the kind of risk
that sustains attention, and then your audience becomes relaxed and convinced as the
persuasive professionalism of the performers
manages to remove this doubt, and it becomes
more and more comfortable (1976:156).

Fernea implies that the potential for risk is an attractive
quality of performance. It is certainly true in the case of music, where all musical styles involve special skills and often
great complexity for correct performers. The performer is a risk-
taker; risking a failure with every performance. This is true
even in societies without fine art musics.

The attractiveness of music may well lie in its very difficulty. Many would-be musicians fail to achieve competence and
remarkable performances are infrequent. This points out a quality of performance which has not been mentioned before. Where specific performance tasks are not communally shared, the performers
of various specific roles such as music-making are demonstrating
difference. They are saying in effect, "I am doing what you cannot or do not do and I am displaying it back to you". This sense
of difference may lie in the complexity -- the risk-taking -- involved in the creation of an art.

Up to this point, concern has been with those instances where
the major aspect of value judgments is competence; now concern is
with those cases where performance transcends competence. This is
what is more usually conceived of as an aesthetic experience; involving the sudden realization that a performance has reached an
ideal which was often unmanifested before it was demonstrated.

In such cases, it is frequently impossible to verbalize the
experience well. There are many examples and the following quote
from King is typical:

There was a performance on Mozart's birthday
by the Budapest (string quartet) in New Orleans.
The Budapest got carried away, and so did the
audience. And it wasn't the Budapest any more.
Everything and everyone was involved in the
performance -- the hall, the audience, the musicians -- and suddenly there was Mozart. But
Mozart wasn't there where you could point. I'm
not a trained musician, but I could see it (1976:224).

The uncommon, transcendent performance is often approached
in this way. Verbalizations fail. Where verbalizations fail,

the means by which people express their feelings is lacking and
may take the form of "inappropriate" behavior.

For example, when Judith Anderson toured in the English
translation of "Medea" in the late 1940's, McLeod was present at
the performance in Salt Lake City. The audience was startled into the realization that the performance was transcendent and when
the curtain descended on the last act, there was total silence in
the audience. No one applauded. After a time, the curtain rose
and Judith Anderson stood in the center of the stage; the silence
continued. Anderson broke the mood by saying, with tears in her
voice, "Thank you. Thank you very much". She then gave an extremely theatrical, nineteenth-century stage bow, as much to say,
"This was a performance and I was the performer". At this point,
the audience stood up and screamed; and after a while, they began
to applaud. Both silence and screaming are inappropriate behavior in a theatre, and here, where the performance was too excellent to perceive properly, the audience reacted with behavior
which did not fit.

In Malta, the authors asked their major informant what he
would do if he ever encountered such a performance. He said, "I
would go to the man and shake his hand". This, too, is somewhat
inappropriate behavior, although it is not verbal and does not
break the verbal canons for indirectness, it does extend the usual gesture of up-and-down approval to direct contact across
space. Thus, he would be breaking another canon, that of allowing performers to have empty space around them.

This concept of atypical response to atypical performance
may help one to understand why such experiences are rarely verbalized. While very little has been written on the state of mind
involved in such experiences, it is clearly a change of consciousness. Victor Turner (1967, 1969) has emphasized the concept of
"communitas" -- a direct, immediate, communal experience of oneness in which an individual senses, if only for an instant, a
merging of his consciousness with all of mankind. While communitas is frequently associated with religion, it may also be a part
of the experience of meeting or listening to music. Mihaly
Csikszentmihalyi has recently suggested a term which is in many
ways related to communitas -- "flow".

"Flow" is a state in which one's actions follow one another
according to an internal logic which apparently needs no conscious intervention on the part of the individual. It is a uni-
fied feeling of flowing from one moment to the next, in total control, with little distinction being made between the self and the
environment, between past, present and future. Wachsmann is
speaking of this state when he says:

> I'm very conscious when my bowing is labored,
> and I am equally conscious when it comes per-
> fectly natural and right. It runs by itself (1976:234).

McAloon and Csikszentmihalyi indicate six elements for distinctive features of the flow experience. These are:

(1) The experience of merging action and awareness, for there is no sense of duality present during "flow". An individual is very much aware of what he is doing; however, he cannot be aware of being aware of what he is doing, since if he is, there will be a break in cognition and a resulting self-consciousness which will make him stumble.

(2) The merging of action and awareness results in and is made possible by a centering of attention on a limited area of action or thought. Hence, consciousness is narrowed, intensified and focused.

(3) The individual experiences a loss of ego as he is immersed in the "flow" of an experience. The suggestion is made that the self is forgotten during the experience, but this does not mean a loss of self-awareness, since when the "flow" experience is broken, recollection of the experience will produce increased consciousness.

(4) A person "in flow" is in control of his actions and the environment. That is, his skills are matched precisely to the demands made on him by the action.

(5) There is usually a coherent, non-contradictory set of demands for action which provide clear feedback to a person's actions. That is, there are explicit rules for action which make the evaluation of action in retrospect and the action, itself, easy and unproblematic.

(6) "Flow" is intrinsic. There seems to be no requirement for any kind of reward outside of the activity itself (McAloon and Csikszentmihalyi, 1975).

Along with the ideas involved in "flow", it is possible to consider another level of analytic awareness about the types of cognition usually dealt with in musical settings. With refinement, the idea of "flow" may indeed prove helpful in ethnomusicology.

When a student is learning to play an instrument, to sing or to dance, it is necessary that his attention be fully focused on the mechanics of learning. Later, as these physical skills improve, it is possible to concentrate on other factors. If a style has been fully learned, it then becomes possible to "flow" with the experience of making music, as it is possible to "flow" with the experience of participating in music as part of the audience.

93

Herndon and McLeod made a recording, several years ago, for a pianist who was applying for a Fulbright fellowship. In the course of the recording experience, the pianist, who knew all his material quite well, began communicating directly with his instrument and "flowing". There was a lack of consciousness of time passing; all those present in the recital hall became aware participants in a moving experience.

"Flow" is an intimate experience of performers. Once competence has been achieved, the pleasure of performing lies mainly in this quality. Here, the mind is freed of the necessity to be totally involved in simply producing the effect. The overarching sense of control over performance is such that some of the attention can then be diverted from mere mechanics. In such moments, the performer can move into a new awareness of the piece being performed which is transcendent of himself and his formal view. Where group performance is involved and all are competent, the concept of oneness in the entire performing group, or "communitas" takes over. In these circumstances, an orchestra may suddenly become a living organism.

Another kind of cognition at a very general level has not been discussed in the literature, but might be called "flash". This is the opposite, in many ways, of "flow". In "flash", there is an intensification of awareness of the entire environment, a consciousness of the importance of the moment and a need to mark it in some way. It has been said with some validity, that all Americans who were old enough to be aware of the importance of the event, can probably say quite easily where they were and what they were doing when President Kennedy was assassinated. This event, totally unexpected, was of such importance that it was almost burned into the awareness of all.

In musical terms, it is not unusual for an individual to have had one or two experiences in which "flash" has occured. A guest on a late night television talk show, for example, noted that his environment on first hearing "Ode to Billie Joe" on the radio was etched firmly into his mind. He recalled with great clarity the traffic intersection at which he was stopped when the song began; the people, the buildings, the odors, the external sounds; all were present in his mind and in some way were connected to his experience.

It might be said that every time people attend a musical event or occasion, they have a certain mental ideal against which the actual performance is matched with certain expectations, which may or may not be fulfilled by the performance, itself. However, the general expectation is that the ideal will not be fully achieved, although it may be approached closely. When the ideal actually does merge with the moment, a sense of "flash" takes place, resulting in unusual behavior patterns.

As in the case of Kennedy's assassination, the awful potential, the unexpected, occurs. Thus, the "flash" experience will take place either as a result of a totally unexpected event, or the achievement of an unexpected degree of perfection in a marked event.

Like "flow", "flash" may take place either for a performer or for a listener. It may be a communal experience or an individual one. One type of "flash" is not reasonable for a performer, but occurs among listeners. This is the state of mind in which the attention is so firmly focused on what is happening that the rest of the environment blanks out, and the listener is totally unconscious of everything else. In circumstances of this kind, he may be immobilized; his arms and legs cease to function. Another common concomitant of this state is the raising of the hair on the back of the neck, the tingling of the scalp and other indications of psychic shock. This state of mind may last for some time after the performance is finished, and may explain the silence of the audience at the performance of "Medea".

There is a "flash" experience in which time is shifted or becomes meaningless into a psychological "now", as Wachsmann puts it. Unlike those occasions on which the environment is burned into the awareness, in this variety, the environment is excluded and concentration is only upon the object or performance. After such an experience, one tends to babble, and again, there are no words to express what has happened. In this case, the atypical behavior is the inability to speak about it.

In all of these cases where transcendence of competence occurs, the states of mind are abnormal and behavior is often atypical. It is not surprising that people often phrase this as being "lifted out of one's self", or "transported". Some of the states of mind which occur in connection with religious experience, may differ slightly from the Western aesthetic experience, but they share the characteristic of the emergence of a changed state of awareness. This seems to be commonplace in association with music. Music is cognitively perceived in the ultimate sense, but it also seems to have the characteristic of changing perception in some way.

CONCLUSION

In this section, the ways in which music, which is primarily aural, is classified and evaluated by the mind was discussed. This is perhaps the most difficult area of all to assess correctly. Elicitation of data concerning the way in which music is viewed, evaluated, classified and experienced is one of the lesser explored areas in the study of music. Music is clearly subject to cultural factors here; but it is also a mark of the individual experience, both for performer and listener. As such, the data elicited are often contradictory and confusing. It is probably for this reason that so little has been said on this subject.

The purpose in this chapter has been to discuss some of the specific ways in which the problems of cognition and aesthetics can be approached. It is not enough to say that music is found in culture, for this approach is too broad, too all-encompassing. It lacks a sense of purpose and definition.

The specific examples given here are by no means to be regarded as the only ways in which to approach these more delicate and diffuse problems. Rather, they are offered as both concepts and discoveries of the authors. It is to be hoped that further study in this area will re-define many, if not most, of the principles discussed here.

The Relationship of Music

To

Social Institutions

In this chapter, focus is placed on three areas of human life which impinge in a major way on music. Although these are not the only areas which may interact with the musical sphere, the inter-relationship occurs sufficiently often cross-culturally to require special consideration. These areas are: economics, politics and religion.

The concept of music as economic or political may seem confusing at first, but the relationship between religion and music is more obvious. In each case, these are general cover concepts for kinds of actions that human beings do which can be grouped together and discussed in isolation from other aspects of human life. Like music, itself, each represents a way of viewing activity which is slightly different from the other. Although these cover terms are undoubtedly Western in origin, they are a means (but not the only one) of cross-cutting and categorizing human behavior.

In terms of value sets like music, economics, politics and religion are aspects of the theoretical view of life rather than hard facts. They are part of the superstructure of one's way of viewing the world rather than truly isolatable elements. The way in which economics interacts with music, for instance, is a variety of theoretical framework. These frameworks are mentioned here because they are so frequent in the study of music, that students may be predisposed to consider one of these aspects of the theoretical approach to human life as a reasonable field of study adjunct to the study of ethnomusicology.

ECONOMICS

Economics as a concept may be helpful in the study of ethnomusicology in that it masses together certain data concerning musicians which can easily be ignored. Concentration upon performance, style, learning, or analysis of music omits account of the ways in which musicians use their music as an economic good or a status good, and the more pragmatic gains (or losses) involved in music-making.

From the point of view of the musicians, music-making may be a way of social interacting, of economic gain, or of achieving a comfortable status if a musician's status is not ascribed. From the point of view of society, the musician may fall into normal social categories and thus fit into the economic system in a particular way. As Merriam stated it:

> ...musicians behave socially in certain well-defined ways, because they are musicians, and their behavior is shaped both by their own self-image, and by the expectations and stereotypes of the musicianly role as seen by society at large (1964:123).

At the present time, more is understood of the economic situation of the musician than in an earlier period in ethnomusicology, where non-literate societies were supposed to be generally undifferentiated economically except for the division of labor between the sexes, a fact which led to the assumption that there were no musical specialists. Merriam has rightly pointed out that the situation is much more complex than that, even in general economic means. The division of labor is normally wider than simply by sex with potters, carpenters, ritual specialists, musicians, weavers and others present in many communities throughout the world. The musician can be regarded in this way as an economic specialist who produces an intangible good (op. cit.,p.124).

The difficulty is not the distinction between the professional and the amateur, where the professional is paid and makes his living from music (although even this is a vexed question, given the number of professional musicians who hold other jobs even in our own society), but rather the way in which the musical specialist is viewed at large.

Merriam has suggested that the true specialist is a social specialist, who must be acknowledged as such by his society. Whether he garners all of his living from the production of music is a secondary question:

> Such acknowledgement may be forthcoming in a number of ways. The most visible, of course, is payment -- either in the form of the abstraction of wealth represented by money tokens, or in the form of basic economic goods -- which, if sufficient to support the musician totally, acknowledges complete professionalism. 'Payment' may also be in the form of gifts given to the performer, in which case total economic support may not be forthcoming; and in some societies, the musician's contribution may be acknowledged only by the recognition of ability unaccompanied by any form of emolument (op. cit.:125).

It has been pointed out for Madagascar (McLeod, 1964) that craft specialization is a more complex factor even than this. If the specialist is, as Herskovits has stated, he who carries on a given craft (1950:273), with the implication that those who have knowledge of a skill are specialists, the situation becomes confusing since, in Madagascar, there are more people who play, sing and dance than there are persons regarded as specialists. There, the recognition of the specialist by the community is clear with three criteria for distinction: (1) music regarded as necessary for certain occasions will be performed only by specialists; (2) such specialists in contradistinction to other musicians will receive gifts for their performances, whether adequate to support them or not; and (3) such musicians will, as a result. carry a definable status in the community in question (McLeod, 1964:278-279).

Distinction is made here between musics designed for special purposes, carried by specialists as defined above, and music for other purposes carried by non-specialists. This somewhat confusing situation is more characteristic of economies without money than those with money. Our own society, wherein the profit motive is supreme and status is defined in terms of money, is somewhat easier to handle in this respect.

Those societies which are partially in the money economy contain elements of social divisions of labor which are differentially rewarded. In Madagascar, there are musical specialists upon whom attention is focused and there are musical persons upon whom no attention is focused. Because of other situations, it is not always the specialists who perform the ritual music in ritual circumstances.

For instance, among the Central Sakalava, the musical specialist is paid to perform the role of diverting the attention of evil spirits from rituals, while other musicians are actually performing the ritual. This division of labor is understandable in view of the Malagasy concept of the supernatural as peopled by ancestors, gods and spirits who are sometimes antipathetic to human life and who will seek at certain points in life history to interfere with the activities of man. While specialists divert the inimicable spirits, non-specialists are invoking the benevolent. Who, then, is the musical specialist? In this case, the presence of payment marks not specialism, but a particular kind of activity. The division goes even further; those who are paid to perform are called musicians, while those who are actually performing vital rituals in the midst of musical "noise" are regarded not as making music, but, entertaining themselves.

The question of social acceptance of a person as a musician is a vexed one. He may be a professional in that most of this income is derived from the performance of his skill. He may be a specialist, in that he is recognized as the proper person to perform certain types of music, receiving some kind of gift for it.

Or, he may be a skilled performer of types of music for which either no payment is involved or there is no social recognition for him as a musician.

William P. Malm recently quoted a case in point. A man was standing in the middle of his field playing a flute. An onlooker, when asked what he was doing, replied that he was farming. Thus, there can be varieties of music occuring which are carried by skilled performers, complex in nature and highly stylized, but which are regarded as a kind of activity other than music. Thus, the American profit-oriented view of professionalism and its ramifications may not always help in finding out what is happening.

On the whole, it is easier to see professionals or specialists at work because their activities are marked in some way. This does not imply that the reasons for marking their behavior are musical ones, or even economic ones. For an overview of such information as is now available on the general implications of the social status of musicians who are recognized as specialists, see Merriam (1964), McLeod (1964) and Ames (1973).

Discussion of the ramifications of the musical specialist as one who is acknowledged for what he does -- gifted or paid in some way, holding a status -- this is dealing with the least difficult area. Payment can be defined and the relative income or status from musicianly activities measured. Attitudes toward one's musicianship can similarly be defined.

Ames points out that, when asked what they did for a living, musicians among the Igbo of Obimo usually identified themselves as farmers. In contrast, Hausa musicians from Zaria regarded music as an occupation and a source of livelihood, yet both receive some payment for their musical activity. The stress laid upon such return was more significant among Hausa musicians than Igbo; this distinction is both between cultures and between an urban and a rural setting.

It is much commoner in rural settings for persons skilled in the craft of music to identify themselves as something other than musicians. Multiple roles are, of course, commoner in rural than in urban societies and this may be a mark of this distinction.

Almost no information is available concerning actual payment for musical activities. In those societies where a money economy is not present (few as they are), livelihood is not determined by the possession of cash or goods. Communities at this level tend to work together for a common goal -- usually survival -- and, if possible, no one goes hungry.

In Tikopia, one of the few societies viewed by anthropologists before the introduction of a money economy, musical specialists are rewarded in the same way as others. Here, gifts of barkcloth called <u>ufi</u> are ceremoniously exchanged in public to mark the honor done by the presentation of a ritual, a song, presence of family at a funeral or wedding and so forth. The barkcloth cannot be regarded as payment for services, since it is immediately exchanged for another barkcloth of similar quality. Rather, honor is conferred by this variety of gift-exchange, a practice common among Malayo-Polynesian peoples (Firth, 1939:229).

Madagascar is also a culture heavily influenced by the Malayo-Polynesian tradition and, as a whole, is a gift-exchange area where allegiances, relationships, honors, kindnesses and economic transactions all depend upon an equal return for every social gesture. A musician, living in a tit-for-tat world, can expect to be repaid for his services in some way. Madagascar has entered into the money economy and for these reasons, two types of exchange take place in every transaction. Fees are frequently set by specialists for performances in public in the tradition of the money economy, with rates varying according to type of music to be played.

Additionally, an elaborate set of exchanges which enhance and honor a transaction exists. When the listeners are happy with a performer who was given a set fee, they will give him something extra. This concept, called <u>cadoa</u> (Fr., cadeau), is identical to the French concept of <u>lagniappe</u> (and may even derive from it); an additional fillip to the delicacy of social interaction. When a <u>cadoa</u> is given, the musician will often reciprocate in the form of another song. Another <u>cadoa</u> will bring forth yet another song until listeners and performers, alike, feel that a social bond has been cemented. Where the relationship is not a one-to-one confrontation, elaborations of this kind cannot happen.

The set fee is an indication of the presence of the money economy; the <u>cadoa</u> is a remnant of the older gift-exchange principle. In rural areas of Madagascar, musicians are usually paid with food; again, in ritual situations, individual musicians receive a set amount. In the less highly patterned situations, the concept of exchange is present; whether the gift be money or food, the interchange is both economic and social. It may be stretching a point to call this "payment", but here, music itself is regarded as something which can be given as a gift for which an equal gift may be received in return.

Ames points out another situation among the Hausa, where professional singers sing the praises of individuals and almost demand gifts in return:

> The musicians themselves tend to have a commercial attitude toward their craft, viewing it simply as the means for earning a living. This craft mentality is quite evident in the typical behavior of the musician. It is reflected in his habit of scheduling annual

101

tours through the countryside just after the
cash crop has been marketed, and in his
practice of consulting musicians when on
tour, in order to learn who, among the
wealthy, are likely to be generous givers
(1973:265).

The Hausa singers tend to urge generous giving on the part of
those for whom they sing and, if not satisfied, may shame the giv-
er in song.

The Igbo musicians of Obimo also receive gifts, but with a
completely different attitude of prizing the gifts, not for monetary value, but for the giving of them. The Obimo are also not as
likely to shame stingy persons in song.

Among the Maltese folk musicians, there is also a distinction
based on pay. The singers of spirtu pront, the song duel, frequently perform at different kinds of functions, and a few make
commercial recordings; however, only those who are regarded as
truly skilled are paid for their efforts. A fine musician often
has followers among the audience, who particularly enjoy his improvisations and who may ask him to assemble a group to perform on
a specific occasion for the standard fee of   l per man for a
single performance. The normal number of performers is seven --
four singers forming two separate song duels, plus three guitarists. In addition to the more formal fee, the Maltese sometimes
give a gift of food to performers; after the legal hour of 11:00
p.m. has passed, singers and guitarists may be invited to partake
of a dinner. This latter is more a gift than a payment for the
giving of food in Malta has social overtones; it expresses friendship, intimacy and appreciation.

The Maltese musician, sufficiently skilled to be paid for
his performance, cannot earn his living from music, alone, but
uses the performing of music as a way of creating extra income.
Many musicians make their living through what Levi-Strauss has
called bricolage, that economic process called "jack of all
trades". The bricoleur of Malta may be a farmer who supplements
his income by any number of other things, music among them. Musicians tend to view music simultaneously as great art, fine entertainment and a potential source of income; but this attitude is
as true of hunting or wine-making as it is of music.

The illustrations given of the way in which music is economically advantageous in certain societies tend to strengthen the impression that the general economic situation will influence music
in some way. The presence of gift exchange in Madagascar allows
music to be an acceptable gift in certain circumstances -- the
praise songs of Hausa musicians are regarded as an economic intangible good; in Malta, music is one of the possible ways a man may
earn a little extra money.

102

The fact that various economic systems place different emphasis on musical styles or performers is an indication of the reasons for the difficulty in understanding musical specialists. In Malta, with its profit motive, the situation is clear: if a musician is not good enough to be paid, he will not be. In Madagascar, skilled people cannot be paid for some of their musical services, because to do so would call attention to them and thus defeat the purpose for which they are singing. In the one case, the unpaid musician is not as skilled; in the other, he is equally skilled, so there is no necessary relationship between skill and payment. This implies that there may be specialists who do what they do musically for reasons that are not monetary. It would, therefore, appear unwise at this time to equate the concepts of skill and specialism until further information on the role of economic systems in musical production is ascertained.

In a broader sense, economics in the sense of _exchange_ is a useful concept in respect to music. In most societies, there is usually some system of exchange which is important. It may be monetary, as in profit-oriented socieites; it may be ceremonial or may denote rank and kinship. Exchange may be a general means of glueing a system together and as such, exchange is one of the grouping mechanisms of human culture. Malinowski has emphasized the concept of commensality -- eating together -- as a highly functional way of cementing social relations between people.

Music, like every other variety of human behavior, may have its place as a means of demonstrating the importance of a given occasion. When a group sits down to a wedding breakfast, music may be necessary to make it special or different. Performances to mark ceremonial points in life are common; but many people use music as a focus for social glue of some kind. McLeod maintained that recreation, where it is public, is not merely an opportunity for people to relax and enjoy themselves (1974). In each society, occasions where music is publicly performed usually indicate the necessity to express social tensions.

The _feasinga_, large daytime recreational performances of Tikopia, are a means for bringing together contrasting social groups who represent opposing social segments within the society. These are the clans, the districts of the island (between whom there is great rivalry) and various villages. Rivals come together at the _feasinga_ to dance together, to exchange personnel in dances, to eat one another's food, thus symbolizing for a moment the relaxation of social tensions.

The all-pervasiveness of music may lie in its close association with the public expression of sentiment of one kind or another. Because music is so frequently accompanied by linguistic texts, statements can be made in public in a highly formalized way, thus giving public validity to certain sentiments which are privately not espoused. Performances, themselves, may be viewed as forms of economic exchange, or, in a wider sense, social exchange.

103

Here, persons come together to express public sentiment and, by so doing may publicly alleviate private quarrels or tensions momentarily.

POLITICS

The study of encapsulated political structures and their inter-relationships with the larger environment in which they exist appears to be a growing concern. F.G. Baily (1963, 1969), has pioneered in this area with his work on the Highland Orissa. In terms of music, which is always found in a context, one might well expect to find encapsulated political structures.

The politics of music has at least two levels: the politics of musicians' groups, whether or not they include the audience; and the wider role politics of music may play in the structure and functioning of a society. Nor should the potential role of music itself as a form of political expression be disregarded. This has been discussed by Betty Wang (1965) for China, where folk songs were used as an indicator of public opinion.

The question arises as to the position of politics and its relationship to a musicians' group. It should be remembered that in some societies, such as the Karamajong (Gourlay 1972), everyone is a musician and there is no large classification called "music". In other societies it is possible that musicians do not communicate to a great extent, although it is probable that in most societies, musicians' groups are formed at some level of tightness.

When a definite musical group is present, it may be possible to derive valuable insights from a consideration of their processes and activities. The musical group may be viewed as a fairly clear-cut accessible entity, a functional organism having most, if not all, of the characteristics possessed by any society. If human behavior, in terms of particular societies, may be expected to repeat itself on the micro- and macro-levels, music provides a convenient, almost universally acceptable area of focus for the study of an encapsulated structure, reflecting numerous other aspects of concern.

The study of politics with regard to musical groups implies that such entities exist; thus, it is first necessary to know what a group is. In the study of social structure, the total configuration, interaction and articulation of groups, care must be taken to employ definitions which reflect analytical goals and purposes.

There are several kinds of general distinctions which may be made concerning the nature and identity of human groups. Contrast between territorial and special-purpose, kinship and non-familistic, voluntary and non-voluntary, or between volitional and ascribed membership in groups may be convenient, depending upon one's goals. Whatever one's specific interest may be, it is first necessary to examine carefully the more general kinds of relationships which identify musicians' groups vis-a-vis other groups.

Often, although not always, musicians' groups will be "voluntary" in nature, rather than being based on kinship or residence. In Malta, there is a level of grouping which might be done on the basis of kinship; many of the sub-groups are residential while the larger entities are not. Membership in musicians' groups might be called "voluntary", although volition is not sufficient cause for admission to the group.

Maltese musicians have a practical necessity for grouping together because the song duel, an impromptu debate, requires an opponent. It is difficult to discuss or debate with one's self for any period of time; it is not easy to sing without musical accompaniment, and most singers have a severely limited command of guitar techniques. On one level, the formation of groups may be seen to be the consequences of practical requirements.

In composition, Maltese musicians' groups are not necessarily territorial, although there is a tendency for grouping to occur according to village of origin. Any grouping by village of residence is usually restricted to what might be called village groups which are of secondary importance, both artistically and politically. Kinship ties, as well, are not a prerequisite to group formation; they do exist in many instances, but are not the sole compositional factor.

Maltese musicians' groups are not status-linked, age-grouped, or related to occupation, but based on a series of variables and a conglomerate of possibilities which may result in temporary or permanent association of individuals -- an association for the purpose of interaction via the means of music and its related activities.

The authors would suggest, after their experiences in Malta, that the term "group" might be used as a generic referent to all types of linkages between musicians. In Malta, there are ideally two groups at any given time but, due to change, it is evident that three or more factions are in operation, although most musicians will insist that there are only two. Given a period of time, the situation may change so that there are only two factions.

Anthropologists comment that factional situations occur frequently. There are usually two factions in community organization (Linton, 1936:229). On the tiny island of Tikopia, there

105

are two rivaling districts, Faea and Revenga; and among the Hopi, there are the "hostile" and "friendly" factions; and Boissevain (1965, 1969) describes dualistic organizations for Malta.

Factions, whether two or more, commonly oppose one another in various activities and boast about their own superiority. Murdoch (1949:90) suggests that ethnocentrism is a possible function of factionalism, which provides a sort of safety valve for the release of aggression.

Additionally, factions are not ever considered to be headed by non-officials (Clark, 1968:151). Throughout all the considerations of factionalism, however, the nature of it seems to have eluded definition, possibly due to the widespread existence of the phenomenon and the fact that it is often impossible to study both factions in a two-part situation. Perhaps the key to understanding the nature of factionalism lies in the concept of opposition. In the study of kinship-based systems, Smith (1956:39-80) and Sahlins (1961:332-45) have discussed the nature of segmentary opposition.

In Malta, factions are not kinship-based; nor may they be considered to be permanent organizations of opposition, although both segmentation and opposition seem to apply. Maltese factions seem to employ the concept of complementary opposition which involves the massing of equivalent segments in defense, exposition, or exploitation of privileges, rights and duties.

There is a long tradition of factionalism among Maltese musicians with a faction headed by a singer of high ability whose expertise is generally recognized. Such a singer does not exhibit the characteristics usually expected of a leader. He does not take any active part in initiating action, nor direct activities, maintain order, nor enforce decisions upon the group. Rather, he sits quietly off to one side, wearing a hat and smoking a cigar (indications of status, since no other musician wears hard-brimmed hats or smokes cigars), and is approached whenever a decision is called for. Then, and only then, does he comment quietly about a situation. His suggestions, while not overly directive, are always followed.

Membership in a faction is continually changing. A man who is a member of one faction may, through various processes, move his relationship to the other faction, then move back to the original faction within a period of two to three years.

With the advent of commercialism in the musical situation in Malta, it was soon deemed necessary for the musicians to form a

106

union. They did so; however, the resultant formation was not a single union, but two musicians' unions, whose membership at any given time strictly parallels membership in the factions. There is only one alteration which is made: the musicians' union has a president who is never the head of the faction. This is done because of the strong myth of egalitarianism; to flaunt one's ability by taking a public office would be inappropriate. To solve the problem, a figurehead president is elected who seeks the advice of the head of the faction before taking any action whatsoever.

In addition to the factions and musicians' unions, "village groups" of musicians exist, as mentioned before. These musicians have nothing to do with the activities of the more formally organized men, but often center their activities around a particular bar in their home village, gathering there to perform almost every night. These are persons whose musical capabilities are not sufficient to allow them to participate in the activities of the factions and unions, whose membership and activities range throughout the islands. Village groups are composed of people who cannot call on friends if asked to organize a performance.

Even within villages there may be factionalism. This is indicated spatially by the presence of two bars in which singing takes place. There are also some remnants of rivalry between neighboring villages; the people of certain villages still assert that they are bitterly opposed to the singers and guitarists of their neighbors in the next village.

It is apparent that factionalism, at least in the Maltese case, is the demonstrating principle of group organization. Since Maltese singing is direct, impromptu and occasionally insulting in nature, there is a certain amount of potential for violence, even if only verbal. It is possible that the presence of opposing factions at several levels of musical organization is indicative of the validity of the statement that factionalism tends to provide a safety valve for the expression of aggression.

Internal politics within a musicians' group is often a matter of the judicious/injudicious handling of gossip. Gossip may be a matter of self-interest -- a cultural device used by the individual to forward himself through impression management. In a widely dispersed community, gossip may be an important method of transmitting what is happening (Paine, 1967:282). Both fiction and fact are to be included under the rubric of gossip, stressing the component of self-interest.

Another focus of emphasis is to be found in Max Gluckman's assertion that gossip acts to maintain the values of the social group (1963, 1968). He views gossip as a "hallmark of (group) membership", in which "the values of the groups are clearly asserted" (1963:313). Although gossip and scandal tend to promote unity through establishment of common membership in a group, they could

107

also potentially destroy it except for the fact that they are regulated.

Louise Lamphere, speaking of the Navajo, claims that "through gossip, individuals not only maintain a flow of information, but control and manipulate it" (1970:6). In addition to self-promotion through impression-management, the unintended consequence of gossip among the Navajo is the definition of appropriate and inappropriate behavior:

> The details of an incident...are not as important as the interpretation or judgment which is passed on the alleged behavior of an individual. What matters is not whether an individual behaved in a particular way, but that disapproval of this type of action is communicated (loc. cit.).

Melville J. Herskovits (1937) first observed that the role of gossip is very similar to that of witchcraft, or as Nadel (1952) would prefer, to witchcraft accusations. Herskovits contends that gossip provides informal and indirect sanctions in situations where an open, formal attack is impossible or inexpedient.

Gossip may be regarded as the interchange of information which may be true or false. The information flow which constitutes communication passes through the cultural filters of an individual, and the nature of his world-view affects his perception both in abstract and real areas. Gossip is culturally patterned and the identification of these patterns may aid materially in understanding music.

The assumption of the existence of patterning of all forms of human behavior with its implications of organization and process may be said to form one of the main raison d'etre of ethnomusicology. If patterning does exist, and if the individual culture-bearer is the medium of information flow, gossip becomes a medium of exchange for interpretation of reality. All communication is a variety of metaphor and the distinction of what is, or is not, gossip becomes a matter of cultural awareness. As such, it provides a vital key to the identification of a particular group's most archetypal pattern.

It does not matter whether or not a piece of information is factual. The implication of a statement varies, depending upon its particular context; however, in order to understand the implications, the individual hearing or conveying the bit of gossip would have to understand the nature of the system and its symbols. The term "gossip" then should be restricted to the conveyance of information which requires prior understanding of the social system and the context in which it is found. Gossip in a particular society serves to identify some of its most basic values.

In Malta, the nature of gossip is predicated upon positive cultural values. Gossip is carried on primarily among the supporters of musicians rather than by the musicians, themselves. Gossip about an individual serves to support his sense of self-value. Collectively, gossip aids in the initiation, maintenance, and re-ordering of factionalism while adhering to a basic two-part model which factionalism is required to take.

In Malta, supporters of musicians move freely from wine shop to bar, to tavern, wherever singers are present. They are given admission to the performances of all groups whether they support them or not. Although they may be considered spies from the other faction, they are treated with equal courtesy by all; spies are welcomed as carriers of information between factions.

The information of the supporters is not accidentally obtained for the central figure of a faction often solicits the services of a supporter. The supporter, selected for the service of spying, maintains close contact with the leader. The relationship is informal with no pressure whatsoever placed upon the supporter to find a given performance, perhaps record it and report back to the leader. By means of the activities of several spies, the leader is kept apprised of any references to members of his group in the song duel or in conversations. It must be noted that spies are not relied upon for complete honesty and their information is often evaluated in the knowledge that supporters really would like to see a serious clash between factions.

Supporters also function in facilitating the movements from one faction to another. When it is known that a man might be considering moving from one faction to the other, he will suddenly be quoted as making fairly nice remarks about members of the opposition. The supporters, who know of his intentions although they may not have been formally stated, begin to make positive remarks about the opposing faction while down-grading their own faction of the moment. Over a period of weeks, comments become so strong that action is finally taken to invite the man to sing with the members of the other faction. Once he has done this, he is cut off from his original group and taken into the other.

In the case of Malta, gossip serves positive, practical purposes -- allowing movement by facilitating the flow of information through indirect channels. It might be suggested at this point that gossip is often a valuable aid in understanding the workings of any society; in many cases, gossip may not be as obvious as in Malta, but the kinds of information transmitted by this route will never be purposeless.

The relationship between politics and music is by no means confined simply to musicians' groups or to the performers and their supporters. In many instances, there is a relationship between the organization of musical politics and organization of the

109

more general political activity within the society. In Malta, there is an almost direct correspondence. The principle of bipolar opposition seems to permeate Maltese society. Boissevain (1965, 1969) reports the same kind of factionalism at the village level which is, at present, island-wide. In the area of national politics where there are actually five or six political parties, only two are regarded as important.

The dual nature of factions becomes clearer in approaching the concept of partiti, which Boissevain equates with factions. In the discussion of festa partiti on the village level, he remarks that, although village unity is an ideal, all villages are divided internally by cleavages which cut across the community at various levels, some of which are only temporary, disappearing when the issues are resolved. Others have become a permanent part of the social scene and, regardless of origin or duration, such divisions are acute to the villagers. He further states that "persons made vulnerable through a network of personal relations are often forced to commit themselves to a particular division. In doing so, they become opposed to neighbors and kinsmen who are committed to the other side". The Maltese call these divisions partiti, a term corresponding not only to "parties", but also to "factions". Partiti are believed to have pika (competition and hostility) between them (1965:74).

Musicians distinguish their factions from partiti, although pika may exist between them. Among musicians who function both at the village and national levels, at least part of the general political concept of leadership has been copied. As mentioned before, factions have leaders or heads but the President of the Musicians' Union is a figurehead. A similar arrangement is purported to be functioning in the Maltese government. Although the factionalism, present in the musicians' groups, exist at what might best be called a national, rather than a local level, there is some indication that factionalism reaches even to the village musicians' groups. The Maltese tendency to group things in twos (whether this is an easy feat or not) is maintained in musical life as well as in wider arenas.

It is not meant to suggest here that the political organization of musicians' groups always parallel the larger political organization of a particular society. Rather, it is suggested that this is an area for careful investigation, since insights gained at one level may be tested at other levels in order to reveal the strength of patterning of decision-making, leadership and other factors of political organization. If musical groups exhibit political organization, music itself may possibly be political as well. The exact nature of this will differ in each case in all probability. While it is logical to expect political organization within musicians' groups, not all music will be political in nature. Rather, it is reasonable to expect that some music will function in a political way.

In Malta, the long ballad form, <u>fatt</u>, sometimes serves as a vehicle for political commentary; they must refer to actual events, but some degree of commentary and interpretation is allowable. Since there is a tradition of indirection in Malta, it is not surprising that a <u>fatt</u> may progress at two levels of meaning; in one instance, a commentary on clothing fashions and their effects on the morality of the country is also interpreted as comments on the political situation. The Maltese song duel is often used as a means of discussing political dissatisfactions at various levels, although usually such remarks are in double entendre, rather than in the surface meaning.

One has only to consider the music of dissent in world perspective to find numerous examples of songs which are political in intent. The cornerstone of the Civil Rights Movement in the United States in the 1960's was "We Shall Overcome". In this case, the song states an intention, a goal and a focus of political activity.

Music is also used in some instances as a means of social control. The moralistic stories of the Malagasy <u>hira-gasy</u> clearly demonstrates how one should behave, serving as a teaching device and a reminder of proper behavior and values. The <u>mgodo</u> of the Chopi (Tracey, 1948) allow for direct insults and comments upon the behavior of members of the community. In some instances, local leaders may be referred to as sneaks, thieves, or whatever might be appropriate; others are similarly chastized for breaches of custom or morality, and the entire community is reminded through public performances that they should mend their ways.

The political ramifications of not only the organization of musicians' groups, but also the various ways in which political roles may be taken by musical sound, constitute an important area of study. Unfortunately, this type of investigation has not received the amount of attention and degree of focus it deserves. However, an investigation of potential political factors within music and musicians' groups coalesces a large segment of the information about music which is necessary to the understanding of the entire system.

RELIGION

The closest bond between music and any other aspect of life is with religion. In all societies, whether religion is a cultural focus or not, music plays a part in ceremonial and ritual. Because this association is so patent, the discussion of religion may be one of the richest for the study of music.

111

The role of music in religion is dominated by the organizational structure of particular religions. Where myth is a prominent part of public religious activities, songs are used as retention devices. Sections of a major myth cycle may be elaborated upon as the basis for highly specific stories in drama and, by this means, the memorization and retention of it is assured. Frequent public presentation allows for wider knowledge of such stories and their transmission through time.

In Tikopia, where ancestor worship is the basis of the aboriginal religion, mythical creatures from the pantheon, or temple, belong to various families. They are venerated by the recital of songs either in the context of special ceremonies celebrating the families' relationship to them, or in the general ritual presentation known as The Work of the Gods, where massive re-statements of the mythical cycle are presented in public. In Tikopia, the songs generally are not mythical recitations, but short, almost theatrical statements which refer to longer myths. In addition, major ancestral figures are remembered by songs (seru) which they, themselves, composed during their lifetimes as part of their ceremonial obligations.

The use of music in connection with the recitation of the stories of culture heroes frequently are religious in nature. In the case of Tikopia, the inclusion of culture heroes in the list of ancestors presented at The Work of the Gods is an indication of their having been raised to at least a semi-divine status.

This is also true of the Epic of Gesar of Ling as presented in Tibet, although this long story of King Gesar is rarely performed as a whole. The total presentation of the Epic would require four to six weeks, with rests for the singer. Most performers choose to sing only one chapter as their religious duty. At present, there is no way of ascertaining whether the ancient Epics were, in fact, religious in nature.

The most frequent use of music in connection with religion is as an intimate part of ceremonial and ritual. There are several possible explanations for the use of music in ritual and perhaps the most logical is also the most simple-minded. Ritual is highly patterned behavior -- and music is also highly patterned. That the two should so frequently coincide is perhaps a mark of their similarity of quality. This relationship might stem from the redundancy involved in ritual speech, music and ritual, itself.

All human action may occur in both highly structured and unstructured forms. Music is always redundant in comparison with other forms of human activity. This is frequently expressed by stating that music is highly patterned; at other times, the repetitiveness (or redundancy) which music represents is pointed out. The distinction which can be so quickly made between music and other forms of human activity lies in the fact that music

112

rarely, if ever, becomes unstructured. Once sound becomes unstructured, it ceases to be referred to as music.

That the patterning of music makes it a natural association for ritual which is already patterned; conversely, whatever is happening in music is also patterning other forms of behavior in a redundant manner. If, on the other hand, the reason for the high degree of redundancy in both ritual and music is sought, there is the possibility of investigating at least one possible explanation. Ritual is a response to anxiety. Is music perhaps a response to anxiety, as well?

Lomax explains the redundancy of music as a group-organizing function that displays the "behavioral norms which are crucial to a culture" (1968:15). In his terms, music has two functions: to organize groups of people into activity; and to demonstrate, within that activity, certain core-concepts which represent a skeletal statement of the major values of a society. Lomax further describes music as a form of communication, in that it signals cultural patterns in specific, symbolic ways.

There are two possible explanations of the redundancy in music. First, that it is a reaction to anxiety; and second, that it is the symbolic statement, a display of the basic cultural values of a group of people. Probably the most reasonable way to examine musical redundancy is to consider the function of music in various ritual conditions. Ritual is often associated with anxiety. What role, then, does music play in ritual?

One of the most striking features of liturgical music is the length of time that forms may be retained. The primary examples must come from those societies with written, rather than oral, history. At one point in Western society, Gregorian Chant embodied all of the fixed sentiments of the Catholic mass. The credo and the other parts of the mass were sung with standard words and varying melodies. Pope Gregory (590-604) codified and arranged the liturgical chant of the Roman Catholic Church. Prior to his time, four different styles of chant had developed in the far-flung parts of Europe controlled by the Roman Church. According to ninth century writings on Gregory, he abbreviated and simplified the Sacrementary of Gelasius which represents the background for the modern Roman Missal.

Some scholars (Reverend Frederick Homes Dudden, 1926:568) doubt that all of the changes and compilations in plain chant were instigated by Pope Gregory, but agree that melodic stabilization took place around his era. While the use of Gregorian Chant deteriorated markedly after the fourteenth century, it is clear that, at whatever period the stabilization was created, it has lasted for at least seven centuries. Even today, the Chant is to be heard in certain circumstances.

113

The example of Gregorian Chant illustrates the longevity to be expected when music is associated with ritual. While in many circumstances, historical records do not clearly indicate the age of given liturgical musics, the assumption from the example of Gregorian Chant that redundancy through time, in the sense of repetition through time, is a mark of ritualized music.

This is a frequent concept throughout the world. For a ritual to be effective, the music must be performed "correctly" or in the proper tradition. Among the Navajo, if any part of the ritual (including the music) is performed wrongly, it must be started over from the beginning. The Kutenai are not so severe as this. If a mistake occurs in the music the ceremony will not be begun again, but the performers will go back a short way to cover up the mistake.

These expressions of correctness are an indication of the way in which people view the function of music in religion. It is a set pattern, often said to have been handed down directly to men by the Gods. This has power; that is, if performed correctly, music reaches the ears of the supernatural.

The idea of music as the communicator with the supernatural is almost world-wide in extent and indicates a relationship which may help to understand the retentive nature of liturgical music. It is a non-human way of talking which can be understood in the spirit world. Among the Central Sakalava of Madagascar, some kinds of music are directed toward the inimicable spirits to keep them busy so that they will not harm participants during ritual moments; other music is directed at benevolent spirits who are asked to bless the proceedings.

While the question of retentiveness cannot always be checked due to the absence of historical records, there are many indications that songs are very old. In the Work of the Gods in Tikopia, some songs use words which are now almost completely unintelligble to modern speakers of Tikopian. The explanation given for this is that the songs are extremely old and have been retained by careful repetition in their original form. While the question as to whether they are now sung as originally composed is unanswerable, the position of unintelligible song texts in the ritual is perhaps indicative: these are the songs of ancestors who died at least several centuries ago.

From these examples, it is apparent that music is regarded as a form of ritual procedure which must be performed correctly. In theory, then, historical versions of earlier musical forms should be preserved in liturgical music. Whether change has actually occured is not possible to determine, given currently available procedures. The point is that constant and exact repetition through time is the ideal for many forms of liturgical music throughout the world. The reasons given for this are varied, but mainly relate to the idea that a particular sound pattern is in some way pleasing to the Gods.

114

In the Blanket Rite of the Lower Kutenai, each spirit only has one song which calls him into the ceremonial province. This particularistic relationship between a song and a supernatural being, while specific to the Kutenai, indicates that a relationship is strongly felt between music and the supernatural. The Kutenai believe that hearing their music is pleasing to the Gods. Spirits like listening to their songs as much as they enjoy smelling tobacco smoke.

Another view of the function of music can be seen in the Jazz Funeral now confined mostly to Louisiana, particuarly in New Orleans. One of several jazz bands may be hired to walk with the funeral procession from the church to the cemetary; large crowds usually assemble outside the church during the service. As the cortege moves out, the band plays slow, walking-hymns such as "For A Closer Walk With Thee", as the automobiles, band and accompanying crowd moves along the streets. After the short ceremony at the grave, just when a ceremonial bit of earth touches the coffin, the band turns and begins to move away, playing fast jazz. The anomolous crowd forms itself into the "second line" of dancers, strutters and actors, waving brightly colored umbrellas, bouncing babies and generally enjoying the music. Young men sometimes drop to the ground to do the "alligator", a dance performed by bouncing up and down on the tips of the fingers and toes.

The scene is one of total release. Those who frequently walk with the dead know this to be a moment in which the past may be wiped away through joyous music and dancing, without regard to surroundings. The heat of the sun, the rain, or the cares of the day are totally forgotten in an expiatory, cathartic form of activity. One comes away from a jazz funeral refreshed, renewed and somehow eased of concerns.

There are many theories as to the origin of the New Orleans jazz funeral. The most peristent is that West Africans believe that the dead go directly to a joyous heaven upon burial. Similar scenes of joy and release are to be seen at the end of West African funerals, where the living celebrate the ascension of the dead to a state of perpetual peace and joy. The jazz funeral may be a retention of this idea in active form. The funeral itself is expiatory. It offers release of tension, a way of cleansing and purifying the mind. It revives hope, temporarily dampens worry, creating new approaches to life within the few hours the event may last.

The cathartic effect of music is not well studied. As participants in many jazz funerals, the authors know, personally, that the psychological effect of temporarily suborning one's personality to the music in a total way is a revitalizing experience. It is not trance, but it is close to trance in the sense that, for a while, the individual allows himself to be swayed by the music and the scene. To the extent that he is successful in letting himself go, he will be more or less relieved. Listening to music and moving with it under such circumstances causes a temporary break in concentration upon the pressures and problems of being alive.

One of the commonest associations between music and ritual is the presence of music in what are called "rites of passage". These are those moments in human life when an individual's change of status is socially marked. Birth, puberty, marriage and death are the most frequently marked changes of status in the life of an individual.

Rites of passage frequently involve changes of states of mind for an individual. At puberty ceremonials, noise, exhaustion, starvation and exposure to fearful situations are frequently used to aid the initiate in changing a state of mind. In the midst of the fear and terror generated by the ceremony itself, initiates frequently pass into a state of mind where they no longer think of themselves in the same way as previously. During the ceremony, the individual is frequently described as a non-person; he has no status, because he is passing between two statuses. Turner (1968) calls this "liminality", the state of being on the threshold. The idea is taken originally from the work of Van Gennep. Turner adds to the concepts of Van Gennep the idea that a person in a liminal state may move from mere shock to "communitas".

In communitas, the individual loses not only personality, but direct consciousness of self, moving into a temporary unity with his fellows. This state, most usually achieved by ascetic monks, often involves a sense of complete well-being and a profound love for all mankind and all living things. While little is known about this state of mind, it is a condition so radically different from normal thinking that it has been commented upon frequently, particularly in religious literature.

It would appear from this that exposure to extreme anxiety and shock may result in a state of consciousness which is difficult to define or explain. The fact that so many cultures in the world deliberately use fear, deprivation and exhaustion to induce shock may indicate that the results of this phenomenon is a state of mind for which all peoples hope. In such circumstances, music is frequently used to create a state of "other-awareness" (something similar to that of the cathartic effect of the jazz funeral). A description of such a ceremony may give some indication of the profound nature of the experience.

Among the Central Sakalava of Madagascar, manhood as a concept is anxiety-producing. This is so because the birth rate of the Sakalava has been markedly declining for some time, due to a

116

decrease in fertility. The Sakalava know that they are losing population and that their very survival is threatened.

The ceremony begins with a temporary altar called <u>hazomanga</u>, ("blue tree"), a large pole the end of which has been cut to a point, is set up. Toward evening on the first day, several groups of people begin to take on special tasks. The women of the village gather together in an enclosure and begin to sing long, commemorative songs and dance, accompanied by a two-headed drum. Songs may refer to the sacredness of the occasion, to Biblical stories or, to other subjects. The women are said not to be performing music, but simply entertaining themselves.

In the meantime, the lad to be circumcised, usually about eight years old, is carried on the shoulders of one of a group of men. They dance from place to place, presenting the child to all the houses in the village and accompany their dance by rhythmic grunting. Another group of men are elsewhere, mystically searching for the two permanent altars which will replace the temporary one, after the circumcision has taken place. These larger trees, also cut to a point at the top, represent the fully-circumcised child and his father.

Another group, headed by the musical specialists of the village, is out searching for the <u>fanafody</u> (medicine) which will be applied to the forehead and body of the boy to protect him from evil spirits during the dangerous moments of the circumcision. The seachers are not singing, rather, they emit a rhythmic set of whoops and grunts which fill the night with chilling sound.

In the early morning, all the participants arrive together at the scene of the actual circumcision. Around 4:00 a.m., bulls are killed and blood is smeared on the tip of the <u>hazomanga</u> and the meat is cooked and eaten.

During the ceremony there is a strict separation of the sexes; women gather under one tree, men under another. The oldest living male relative of the family is the leader of the ceremony and gives the feast, as "father of the sacred tree", which symbolizes family continuity through the male. His wife is the "mother"; around her head are twined the <u>fuli velu</u> (threads of life), twisted cotton strands used by the Sakalava as magical representations of the continuity and stability of life. Such threads have a protective function; they are also worn by the father and by the boy, himself, who is in the most danger.

The most important aspect of the circumcision is the way in which all participants involve themselves in music at every point. Each person has music and/or noise to accompany his travels throughout the night and during the playing-out of his position in the ceremony on the following day. Sometimes, the sounds overlap in such a way as to create almost total sound confusion.

Two basic principles arise out of this example. First, whenever noise and confusion are at a high point, some bit of ceremony takes place. The madness of the scene of the surgery, the singing, the crowding, the noise and hysteria effectively mask both circumcision and the arrival of the men with the two true hazomanga. This is done so as to confuse the evil spirits. The truly important aspects of the ceremony are performed with a high degree of casualness and, by supposedly the wrong persons. Musical specialists are to be found leading the distracting music, while women (who are not regarded as making music at all) are actually performing the most essential part of the ceremony. The kolondoy is for the spirits, yet it is performed by women, who are only "entertaining themselves".

Aside from its supposed effect on the spirits, the effect of the use of multiple musics and noise on the boy is startling. He is exhausted, frightened and hungry. At the beginning of the morning ceremony, he is already in a state of shock. By the time the actual circumcision occurs, he is deeply unaware of his surroundings. His eyes no longer focus; his musculature is completely limp; his jaw is slack. His personality seems driven out of him and the liminality of his state is very apparent. The Sakalava would not describe the boy as in a state of trance; this concept is reserved for other behavior.

The common association between music and noise in rites of passage has been noted previously, particularly by Needham (1972). While not nearly enough is known about the role of music in rites of passage, theory at this point can state that there is an intimate relationship of some kind between the production of overwhelming sounds (be they musical or otherwise) and the liminal state of mind.

The shock produced by this may be purposeful, although its function may not yet be established cross-culturally. The personal limbo produced by massive sound is so evident as to be one of the most easily observed characteristics in rites of passage. One of the factors in the production of this state of mind is music.

Yet another view of the function of music is widespread on the North American continent. As a general rule, American Indians regard music as a special form of communication with the supernatural, which has power. While music is made by human beings, it is the vehicle for the transmission of information to and from the supernatural and the means by which situations may be changed. The function of music is essentially magical.

In the Vision Quest, a young man is given a vision by his guardian spirit, usually in the form of an animal who gives him power through the use of a special song. Vision Quest songs are subsequently used for whatever purpose they are best suited to. Among the Kutenai, the shaman who is to perform in the Blanket Rite where the shaman, himself, is said to dematerialize and carry messages directly to the spirits, must first have a Vision of Strap before he undertakes the role. Strap is the guardian spirit of the piece of rawhide with which the shaman's thumbs are tied behind his back.

At the high point of the first part of the ceremony, both Strap and shaman are said to have completely dematerialized and to have taken on total spirit form. In this condition, the evanescent shaman flies through the walls of the lodge or teepee, guided to particular spirits by Strap, with whom he will return into the ceremonial precinct. The relationship between the shaman and Strap occurs through Vision of Strap which takes the form of the Strap song. Among the Kutenai, each spirit has only one song. The power of a shaman is derived directly from the singing of the Song of Strap to the spirit, who comes when called and invests the human agent with the power to become evanescent.

This is a common association among American Indians. Music communicates with and transmits power from the supernatural. It is thought of as another form of language which is directed, not toward men, but toward the Guardian Spirits or pantheon believed to be in control of the universe.

In order to emphasize this, there is a frequent association between music and what has been called nonsense syllables. The texts of secret songs among American Indians are frequently not in a recognizable language; rather, they appear to be isolated syllables without meaning. Herndon (1971) and Halpern (1976) have reported for the Cherokee and the Kwakiutl, respectively, that the accompanying text for religious songs or chants are, in fact, a form of coded message. This accords well with the American Indian concept of a "spirit language" as opposed to human language. The full extent of the use of nonsense syllables as a coded message is as yet unknown, since the sacredness of the messages has precluded their translation to ethnographers.

As yet, the ways of speaking to the supernatural have not been fully investigated in North America. At the present time, the only information available is from the Cherokee where four forms of ritual chant occur: thinking, muttering, speaking and singing. Thinking a ritual chant is the least effective and least powerful. This form of chant is used in those cases where great force is not considered necessary to the solution of the problem. Singing a chant is regarded as the most powerful form of communication with the spirits; it is reserved for use in dire emergencies.

This concept of music as power among American Indians has led to a close association between ritual specialists and music. Those who sing are not musicians; rather, they are shamans or diviners. The function of music in this case subsumes music under religious categories so firmly that there are almost no power-free forms of music.

From a functional point of view, the relationship of music to ritual and ceremonies involving music has been seen as a device for retention; for catharsis; for the succinct expression of basic religious values; and for the creation of shock and noise in rites of passage and as a vehicle of power. In each case, there is an expression of the value of music as a carrier of something else -- a participant in holiness or sacredness. While these do not represent all of the major associations between music and ritual, they seem to be major factors. This description has omitted an account of one of the most dramatic of music's associations -- that of trance -- which is the ultimate binding of factors in religious expression.

There is no reasonable definition of trance. This human activity so removes the personality of the individual from the everyday social sphere that it is difficult to discuss its nature. Trance does not take the same form everywhere; appropriate trance behavior, although seemingly anomolous as a concept, is apparently the norm rather than the exception. Trance is at once ecstatic and culture-bound, seemingly withdrawn, yet profoundly and deeply culturally patterned. Although an extreme form of human behavior, trance is, nevertheless, human behavior. As it is the nature of our species to respond to basic patterns which are learned and transmitted from one generation to another in other areas, so it is in the case of trance.

Generally, trance might be described as a variety of atypical cultural behavior which signals a special condition. The actions which take place while an individual is in "trance" range from quiet introspection to violent, uncontrollable muscle spasms. What seemingly binds the various behaviors together is an assumption of "otherness", in which the consciousness or awareness of an individual is severely transmuted from the norm. Basically, trance is a state of mind into which an individual may either slip unaware (as in the case of trance possession) or which he may induce.

The close relationship between religious states and trance states reflects an assumption of the otherness of the supernatural, which requires otherness on the part of the individual facing the supernatural. The rationale behind the assumption of this behavior is as varied as is the behavior itself. What all descriptions of trance seem to have in common is that the individual is acting in ways which are beyond some norm, yet symbolically comprehensible.

Among the Central Vezo and Sakalava of Madagascar, two varieties of trance are commonly found. Both involve possession by spirits. The variety of possession called <u>tromba</u> results from possession by the "Spirits of the North". The Spirits of the North is a general term for the spirits of dead kings. Nobility are considered to have special powers after death, as well as individual and special needs. They long to hear music and to assume their vaunted earthly positions. To accomplish this, they possess living persons and, through them, experience what they may not know in the ancestor world.

The Spirits of the North need not come alone. They sometimes bring other spirits with them, such as the spirits of dogs or slaves. An incident of possession occurred at the town of Belo-sur-Tsiribihina, the court of the king of the Central Sakalava, where one man was possessed by the spirit of a king, and another by that of a king's dog. The latter was licking the feet of the former.

The commonest association between Spirits of the North and men involves players of the case zither (<u>salegy</u>). The zither music of the West Coast consists of a rhythmic, harshly harmonic accompanying figure repeated over and over, interspersed with melodic interludes of great virtuosity.

The most important aspect of zither playing is its intimate association with the spirits of the dead. Zither players are said to be possessed by one of the Spirits of the North. Players are not taught to play by the spirits; rather, the spirits play the instrument <u>through</u> the player and afterwards the player's fingers "remember" the song. The players claim to be in trance.

Not only zither players are possessed by a Spirit of the North. Anyone who asks to hear case zither music is always willingly accommodated, since it is assumed that such interest is always instigated by a dead king.

<u>Salegy</u> players exhibit a serious demeanor, for to them, their introspection is a form of possession. The expression of a sober, dedicated interested player and a quiet, intent listener as two possessed persons is a way of acting out the closeness which life and the after-life have for the Malagasy. In the midst of a truly amazing artistic style with its trembling runs, ecstatic falls of sound and intricate musical improvisation, listener and player, alike, are caught in a mood of introspection in which the music is the central focus of attention. In Western terms, it is difficult to say that <u>salegy</u> players are indeed in trance; during performances, they are capable of answering questions and otherwise distracting themselves from the music.

In contradistinction to this gentle, introspective statement of awareness, the Vezo and Sakalava have another form of trance, called <u>bilo</u>, mentioned before. This term refers to a feast for the spirits; called a feast because in the more extreme cases, it is necessary to sacrifice bulls. The word <u>bilo</u> applies equally to the state of an individual, to the individual himself, to the rites occasioned by this state, and to the spirits present (Faublee, 1954:39). Because this is trance possession, the spirit (bilo) becomes the individual when he possesses him. The bilo usually takes the form of dancing madness, and is an extremely dangerous and incoherent form of trance possession.

The ferocity of behavior in persons possessed by bilo is said to be exorcised only by "dancing them out". The spirits must be made to go away by the process of regularizing the motions of a possessed person. Musicians are absolutely necessary for this purpose, since the presence of rhythmic music reduces the arbitrariness and incoherence of the body movements of possessed persons. As the sound of music penetrates the mind of the possessed, he or she begins to regularize motions of feet and hands until they are actually dancing. When the individual drops to the ground exhausted, the bilo has been chased away.

In this exaggerated form of trance, one sees a relationship to the activities of the circumcision ceremony where the kolondoy is also played. Just as this form is used to drive spirits out of the possessed person in the bilo, in the circumcision ceremony, it is used to prevent possession of the initiate by evil spirits.

These two examples of trance within the same society, different as they are from one another, indicate the range of behavior which may be involved in the concept. In the case of the Sakalava, the diversity of behavior is supported by a belief that there are benevolent and inimicable spirits. Thus, two different approaches to the supernatural result from an assumed difference between types of spirits. From these examples, it is possible to determine the cultural patterning involved in the concept of trance.

It is interesting to note that in Madagascar, dancing madness is a response to upsetting situations. Epidemics of dancing madness in which entire villages or towns have been seized with the impulse to dance have been mentioned in the literature. In each case, the individuals have been upset by political or religious decisions on the part of their rulers. One can speculate, therefore, that dancing madness serves two purposes, only one of which may be religious. As an attention-getting device for an individual who is troubled, dancing madness is unparalleled.

Dancing madness is an exceedingly dangerous state. If the bilo cannot be driven out of the body of an individual through the exhaustion of dancing, they may die, for the general musculature of the body seems to lock, resulting in uncontrollable behavior. Among the Betsileo of the Central Plateau, an episode of dancing madness which is not quickly cured is regarded as a sign of supernatural power. If the spirits will not leave an individual's body, the individual becomes theirs. At the same time that the bilo is a mark of social anxiety or personal upset, it is also an indication of the possibility that a person may be the vehicle for communication with the other world.

The concept of trance as a vehicle of communication with the other world is common in West Africa and in Afro-American communities. In West Africa, most cultures do not have a centralized religion. Rather, each god his its own cult. Individuals are "called" to become members of one cult or another by special circumstances which indicate the god which has chosen them. For example, Shango is the god of lightning. Those who are struck by lightning and survive know that they have been called to his cult. Cult worship in West Africa involves possession of cult members by the god or gods involved during established rituals. Percussion orchestras play the music of the god, and he or she "comes to the head" of various members of the order. The god is believed to physcially enter the body of his worshippers through the head during such ceremonies; the people in trance then dance out the desires of the god.

This form of trance possession is not as chaotic and uncontrolled as that of bilo. Each cult contains some persons who do not go into trance and who are designated as helpers of those who do. Those who go into trance generally act out certain characteristics of the cult god through body motions. Trance is controlled by the ritual setting in which it occurs and ends when the ceremony ends. This more controlled form of trance, the commonest form throughout the world, still involves both music and dancing.

The shamans of the Kutenai Blanket Rite are also considered to be in trance. The songs of the Blanket Rite Ceremony are in three sections. In the first section, attention is focused on songs which will cause the shaman to dematerialize. In the second section, his dematerialized spirit, guided by Strap, is said to be seeking out spirits to bring into the ceremonial precinct to answer questions and aid members of the community. In the third section, songs are directed toward spirits who help the shaman to dematerialize. At the end of the ceremony, he has been returned to human form.

Informants described the shaman's condition as similar to that of hypnosis. He is taken over, guided and controlled absolutely by the spirit world. His body melts before him. First his thumbs dematerialize and the strap falls through them. Then, he becomes light and begins to float off the ground. Third, he comes in two in the middle, and the ropes tied around his waist fall away. Finally, he disappears altogether. In the process, the shaman, himself, undergoes the metaphysical shift from human to non-human. He is a will-o'-the-wisp with no mind of his own. His whole being is put at the service of his community and of the spirit world and he rides upon the wind, guided by Strap, to seek out the forces of the Universe.

Is this trance? It is so described by the Kutenai; yet it differs markedly from the other examples given here. The individual induces trance in himself. He places himself at the service of the supernatural, rather than the other way around. His function as a ritual specialist is an important one in the community and the position of shaman is both feared and revered. Like all shamans in the Circum-polar cultures, he is regarded as different from other men, in that his special powers remove him from normal human life in many ways. In those cultures exhibiting shamanism, persons who do not fit well within the social fabric frequently become shamans through the acceptance of their difference from others.

Whatever specific forms it may take, it is clear that the relationship between music and ritual is extremely close. This provides an intensely fertile ground for ethnographic investigation, one which has long been utilized productively.

CONCLUSION

The relationship between music and culture, which has often been asserted, is indeed present. What scholars have mainly referred to in these statements is the close association of music with economics, politics and religion. This association can be viewed in three ways: (1) That cultural institutions limit musical expression; (2) That certain cultural institutions provide organizational models for musical groups; (3) That music functions within culture as a means of shifting personal awareness.

FIELD METHOD

Undoubtedly, the most important aspect of ethnomusicology today is the actual gathering of information in the field. This is so because ethnomusicology, in contrast to historical musicology, places most of its emphasis on synchronic rather than diachronic studies. The reasons for current studies of living people are obvious: (1) many groups studied are preliterate and lack written histories, depending instead on oral history and tradition to account for their past; (2) among all peoples, there is a difference between what they say they do (or did) and what they actually do (or did). As a result, ethnomusicologists have tended toward the position that studies of music must be done with living people in current situations.

Also, there is a tendency to consider it best not to use material collected by others, where possible. Although Curt Sachs (1962:16) separates ethnomusicological research into two distinct components, desk work and field work, later scholars such as Bruno Nettl (1964:62), feel that such distinction should not be made.

While some still use the materials of others, it is imperative for the full development of an ethnomusicologist that each individual accomplish his/her own field work for many reasons. The most significant reason is that, without personal contact with musicians in a field situation, the scholar is unable to formulate new hypotheses, either working with theories already expounded or resorting to speculation.

It is a truism that one learns from one's informants, although the specifics of that knowledge are naturally subject to great variety. Because of the diversity of human musical behavior from one society to another, each society offers the scholar a special opportunity to re-visit aspects of the art called music.

It is impossible to delineate specific condition and prospects for each and every musical group in the world. Preparation for work with each culture must be slightly different; however, some generalizations can be made. The common ground is music; the common goal is fuller understanding of the phenomenon. The situation in every "field" will be in some way different from all others; if this were not so, field work would soon become unneccessary.

It is presumptious to assume that all aspects of all field situations can be covered; indeed, they cannot; but it is imperative that each scholar be given some general preparation, so that mistakes may be avoided. In this matter, the authors walk a special tightrope, for many of the remarks made in this section will clearly not apply to all field situations. It is hoped to inform the reader as fully as possible about the joys and pitfalls met. Although specific instances may differ, some related patterns will inevitably creep into human situations, particularly in cross-cultural contacts.

Field work can be defined as the gathering of primary information for consideration by others in the future. It is the process of first-hand investigation and direct experience of the behavior of others. Both during and after the gathering of field data, the investigator expects to interpret the material, question it, and present it to the scholarly community and to the world at large in various traditional forms.

Field work can be undertaken either individually or in groups. Most field work is the product of individual scholarship. The authors have engaged in both types of research and find that there are problems and benefits unique to each. Field work undertaken alone produces a higher level of anxiety, more possibility of omission of crucial questions or observations; however, it forces the scholar to integrate more deeply with the group being studied, permitting certain kinds of work not otherwise possible.

Group field work has the advantage of allowing multiple observation of the same events, styles and structures; it has the distinct disadvantage of possible disaster if scholars who are under intense psychological pressure, cannot complement one another, and also the possibility that more than one investigator will overwhelm informants by posing a threat to them.

The first questions which arise in a consideration of field work are "What is a field?" and, "With whom do I work?" The answer to the first question is much easier than the answer to the second. A "field" was, historically, any type of music except Western art music; however, current thought would seem to include all music, however defined.

A "field" may be a geographic area; a linguistic area; a particular village, town, city, suburb, or rural area. It may involve the study of a single style of music or aspects of a single style; equally, it may be concerned with either homgeneous or mixed ethnic groups. It may be either a survey or an in-depth study. Depending upon the manner in which a "field" of study is defined, the answer to the second question will vary. In any case, the people with whom the scholar works are called "informants".

Field work involves the delineation of a "field" and the gathering of data from "informants". Since music is always in a state of change, each field study represents not only a study of "The Music of X", but also a statement in history. What one scholar finds to be true at one time in one place may be essentially the same for the second scholar who visits that same place, or it may be quite different. Statements made by Densmore about various American Indian musics are often quite different from the findings of scholars in the last ten to twenty years. This is true of other early scholars and will probably continue to be true of those who are yet to come.

It can be safely said that no matter what time period being considered, no matter what field situation being investigated, the information gathered is a one-time validity which can never be quite replaced by the work of another at any other time or place. It is equally true that material gathered on an initial field trip will probably not be of the same nature or quality as that obtained even by the same scholar on subsequent trips.

While one village of a particular culture may have been well investigated in the past, this does not negate the work of any later student in the same or another village. This is so for two reasons: (1) The personality of each scholar is individual and different, so reactions to situations and events are therefore subject to a wide range of interpretation. What appears depraved to one scholar may be charming to another; what appears to be illogical to one will assume logic for another. Responses of informants to one researcher will not be the same as those of the same informants to another, often even at the identical time and place. (2) Regional differences may be extreme, requiring the work of several people. Simply because one village or group views a dance, style, or instrument in a particular vein does not necessarily mean that nearby villages or groups will feel the same.

Because of the many problems involved, it is understandable that little attention has been paid to field work in critical articles. Previous work on questions of field method has sometimes been incorporated into studies of general ethnomusicology, such as Hood (1971) and Nettl (1964), or has been assumed as a general background competence acquired elsewhere (Merriam, 1964).

PREPARATION FOR THE FIELD

Before leaving for the field, it is advisable to read general works on the area. Though most information thus gained may be of little significance to musical study, much helpful knowledge is available. For non-European societies, this information will be found generally in monographs and articles by social and cultural anthropologists, political scientists and historians. While the musical information is frequently sketchy and often misinformed because of the inability of the author to handle the material, certain scholars such as Speck (1909, 1911), have been extremely specific about music and offer a fair outline of the area to be studied.

The problems posed by language barriers must be carefully considered because the group to be studied may speak the same language or be bilingual with a language spoken by the scholar. If this is not the case, it may be possible to learn the language before departure. At the present time, most trade languages and many specific languages can be studied either at major universities or through various tapes or recorded courses.

It is always possible, however, that a particular language will not be accessible to the scholar prior to departure for the field and it may have to be learned before serious work can be undertaken. Depending on individual ability to learn another language, considerable time might have to be added to the length of the study in order to allow for the acquisition of linguistic competence.

It is also necessary to consider those problems of language which may be posed in the ethnomusicological investigation. Since much music is sung, a high level of competence in the language may be necessary in order to explore the symbolic and contextual aspects of songs. In such cases, it may be wise to choose and train a translator who is a native speaker of the language. These translators, if selected carefully, may in turn become most valuable informants.

Before going into any area, it is necessary to contact personally those scholars who have worked in the area before, whether they are ethnomusicologists or not. While this is only common courtesy, it can add immeasurably to a scholar's work if persons who have previously visited there are willing to offer advice and information.

Prior to working with the Cherokee, Herndon contacted Raymond Fogelson at the University of Chicago. As a result, she discovered that he had worked with the same ceremonies and informants about ten years previous to her own work. Although Professor Fogelson is not an ethnomusicologist, an intense and fruitful collaboration followed this contact which led to the publication of parallel articles on the Cherokee stickball game (Fogelson, 1971; Herndon, 1971), which demonstrated many similarities in the ritual and musical organization.

If one is planning to work in one of the less accessible areas of the world, it is advisable to write to any churches who have active missionaries in the area. Information which is important for comfortable living will not usually be found in readily-available form, such as State Department reports of foreign countries. Data on climate, prevalent diseases, economics and politics are often restricted in such reports to the capital city.

This is not to say that such reports are not helpful, but that they may provide only partial information. Many researchers heading for more remote areas have found themselves mis-clothed

128

or otherwise deceived in their expectations of living conditions. For example, before doing field work in Madagascar, McLeod read the State Department reports of conditions there and perceived Madagascar to be a temperate climate with a mild winter and a relatively mild summer, with major health problems involving only malaria and polio. Missionaries living in other parts of Madagascar, however, revealed that the climactic shifts on this island are extreme. In addition to malaria and polio, amoebic dysentery, bilharzia, Bubonic Plague and bacterial dysentery are health problems. Without the aid of missionaries with respect to climate, disease and proper clothing, McLeod would have been ill-prepared for Madagascar by reading the State Department reports, alone.

Once basic information on the country has been gathered, it is wise to obtain those immunizations which are available. Unlike library research, disease and discomfort are actual possibilities in the field environment, so the risk of losing valuable time and energy should be minimized.

Proper clothing is a definite problem, since one is often stereotyped into role behavior on arrival in a foreign country which requires one to wear certain clothing. Safari gear is generally not acceptable clothing in the tropics, particularly for women, even though it is extremely suitable from a practical point of view.

In Madagascar, the wearing of a pith helmet is ludicrous since this is the mark of the midwife. Ethnographers and others who have been so incautious as to wear a pith helmet on this island have found themselves taken to the scene of an imminent birth and expected to perform obstetric duties. While slacks are extremely comfortable and practical in mosquito areas, local custom usually does not allow European women to wear European male garb.

It is advisable to follow local feeling whenever possible, although direct assumption of local modes of dress is often unwise. McLeod was required to dress not only as a woman, but as a missionary woman in Madagascar, because this was the only available role for a white American woman. While it cost something in mosquito bites around the ankles, the wearing of the proper clothing in the eyes of the local inhabitants led to an immediate rapport. This was true because missionaries in Madagascar have been extremely successful in establishing rapport.

In less remote areas, the picture is not so grim. It is still wise, however, to contact local inhabitants of European or American origin who may be helpful in the selection of comfortable clothing which is still acceptable. The subtleties of proper appearance are not restricted to remote areas. A few years ago, Dieter Christensen, respected German ethnomusicologist, stopped in Berlin enroute to a conference of the International Folk Music Council in Spain. He bought a used car to drive to Spain which

129

soon began to consume much oil. The car situation became so extreme that, on his return trip to Berlin, Christensen bought cases of oil, stopping frequently to add oil to the engine. By the time he arrived at the German border, his body and clothing were covered with oil stains, his hair disheveled, his hands filthy. The border guards completely searched the car for drugs and other illegal items, since they regarded him as a "hippie" of the worst kind.

When working in American or European situations, it is wise to remain neutral in dress before deciding what specific clothing to be most valuable. Many Americans who have an affinity for Navajo culture imitate the dress of local Indians and wear silver jewelry of Navajo manufacture. Imitative behavior of this kind can be extremely dangerous where individuals who have previously adopted the style have established a poor reputation.

For men, it is advisable on entering any community to get a local haircut, as a general rule of thumb. The primary reason for this is that local barbers often have valuable information on what various styles of dress and etiquette might be. It is best to avoid the more comfortable type of American clothing such as blue-jeans and tie-dyed shirts, since all types of clothing tend to carry overtones of some kind and American comfort-wear is generally looked down upon in many areas of the world.

The old dictum that a person is judged by the clothes he wears is best not forgotten, especially when making initial contact with members of another culture. As time passes and familiarity grows, it is possible to ascertain the extent to which care in dressing may be relaxed; however, at first it is best to proceed with extreme caution in order to minimize difficulties in establishing rapport.

OBSERVATION AND AWARENESS

People are basically observers. There is no specific way to prepare an individual to observe the music of others because of the immense diversity of music and musical behavior. However, there are some general areas which should be considered when preparing for the field. The level of rapport which one gains in any area defines the limits of the data. Good observations and sensitivity aid in establishing rapport with other human beings which, in turn, enriches the ensuing data.

Body posture is a common indicator of role in any society. Imitating various body postures is useful in preparing for field work. If practiced in private, it can also be an aid in delineating various roles while in the field, as well. Body posture, gestures and facial expressions are revealing and characteristic, not only of individuals but of groups, roles, statuses. McLeod (1964) noted that Malagasy musicians were to be distinguished by larger and wider arm gestures, more pronounced facial expressions, the wearing of special clothing and the carrying of distinctive nicknames.

The size of the space envelope which each person carves out for himself may be a means of role definition. Maltese musicians tend to require more space around them than do non-musicians. This may arise from the nature of the song duel, however, one Maltese musician declared that he desired to become a singer in order to have more space.

While it is possible to view behavior in isolation, one should always remember that human relationships are based on interaction. The same person may display completely different behavioral characteristics in different situations; such distinctions are always meaningful and sometimes helpful in defining musician vs. non-musician.

Meaningful behavior may take place at many levels. In Western culture, taking off one's shoes in another's home denotes trust, self-confidence and informality and the relationship between comfort and trust is very clear. In Southern Germany, when men wish to indicate friendliness to one another, they display their stomachs by sticking them out and patting them to call attention to the behavior. Actual items of behavior will differ from one society to another, but each society will have marked behavrioral syndromes which will be significant.

It is necessary to act out roles if one is to study successfully in another culture. The behavior of the ethnomusicologist is as well observed as that of the informants. It is wise to learn to act out roles without living them, before leaving for the field. In this way, a certain level of objectivity may be achieved which is not necessarily easy to attain under strange circumstances. It is therefore advisable to imitate roles that one sees around one, which are not fitting. A young man, for instance, may try to imitate the behavior of a middle-aged woman, knowing that he is not middle-aged nor a woman, simply to sharpen his awareness. This ability becomes particularly pertinent in field situations.

Both authors fell, quite automatically, into the role behavior of young women in Malta without ever having seen or observed the behavior consciously. Once this role was adopted, then other roles could be added to it by slight alterations or shifts of behavior as observed in more marked situations. One should not assume a role, but only its external characteristics, so that informants will be comfortable and receptive.

No matter how well trained, no one will be able to act out or to accept certain patterns of behavior without conscious effort.

While total elimination of all hindrances to objective observation is impossible, conscious observation and imitation aid not only the informants but also the researcher. The resulting relaxation in the observer allows informants to be more confidential than they otherwise might be. In the field, it is unsafe to assume that one can ever totally cease being observant, although one can often relax. Unfortunately, much valid information comes in moments of theoretical relaxation. The sharpening of observational powers is an absolute necessity in field work.

ETHICS

In recent years, the Federal Government has become concerned about the role of persons engaging in scientific research involving humans or animals in any way. As a result, most research proposals now require a statement and verification that the intended research will in no way be harmful to human subjects, physically or psychologically. This raises the hoary and overdone question of ethics, even in ethnomusicology which might seem, on the surface, to be the most harmless type of enquiry.

However, scholars have a three-fold responsibility: (1) to their informants; (2) to their profession; (3) to themselves. It is clear that any work should be so conducted that it leaves behind good will and open hearts for the next person who wishes to work in the area. For this reason, the authors spend much of their time in the field developing rapport with their informants, often above and beyond the levels necessary to acquire the types of data each was interested in studying.

Everything that is learned from any group of people ultimately belongs to them, not only for their comfort and safety, but also for the history of the group. The arts will change, shift their emphasis through time, and it may be that the music of a former time will be unrecognizable to the descendants of those studied. It is therefore the ethnomusicologist's responsibility to see to it that the best possible description and evaluation of the material is done within the limits of an ethical system of behavior.

During field work, a sensitivity must be developed to that which is locally regarded as sacred, holy, confidential or important. Within the field notes of every ethnomusicologist, there are probably items which his informants prefer to be kept confidential. In some cases, an individual will specifiy that he does not wish certain material to be published, or that it is solely for the information of the ethnomusicologist. In other cases, the informant may not want to be known as the source of information. In both cases, one feels duty-bound to conceal the information so achieved. While the "need to know" is the major impetus of the work, where the informant wishes the material to remain confidential, it should not be revealed.

The more difficult situations occur when the scholar is not sure what his responsibilities ought to be vis-a-vis political or confidential information. Whenever a piece of information (however arrived at) could be injurious to the informant or the group under study, it should be suppressed. While this seems easy on the surface, it is not. Knowing what might be injurious to an informant is a mark of one's ability to understand the culture in question, and many mistakes may be made before full knowledge is available. If the situation is not clear, it is best to do nothing.

A major rule might be, "Do not take advantage of informants in any way". What is important to them -- what is significant or sacred to them -- must become important, significant and sacred to the scholar. This is not to say that the scholar must completely embrace a philosophy or belief system; rather, it is understanding sensitivity to the ways of others which is called for.

It would be wrong, in the authors' opinion, to ask a group of people to "stage" a religious ritual using proper paraphenalia at the wrong time of the year. It would be equally unethical to ask Indian musicians to play a time-oriented raga at the wrong time of the day. This might lead to repercussions, particularly if social time were a significant factor in ritual activity.

While it is difficult to observe rituals in progress, it is probably the only ethical way to observe them, unless the informants suggest and are willing to accept the idea of staging a ritual. However, when rituals are staged for visiting ethnomusicologists, much which is symbolically significant is often left out. This should be taken into account in descriptions.

For the authors' purpose, the most difficult situations are those rituals in which noise is a significant factor, as mentioned by Rodney Needham (1972). Since the purpose is the capturing and understanding of music, the presence of heavy noise may well force a recording of some songs out of context. Such songs cannot be depended upon for accuracy, since performance out of context often involves either change of text, abbreviation of the music, or actual musical changes. In Tikopia, funeral dirges, sung out of context, are rhythmically re-structured and thus do not represent a true picture of funeral dirges in context.

The most difficult ethical problems arise after the return from the field, when it may be possible, or desirable, to produce records. The problem here is payment. Some informants are hesitant to make recordings for ethnomusicologists and take great satisfaction in assuming the worst after those ethnomusicologists have left the field.

Alan Lomax (personal communication) has suggested that all monies received from records, beyond the personal costs incurred in production, should be returned to the informants. While agree-

ing with this in principle, it is felt that this might not always be the wisest course of action. It might be best to return
the money to the entire community, particularly in communities
where goods and services are shared.

The effects of commercialization can be deleterious to continued rapport with the informants. It is perhaps best to regard
any money garnered through commercial efforts as the property of
the performers; after all, ethnomusicologists make reputations on
the basis of their artistry. In any event, the future disposition
of recordings should always be made known and agreed to by the musicians before recording begins -- for the protection of both the
musicians and the ethnomusicologist.

Where it is possible to concertize the artists in addition to
recording and studying them, more complex problems arise. In the
past, some jazz musicians have been taken away from their usual
context and displayed throughout America. The tragic results of
this form of exploitation are well documented in many cases.

While the performer gains an opportunity to be heard by a
wider audience, there is always the potential pitfall and consequence of being plunged into urban society. Booking agents and
others have not always been honest; managers and recording studios
have frequently written poor contracts; many folk and jazz performers have learned to their sorrow that the commercial world does
not necessarily imply either monetary gain or personal well-being.

The question is a moot one: how shall great music be best
exposed to the world, without exposing the performer to situations
potentially damaging or exploitative? While there is no answer to
this, total paternalism on the one hand is certainly to be avoided;
while allowing the promotional world its way with a performer is
also not in his best interests. Many folk performers harbor a sin-
cere desire to become commercial performers, no matter what the
consequences may be.

Relationships to the profession is equally complex. On the
one hand, since ethnomusicology is new, one is required only to
act in a scholarly manner. On the other hand, the people from
whom data have been taken may feel victimized by the entire profession because they have received ill treatment from a single
person.

Various American Indian groups are asking reparation for past
exploitation, as in asking linguists to aid them in preparing materials in their language. Ethnomusicologists may well be asked
to aid in the reconstruction of ceremonies or musical styles now
almost lost, and should keep this in mind when preparing and collecting materials.

The process is already beginning. Several ethnomusicologists
have been assisting individuals informally for years. Thus, the

sense of professional responsibility is also an extension of responsibility to the informants. It is a mark of scholarship that
one should at all times attempt to describe and analyze material
so that it can be used by others in the future.

There is another responsibility to the profession: to so
conduct one's self in the study of music so that nothing is done
to injure the wider reputation of the field of ethnomusicology.
In recent years, Russian expansionists have been using all kinds
of folklore (including music) for political ends. It has been revealed in the past that the CIA was using anthropologists and others who worked in rural areas as spies in order to locate and
assassinate anti-government figures. The weight of blame is
spread equally over all.

In order for scholarship to remain a viable entity in any
time, place or locality, it must absolutely eschew any such prac-
tices and activity. The aim of scholarship is clearer understanding; not to change the world or even improve it. Scholars are
seekers after knowledge and knowledge should be the only goal. In
times of economic turbulence, it may be tempting to take money under shady circumstances for shady activities. In some situations,
this may seem to be the only way in which work could be accomplished at all. It is the authors' opinion, however, that it is better
not to know than to be party to any scheme of political intervention on the part of any nation, for any purpose, whatsoever.

This profession must protect itself from accusations of inter-
ference, as must every other. Ethnomusicologists are the intruders
into the art forms of others -- the strangers -- and therefore, always suspected of something even in the easiest of times. To maintain an ethical posture, one must keep faith with scholarship as a
whole.

Ethnomusicologists must also keep faith with their profession
in other -- less dramatic -- ways. It should be a personal responsibility to keep up with all the latest theoretical, technical materials which might aid in developing more profound theoretical insights into music. To do this, one must avoid amateurish and undi-
rected field work. At the present time, it is apparent that the
tape recorder and camera, alone, will not provide answers to the
questions posed. There is need to see more; therefore it is possible in the near future that many professionals will have to become
intimately acquainted with videotape or some yet-to-come device of
technology which may be an aid.

Familiarity with both concepts and equipment is a must, since
one passes but briefly into the lives of those studied and must be
well-armed as possible with both theoretical and technical information. Tomorrow's scholar will do better than those of the past,
but those precious moments of time studied must not be wasted and
the current traditions -- which might possibly change or vanish --
should be studied and understood to the best depth to which it may
be theorized.

Finally, one should so conduct one's self in the field that the lessons of humanity -- which are available to all in all times and places -- become an owned asset which is carried away for personal benefit and improvement. To this end, no scholar should work so hard or with such dedication that he does not have time to relax and view himself as a human being, to learn his own limitations and capabilities, to assimilate what he has learned from the people with whom he is working.

The deepest moral and ethical lessons of the authors' lives have come, not from churches or schools, but through direct work with musicians, artists, priests and witches. It is to them that is owed the maturity, understanding of humankind, the firm belief in the dignity of all people and the right of all people to conduct themselves within the bounds of their own system of thought. This is, of course, the ethic of anthropology and not ethnomusicology, but until a better ethic or a better means of approach is found, this is proclaimed as the authors' own.

METHOD AND TECHNIQUE

Merriam has maintained that there is a difference between a field technique and a field method:

> "Technique" refers to the details of data gathering in the field, that is, to such questions as the proper use of informants, the establishment of rapport, the importance of vacation periods, both for the investigator and those he investigates, and so forth. Field method, on the other hand, is much broader in scope, encompassing the major theoretical bases through which field technique is oriented (Merriam, 1964:39).

Merriam equates "method" with "research design". While this is proper in a strict sense, ethnomusicology as yet lacks a well defined theoretical base. Consequently, theoretical frameworks are drawn from a wide range of sources, making it impossible for any general book to cover "method" encompassing every current research design.

In the usage of the term "method", the authors refer to more general methods of approach to field work; "technique" concerns technological and mechanical aspects. It is inevitable that, at times, elements of research design will creep into the discussion, since field methods are not truly isolatable from the theoretical premises which takes the student into the field to study. However, many situations are parallel from one society to another, and will require some method of approach in order that work can proceed. It is to these types of problems that attention is now directed.

SELECTION OF COMMUNITY OR POPULATION FOR RESEARCH

In today's world, where the vast majority of people have been deeply influenced by Western music, even the study of folk music often requires the location of the least acculturated portion of the population in order to determine a base line for present change.

Locating the least acculturated segment of a population is never easy. One approach is to assume that strangers will not be welcome in whatever town or village which has most closely retained its original base; however, this is certainly untrue of a number of societies. For instance, that portion of Switzerland which still makes animal masks for the Winter Solstice celebrations welcome tourists as well.

While the situation is far from clear, it is frequently possible to assess likely locations by discussions with acculturated individuals who will usually indicate those areas of their country least like themselves through some perjorative statement. In areas where the base line is known and the research design involves the study of acculturation, this would not apply.

The major problem in dealing with unacculturated areas is finding informants willing to discuss their art forms. This does not imply that they do not talk about them, but that they may prefer not to talk about them to an outsider.

Another major difficulty is the establishment of a most typical area, in the case where one's design involves the study of the folk music of an entire region. Cornelius Osgood (1951:3-12) is one of the few writers who discusses this rather difficult question.

INITIAL CONTACTS

Moving into a new community generally requires acceptance at a number of levels. A good way is to follow the suggestions presented in Notes and Queries in Anthropology (1954) by starting at the top of a governmental chain and working down. This usually means a courtesy visit to the office of the President, Prime Minister, or chief political figure, followed by the usual visits to the proper officials to verify all necessary papers. At some point along this chain, one is usually directed toward an artistic figure who is known and well-regarded in government circles. This process is sometimes called a "chain of introductions" and represents the formation of a hierarchical network of connections.

137

If one is working in a new area, there is no choice but to follow such chains, although they rarely lead to the informants or to musics one has come to study. This is so because of the tendency of governmental officials to be Western-educated elites in most parts of the world, and who are more likely to know acculturated artists. However, such visits represent a courtesy as well as a political necessity and so is not wasted time. At some point in the chain, one will learn of the existence of individuals whose talents are devoted to the style or styles of interest.

Once introductions of a tentative nature have been made, it is necessary to begin the tedious process of working through the etiquette levels which represent the buffers between a group of people and strangers. It is at this point that the selection of one's role or roles becomes vital.

A number of suggestions have been made as to the proper roles to assume -- the role of scholar is often used where respect for scholars is great -- however, as each situation is different, no standard rule applies. Both authors have assumed the role of initiate, tourist, dilettante, trainee, scholar or friend in different types of situations. While it is crucial to choose a role, it is often better to observe how one is being treated, as well. If one is given a role that is workable, no matter what it is, it is best not to try to change it.

RAPPORT

The level of rapport is generally indicated by the level of etiquette used in given situations. During the initial level, little can be done to ask pertinent questions or discuss subjects of deep interest; it is necessary to proceed to another level as rapidly as circumstances permit.

In Malta, strangers are usually offered a shot glass of whiskey and a cookie and placed in the hall on stiff-backed chairs. One device for overcoming this level of etiquette was to ask the hypothetical question, "Suppose I am friends with someone. Could I ask for something else besides whiskey?" Having indicated the desire to abandon the role and the level of etiquette implied, the authors next found themselves in the kitchen, eating whatever was available. At first, reciprocal invitations to dinner were necessary. Later on, this behavior changed entirely, resulting in picnics and other forms of freer association.

In societies such as Afganistan, where levels of etiquette are so complex as to defy description, one may never reach the bottom. There is a continual process of re-education into the nature of relationships between people. At each level of identification, new kinds of information become possible. In some cases, these levels are highly organized and require test-passing.

For example, among the Cherokee, Herndon was placed in the status of initiate in the divination system. At each stage of data revealed, she was faced with the situation which had just been described to her. After a discussion on the nature of snakes, she found her way on a mountain trail barred by a coiled rattlesnake. After learning the proper way of speaking to a bear, she found herself confronted with a bear to which she had to say the proper ceremonial statement.

In McLeod's training as a Transylvanian witch, similar tests were put forth in a logical order. First came tea leaf reading, then card reading; finally, the simpler love charms and good luck potions were revealed. As she learned to perform and appreciate each level, a test of strength of character was involved. In one, she was required to drink an entire quart of whiskey at a single sitting; in another, to learn to blush on command.

While not all situations will be this well-organized, every culture has its means of determining the honesty and trust-worthiness of the individuals with whom members of the culture are interacting on a day-to-day basis. In view of this, it is wise to assume the role of language-learner, even if one knows the language fairly well. In dealing with language, many people abstract situations rather than act them out. In this way, personal situations which involve complex behavioral responses unknown to the individual are frequently avoided.

The most significant concept concerning rapport is that it is a learning and unfolding process. Just as one learns to play an instrument according to ability, a culture is revealed according to the same criteria. Rapport is an open-ended process full of subtle nuances and limited by the amount of effort put into its development.

WITCHES, LOCAL EXPERTS AND OTHER PITFALLS

Whenever an outsider moves into a new group, he will be confronted by those who believe themselves to be allied with him in some way. The concept of the "local witch" is the authors' code name for those individuals who first approach a stranger. Every society has its deviants and outsiders and, since they have few social contacts with their own people, it is generally these who welcome strangers.

Close association with local witches is obviously to be avoided for lengthy periods of time, but this is not to say that they should be completely ignored. An individual who is on the fringes of his musical milieu not because of inexpertness, but because of personal tendencies, may well talk about items of interest to a stranger when others better incorporated into the system will not. It is well to recognize in-group and out-group members for what they represent -- either a danger to the completion of the field work, or a handy source of information where others refuse to speak.

Accident may lead one to an angry man. Working with the Kutenai, McLeod visited a lady of senior status who threw her out of the house. The lady had previously had her son-in-law put in jail because he became intoxicated and beat his wife. When he learned that his mother-in-law had refused to talk to McLeod, he talked freely about the "Blanket Rite" ceremony, a ritual which had previously been kept fairly secret.

The "local expert" is often an outsider to the system which interests him, as well. Local folklorists and folk music students are frequently educated men and women who are not of a different class than those they study. In many cases, their information is to be regarded as scant, since they carry with them into their investigations the natural prejudices which they feel for members of other classes in their own society. In addition, they frequently accept the myths about musicians which are so prevalent in every society. They represent an exceedingly good source of myth, but not necessarily a good source of information. While many local folklorists are superb at their job and have the confidence of the musicians with whom they work, it is enough to say that this is not always the case.

In Madagascar, for instance, the most interested scholar frequently found himself unable to acquire the data he wished, since he was a member of the Merina culture of the Highlands, the educated elite of the island. Recent political events had made his work difficult, since a political party massing the anti-Merina factors on the island had won the first Presidential elections. He was frequently mis-informed by his informants and felt himself to be at a great disadvantage.

Other types of local experts exist, in radio or rediffusion stations, universities, or scholarly societies. Each has some variety of information about musical forms, although myth and prejudice are to be found. While their information is useful in many cases, it is not substitute for personal knowledge. A useful technique has been to employ the information given by local experts in the wrong places. Sometimes, by asking the wrong questions, one can arrive at some surprising new answers.

THE FLY ON THE WALL

At the beginning of any field trip, it is best to start qui-

140

etly and to observe widely. Many scholars maintain that what one sees in the first three or four weeks is the most vital information. This is not necessarily true, but initial data usually has a modicum of value. During this time, the authors tend to use a method named "the fly on the wall", in which the observer does nothing much except to use his best effort to fade into the woodwork. The more prominent the investigator, the more likely the information is to be skewed toward him, often as a favor.

As an example, the authors' first recordings done in Malta contain numerous texts about them, which were less than useless until the involved double entendre was understood. In the "fly on the wall", the scholar should do absolutely nothing to attract attention, even if that means refraining from running a tape recorder. Social responses should be minimal -- one's general attitude quiet and pleasant, not attempting to direct anything. Once this behavior is learned, it proves extremely useful in tense situations. Unless one is asked to mediate a quarrel, it is best to slip away from it quietly.

The "fly on the wall" is particularly useful in cases of factionalism where each side wishes to enlist the allegiance of a stranger. There is a distinction to be made between "just being a tourist" and being a "fly on the wall"; both are observers, both are pleasant, both are out of place, but the difference of attitude is profound.

PARTICIPATION

No matter what research design has been chosen, a student will be a participant in events. In view of this, it is best to live in the culture as much as possible. Malinowski (1948:38-63) finds that living closely with one's informants is more valuable than living in town and visiting. Things tend to happen directly and there is less hearsay involved. In some situations, this would be impossible because of the ferocity of participation required.

While a certain degree of participation is beneficial, total immersion in local activities is to be avoided. The scholarly participant should remain a "participant/observer" -- retaining an internal stability under what are sometimes most severe conditions.

A recitation of a typical day in Malta, in a group field work situation, will indicate the level of activity which may be brought about by living in a village. Since musicians generally sing in the evenings in taverns, the day was structured by their work hours and recreation times. At 4:00 A.M., one member of the

141

group left the house to go out with the fisherman he was studying. Fresh vegetables were available about 5:00 A.M. The garbage, collected daily, could not be set out too early, since the first garbage thief took only material for his compost pile; the second garbage thief was neat and desirable, with the regular garbage pick-up of uneven quality. At 8:00 A.M., a gentleman arrived to give McLeod guitar lessons. At 9:00 A.M., the translator usually arrived and worked until 5:00 P.M.

During the day, any number of other events might occur. It was common for someone to drop in for something to eat or drink while chatting. The weekly grocery order included four cases of beer, six cases of soft drinks, about 50 pounds of meat and fish, four fifths of gin, four of scotch, plus the requisite number of vegetables for the meals. After cooking an evening meal, the authors usually went out for a musical performance and worked until 10:00 or 11:00 P.M., after which time, the bar owner frequently served dinner. At about midnight, there was a return to the house where field notes for the day were written up; then, a few hours' sleep until the routine began again. This was a normal day. On abnormal days, there were 27 for lunch and 35 for dinner.

While the extent of interaction will differ from one situation to another, it is necessary to find a means by which one continually observes while living in a new situation. This is not always easy and the basic reasons for indicating as many techniques as done here is to give scholars some means of handling themselves where participation is a necessity of field work. The culture naturally limits the amount of participation/observation possible; further, as can be indicated by the preceding passage, there are hazards to participation. The end results, however, seemed more preferable than the more prosaic library research. The vitality of the creative individual is brought home more strongly and the reasons for being creative are usually only revealed to those who are willing to follow them closely in their behavioral as well as their musical pattern.

One of the most useful of all participant observation techniques is sharing a meal. In many cultures, particularly those with a peasant base, the giving/receiving of food is a major device in the establishment both of initial rapport and friendship. One gains more than weight from this; the act of eating and drinking seems to expand confidence, creating a situation in which the more delicate subjects related to artistic behavior can be discussed with the greatest introspection. Nothing seems to inspire confidences so easily as a full stomach.

To a musician, it is often tempting to abandon participant/observation for participation. It may be desirable to join in a performance at times; however, the scholar should maintain participant/observation in order to maximize the situation. In Malta, Herndon sang a reply to the leader of a faction, ending both an

142

impromptu song duel and the difficulty the authors were having in achieving a depth of rapport with both musical factions.

In a number of cases, it is literally impossible to learn anything from participating in a sequence of events. This is most true of rituals, where the richness of symbolic behavior as well as musical behavior mitigates against using it as a learning situation. The most useful comment is that the student should learn the ritual beforehand from a participant who is able to describe the general order and configuation of the ceremony to be viewed. In some cases, even this is not enough, especially where noise restricts recording to such an extent that the subsequent record is unintelligible. This represents a severe problem and in many cases, songs sung out of their contexts are distorted and thus no record is possible.

GOSSIP AS A MECHANISM

In a previous publication (1972), the authors mentioned the concept of "cultural routes" whereby each culture presents to individuals a number of alternate means to arrive at solutions to problems. One of the commonest cultural routes for establishing the reputations, disseminating information and establishing rapport is gossip. Gossip is not merely the re-telling of events; it is the re-phrasing of events into a culturally acceptable pattern, along with the statement of what the behavior means. While gossip rarely details factual events, it is a major mechanism for the revivification of cultural patterns.

In gossip, the reputations of artists are made or broken, depending upon not only their artistic ability, but also their other social activities. A man may be the finest guitarist in the culture, but if he does not play the cultural game correctly, he may find himself without an audience. Thus, he is a cultural man, whose artistic activities are to a great extent controlled and defined.

It is to gossip that one may turn in order to learn the kinds of limitations which are placed upon creative individuals by the societies in which they live. There are caveats here; learning to re-phrase events in a culturally acceptable pattern means tampering with the reputations of the individuals one is describing. This endeavor should be approached with the greatest care and with the full fore-knowledge of how the system works. But it can be one of the most useful mechanisms of musical study, since each individual re-phrases the activities of every other.

In cases where gossip is possible, it is best to tell of events as nearly exactly as one saw them happen. After a period

143

of months, the story is usually re-told in its transformed version. By comparing the two, cultural patterns can be assessed. Frequently, gossip of this kind refers to the competence of individual performers and uses the highly distorted examples to indicate what they did right or wrong in a given situation. This is, of course, the rules for music-making in a transmuted form. If the authors owe their understanding of Maltese music to any particular mechanism, it is to gossip.

TYPES OF INFORMANTS

All people are potential informants. In the study of music, there is a tendency to devote the majority of attention to one or two particular informants who are experts in the style. This concept, sometimes called the "best man", often leads to a highly individualistic description of a musical style. There is a danger in this; coming as an outsider, one is frequently led to highly acculturated individuals who are not representative of the style. Perhaps more significant is the fact that if one does find the "best man" and works with him successfully, the nature of the changes and the development within a musical style may not be apparent. Unless one is in a society with recognized professionals, it is best to use a wide range of informants from novice to expert. This becomes particularly significant for the learning process; in many cases, the styles sought to study are sufficiently complex that they are too difficult to learn from an expert. Thus, the investigator frequently needs novices in order to inform himself about the more basic and simpler aspects of a style.

For example, McLeod studied guitar initially with a man who was by no means an expert in the style. It was later discovered that he represented a style of playing which was no longer in vogue; since the innovations of a fine guitarist named Cardona, most guitarists on the island were of the new breed. Therefore, it was from the less expert guitarists that McLeod learned the basic patterns which led to the later innovations. This was a procedure which could not have been accomplished backwards; more expert guitarists no longer knew the nature of the older style.

It has been the authors' experience that the use of a wide range of informants, including even liars and failures, allows the best initial view of the range of a style. The process by which a group of people reject a particular musician as inept will remain cloudy until one has examples of bad performers. This means that until such information is available, the outer edges of the style are unknown. On the other hand, when one deals with truly gifted informants, there is always the danger that they are moving out of the style at the other end. The process by which they are regarded as too extreme in a musical style is one which

144

can only be determined through the study of the behavior of some musicians toward others.

By now, it is probably true that most ethnomusicologists are aware of the dangers of the "oldest man" as expert. First, he is not necessarily an expert; second, cultures sometimes change from one generation to another. Thus, it is common to find age group-ings of opinion and style in most musics.

In the same way that there are levels of etiquette and lev-els of rapport, levels of information also occur which take two forms. First, novices have a more simplified version of the rules of singing than do experts. Each musician operates upon the assumptions that he has been taught and can understand, and his music is produced accordingly. Thus, while a novice guitar-ist knows there is a distinction to be made between the bottom three strings and the top three; that these are ranges of tessi-turas, he is unaware of the refinements of switching from one to the other. His management of range is different than that of an expert. Second, there are levels of information which are only revealed as the informant is regarded as more and more trustwor-thy.

At first study of Malta, the authors were told that the mu-sical texts only required rhyming and syllable control, and that the first line might mention the subject but not repeat the word. Later it was learned of the existence of doppiu sems (double en-tendre) in singing. Thus, the depth of information received is a function of generation, ability and levels of rapport. Informa-tion of a delicate or secret nature will eventually surface, but may depend upon the level of trust invested in the scholar.

Many examples abound -- the best, perhaps, is the story of The Golden Mare. At first, Malta revealed a general fear of the Evil Eye with members of the upper class seemingly more affected by this than those of the lower. While upper class people fre-quently spoke of the Evil Eye, lower class people generally de-nied belief in it.

It was only during a second field trip that it was learned from one informant -- who had firmly denied belief in the Evil Eye -- that he, himself, had been a victim. His father had bought a beautiful golden mare for plowing his fields. One day, his son (the informant) was plowing in a backfield of the farm. Around noon, he hitched the mare to a cart to return to the house and on the road, met a neighbor. The neighbor's eyes widened; he sucked in his breath and said, "Where did you get that beautiful mare?" The boy was stunned; the neighbor clearly coveted the mare. At that point, the mare fell down and broke all four legs without even moving and had to be shot. Later, the informant went through the ritual by which one removes the Evil Eye from the family. This is a typical incident in the sense that most people will not vouchsafe information of this kind to anyone with whom they do not feel comfortable.

It is a matter of intuition in some cases to know when an informant is ready to talk. Many musicians feel uncomfortable in the presence of persons who do not represent their style of living and, it is only after repeated efforts that the scholar finds himself in the position to ask the proper questions of such people.

In Malta, one man refused to join either faction of musicians definitively. He was a "floater", moving about the musical scene without being deeply involved in it. While he had his favorite singers and had studied intimately with two of them, he was sufficiently good that each faction desired his presence. Unfortunately for the system, this man was not willing to cast his lot so easily. His sense of individuality was so high that he felt uncomfortable in concert with others.

About eight months into the field trip, the authors learned that he had lost his job and immediately went to ask him if he would allow them to hire him. He said he would be glad to talk "now" and, for the next six weeks his comments were typed directly onto the typewriter for eight hours a day. He was the most introspective and careful of many informants and the depth of information received from him was so great that the authors blessed the day he decided to talk.

This man is an example of the atypical individual. Most works on field methods advise against working with atypical individuals, since they rarely represent full knowledge of the social situation. In this case, since all Maltese musicians are geniuses by definition, the level of introspection of this man was natural to the breed. It was his atypical behavior that made it impossible for him to talk objectively about factionalism as a component of music in Malta. On the whole, however, atypical individuals rarely reach the level of proficiency to become good informants.

A common denominator in all field situations is the "yes" man. Elements of politeness in any society may force an informant to give an affirmative answer if the investigator's question is put incorrectly. It becomes exceedingly important to know, before beginning the investigation, the proper form of question.

Among the Cherokee, anyone who asks the proper question must be given the answer, especially if he recites a ritual phrase beforehand which binds the informant to telling the truth.

In Malta, the situation is extremely difficult; it is considered improper to ask questions. However, there is again a formula -- in this case, the use of the "hypothetical question". A typical hypothetical question would begin: "Suppose a man wants to learn to sing..." Once the statement is placed in the hypothetical realm, everyone feels free to answer any question. This form of questioning is a mark of initial etiquette stages. Once one has a level of relationship which is secure with an informant, it can be abandoned. However, it is significant that the "fly on the wall" method was exceedingly useful in Malta, in that it led to the use of the "hypothetical question". Later, it was found that this was proper behavior, in that direct questions would have brought accusations of witchcraft. Once people noticed the caution, someone explained how to be polite.

The types of information-gathering and interviewing techniques in use vary widely. Question and answer types are regarded as best by a number of investigators, including Gladwin and Sarason (1953:19-24). Formal interviews -- where an informant comes to the house and is paid -- are also common. Informal interviews, where a friend is met on the street or casual questions are asked, is also useful. In general, most investigators agree that the best questions are open-ended, leaving the informant with a chance to answer in any way he wishes. Perhaps the least useful form of questioning is the questionnaire. Unless the musical situation is well-known beforehand, questionnaires usually define only the investigator's point of view, leaving no room for discovery of the way in which a particular system works. The authors tend to feel all questionnaires as a priori reasoning, in printed form.

ETHNOLOGITIS

It was Margaret Mead who first remarked that any observer living in a culture, not his own, would eventually go stale. This is a disease; it is a result of the strain of psychological accommodations caused by living with a culture other than one's own (see Mead, 1952:343-46, and Paul, 1953:430-51). After a period of ferocious activity, it is common to miss cues and feel drained. Dejection, depression, anger, or nostalgia for items one never liked initially are clues to the presence of ethnologitis. Mc-Leod usually develops an insatiable craving for chewing gum and root beer, neither of which she particularly likes. Herndon often becomes ravenous for corn on the cob. These are mild psychological signals that something is reaching its uppermost level and that it is time to stop for a while. Everyone has a different solution for the problem; some people go into a large town and have an alcoholic binge or go to see four or five bad movies.

Many people suggest that, before leaving, one pack the four or five books most desired to have on a desert island. Bohannan took Shakespeare, the Bible and "a terrifying handbook of tropical diseases" (Bowen, 1964:3). Each individual will have his own selections; in addition many investigators take mystery novels or science fiction or gothic novels of no particular import to while away the hours while the body returns to normal.

It is axiomatic that it is practically impossible to relax with informants, but from time to time, one should try it. Go out to a musical performance with the firm conviction not to take notes, but with a notebook tucked away on your person, just in case. Attempt to relax into the situation. Frequently, under such circumstances everything is seen with a new eye and suddenly note-taking becomes essential. If one feels that an informant has run out of things to say, it should be assumed that the scholar has run out of questions, not that the culture has run out of answers. Under such circumstances, it is entertaining to take an informant into a non-musical situation. Go to the beach; go fishing; go to a festival or for a drive.

It was during such an outing that it was learned that Boissevain (1965) was quite correct in his assumption that somewhere behind every Maltese church there is a singing bar. While unsure of this, because many of these bars have no guitars hanging on the walls, the truth was learned by asking casual questions of an informant in one of the excursions into non-music, a festival of the patron saint of Qrendi.

In some cases, the strain on the investigator can become critical. McLeod once found herself at a point of psychological crisis so extreme that she was forced to retreat from the situation for several weeks in order to re-stabilize so that she could continue the work. Herndon once abandoned a field situation entirely when she found that her moral, ethical code could not accommodate exhumation of the recent dead in order to dance with them and other ritual activities. This happens frequently when the context, subject, or informant is thoroughly disliked or feared. In such cases, it is easy to say that the investigation is not worthwhile and should be abandoned. However, one's personal feelings about a subject are yet another example of one's own cultural patterns.

The feelings about the informants or subjects do not validate or invalidate them: in extreme cases, they merely serve to indicate severe cultural differences and necessitate a re-thinking of the scholar's value system. Although the procedure of re-thinking one's life style is unpleasant, it has the benefit that, providing one can solve the problem intellectually, future investigation is usually easier.

CLOSED SYSTEMS AND OPEN MINDS

The book of this title, edited by Max Gluckman (1964), is the best essay on the problems created when an investigator moves outside his area of expertise. Each intellectual discipline has its own preconceptions about the nature of reality and students come prepared, primarily, to investigate factors previously dealt with and formulated by that discipline. This produces certain problems for ethnomusicology, which is not yet by any means a discipline of its own, but has many features which are basically interdisciplinary.

While the type of training and orientation is interdisciplinary, the subject of investigation -- music -- is highly patterned. However, the vast variety of music and musical contexts at the present time means that while one investigator will be dealing with religion and ritual (as did Herndon among the Cherokee), another may be dealing with politics (as in Malta), or with pure esthetics, folk tradition, secular stage performance and so on. Provided the investigator is interested only in the music and plans to analyze only musical sounds and describe instruments, no problems will ensue.

Once one moves into the study of context, however, religious, political, economic, or philosophical issues may come to the fore as the shaping forces of styles or traditions. Anyone interested in the study of music in context, therefore, must have a different approach to music in every society.

The message of Closed Systems and Open Minds is that no one can deal with all of the material successfully, mainly because of lack of expertise. It is often necessary to recognize that everyone has educational limits and to admit that no ethnomusicologist is competent to deal with all issues and events. A simple example would be that a wind player could not deal with stringed instruments, and vice versa. The rule is to try to get as much information as possible and, to get help if needed. The authors' study of bagpipes in Malta will probably always be a poor one, since neither one understands bagpipes well; however, the lack of expertise did not eliminate bagpipe music from the data.

DEVICES FOR CHECKING DATA

Every informant will give a different version of the same information. Frequently, informants lie or tell half-truths. Some informants know only part of the truth. It is often essential, therefore, to review data in order to determine its relative significance.

The most reasonable method is what the authors call the "Friday Meeting", simply because that tends to be their day of reckoning. Once every week, the investigator should review the material to date and determine which areas have been left in con-

tradiction or require further investigation. It is a good idea
to list new questions which might answer old problems, to establish new hypotheses about the meaning of the data already gathered and to assign one's self one week to solve the problems or
check the hypotheses. Essentially, this is a progress review.
One should list goals and decide priorities of significance for
the coming week, taking care not to assume their validity.

This is also a good time to let out any hint of emotions
from the week in private. It is also a good time to re-vitalize
one's self, to re-dedicate to the project at hand and to stimu-
late new ways of approaching data. Herndon had great difficulty
in visiting various of her informants among the Cherokee because
households often have two or three vicious dogs. On approaching
a house, she would find herself surrounded by snarling, snapping,
filthy dogs. A few days of this would reduce her willingness to
visit people and about once a week, she had to review her feelings about dogs in order to present to these animals the calm
face necessary to survival.

McLeod found herself extremely unhappy with officials, particularly minor officials, in Madagascar. For the most part,
they were strangers in the areas they directed and seemed always
to assume themselves better educated and more elite than anyone
in the region. Their snobbishness and obstructiveness were exceedingly burdensome, and she found herself shouting at the wall
about once a week in order not to tear them apart in person.

A major problem in any field study is divergencies in opinion on the parts of informants. One solution to this is to get
only one opinion; unfortunately, this can lead to an exceedingly
aberrant view of the musical system. Any single opinion should
be verified, especially if it is attractive. The scholar is fil-
tering the information through his own cultural system and it is
easy to misunderstand information. Unfortunately, checking opinions on a subject will frequently lead to more divergence. The
only reasonable way to solve this is to form a hypothesis which
will confirm both opinions and then develop a set of questions
which will test the hypothesis. Although this is slow and awk-
ward, it is sure. Looking back on the half-formed hypotheses
from the center of field trips, both authors agree that if further work had not been done, some extremely silly ideas would
have found their way into print.

Perhaps the best approach is to assume a hypothesis is false
and attempt to destroy it. Popper states this point of view very
well:

> The point is that, whenever we propose a solu-
> tion to a problem, we ought to try as hard as
> we can to overthrow our solution rather than
> defend it. Few of us, unfortunately, practice
> this precept; but other people, fortunately,

will supply the criticism for us if we fail to
supply it ourselves. Yet criticism will be
fruitful only if we state our problem as clearly
as we can and put our solution in a sufficiently
definite form -- a form in which it can be cri-
tically discussed (1968:16).

DEFINING A SYSTEM

When one moves out of his own cultural pattern, he is faced
with data which is based on assumptions unknown to him. Unfortunately, despite all the care one may take, the information one
acquires is filtered through one's own culture. As a result,
most are faulty reporters. For some years, this problem of how
to describe a system of thinking differently than one's own has
been a prime concern in anthropology. The only reasonable new
approach available today is that of cognitive studies, where the
emphasis is upon the ways in which information is categorized and
patterned in a given culture.

It is included here only in order to point out the usefulness of cognitive studies for the discussion of music. The patterning of music is sufficiently rigid that many musical systems
consist of set pieces, that is, pieces of music which can be repeated. The rigidity of the system implies the existence of complex and strict rules for performance which, if followed poorly,
will result in poor performances and, if followed well, good performances. Although this has not been a subject which is well
investigated, musical terminologies and performance conventions
seem to exist in greater or lesser degree in all societies. In
some cases, it is possible by tracing the implications of terminology, to determine the rules for music-making.

The terminology of music and the rules for music-making fall
into "Cognitive Sets" and represent a logic of their own. It is
possible to operate upon these ideas with the same principles used
in the study of kinship terminologies, decision-making maps and so
forth. Such studies may represent a future good for ethnomusicology particularly since, in the past, most investigators have maintained that performers cannot talk about their music. This myth,
now well-known to all ethnomusicologists, may well have led many
to neglect the study. There is a danger, however, of previous
assumption. Music does not always follow the rules which are verbalized. This is a factor to be watched for. For example, while
a raga states a set of pitches, it is not necessarily true that
only those pitches will appear in a piece of music based on a particular raga.

All people are logical. Each logic will differ, of course,
but it is possible to map statements concerning genre, repertoire,

ceremonial order, tuning statements and other technical factors. It is possible to determine how competence is defined. In this area, one can learn what ought to happen in a performance by asking questions concerning the competence of different performers. These are ideal logics; they do not necessarily mirror reality.

In Tikopia, McLeod found that the category _fuatanga_, supposedly the funeral dirge, actually contained a number of different musical styles, depending upon the context in which it was sung. In addition, statements concerning musical styles usually do not incorporate change; they often represent a system which is no longer in existence.

Perhaps the most difficult area is what is now being called the non-verbalized cognitive area. While a number of investigators feel that they can properly talk about cognitive areas which are not verbalized, both authors recommend that only verbalized statements can be regarded as valid at the present time. Since so much of music is learned subliminally and, since those cognitive maps available are frequently unrealistic, this represents a very real problem. A purist point of view is the cautious approach here. It is frequently to be noted that any re-statement of other cultures which is not verified by verbal comments from informants is a pure fabrication of the investigator's culturally bound mind.

TEXTS AND TRANSLATIONS

It is wished here only to point out methods found valuable in the recovery of texts and in their translation. The problem of musical texts is vast, and no one person can conceivably advise all investigators as to what might be found. Therefore, the remarks that follow are based only on limited experience.

Among the Malagasy, Maltese and the Kutenai, text squeezing is characteristic. For the Kutenai, this is extreme; texts are presented in a syllabic code. The problem of hearing what has been sung is extreme in many cases. In the highly melismatic _bormliza_, text syllables -- particularly the vowels -- are severely altered. As a result, it is often impossible to recover the words, even for trained Maltese singers. The recovery of texts from taped examples is a major problem. In Madagascar, McLeod used a young informant who spoke two of the major languages of Madagascar; Merina and Sakalava. This bilingual man was able to recover texts of six of the major language groups studies, but was unable to understand other, mutually unintelligible language texts.

152

In Malta, a village boy proved extremely successful in dealing with the highly proverbial idiomatic and metaphorical texts
he was presented with. At one point, however, severely difficult
texts were submitted to a committee of four people (one, a singer) in order to recover texts sung by three people whose dialects
were radically different. Texts represent problems of dialect,
metaphor, idiom and proverb. For this reason, it is probably necessary to employ someone who understands the local dialect involved and its metaphorical and idiomatic nature, to pull texts from
tapes.

Translation presents an even more difficult problem; it is
axiomatic, however, that translations cannot be done after one
leaves the field; much time must be spent in translating texts.
What is learned from the study of texts can be returned to informants to enrich information on other levels. In dealing with
the highly metaphorical songs of the Vakinankaratra, McLeod once
drove 125 miles to ask the singer the meaning of a single word.
It is therefore best to do translations on the spot, where possible.

No translation will be totally adequate, but some attempt
should be made. One pattern of translation is, first, a word-by-
word translation in order to preserve the grammatical order, followed by a free or literary translation. One verse per page
leaves sufficient space for comments concerning proverbial or
metaphorical statements. The end of the translation of short
songs should be followed by a statement concerning the meaning of
the entire song, plus any special reference necessary. The major
problem is to get a good translator. This means finding someone
who speaks a local dialect and who is bilingual in a trade or
European language.

LIES

As mentioned before, lies are cultural statements also. As
a result, lies fall into patterns. They may be a matter of etiquette, a lack of knowledge, or deliberate deceit. Recognizing
the lie is sometimes exceedingly difficult. Perhaps the best
test of a lie is the development of confidence in a particular
informant known to be expert, who can comment on statements made
by others. Non-conformity to the statements of a trusted source
are a reasonable means of identifying lies.

In some cases, it is easy to detect the liar and, subsequently, his lies. Such persons should not be refused entry; they often have something valuable to teach. The deliberate telling of
a lie is often accompanied by kinetic indicators. In Madagascar,
McLeod noticed that an informant in the village of Bekily occasionally exhibited a trembling in both little fingers when he was

talking. Observation of others showed that whenever someone deliberately set out to lie, their little fingers trembled. To verify this, McLeod asked her interpreter to tell her a lie. The trembling of his fingers indicated the presence of a clue to reliability.

Each culture has its own signals and frequently, they are sufficiently noticeable to be seen. Most lies, however, are half-truths. They depend upon the level of a rapport one has and the level of expertise of the individual. Among American Indians, for instance, the level of rapport dictates the information absolutely, since most information is sacred in nature. In addition, there are frequently surface and deep meanings through every phenomenon. Some people will know only the surface interpretations. Sometimes, information comes in layers.

CONTEXT

Whether an individual is anthropologically or musicologically trained, it is still true that music takes place in a series of contexts and is, therefore, context-sensitive. Repertoire is a function of context, as is the order of presentation, the rigidity of that order and the selection of personnel. In some cases, internal form may be affected by context. While the style is the same, interpretation may differ. Thus, while it may not be a major methodological focus to study context, even those whose interests are mainly musicological can learn a great deal by recalling that music may shift from one performance idiom to another.

In Tikopia, true musical expertise is combined with the concept of the proper persons to perform in a given context. In the Anga feast, in celebration for the loss of a chief's first adult tooth, the chief -- whether creative or not -- is required to compose a number of songs. These songs, Sore, are later presented in the Work of the Gods (Te Fekau Nga Atua), the yearly cycle of ritual celebration of the major gods of the island. Someone else frequently composes these songs; however, they are always known by the name of the chief who is supposed to have created them. Thus, context often dictates both form, style and even the definition of expert.

Since context is significant in the creation of repertoires and the development of styles, it is commonsense to determine the various contexts in which music occurs and to, at least, venture a short description of the characteristics of the differing contexts.

LEARNING TO PLAY, SING, OR DANCE

It may become advisable within the course of field work, to learn to play an instrument, sing in a musical style, or to learn to dance. In so doing, it should be remembered that the responses of the teacher may be quite different toward an ethnomusicologist, or other outsider, than toward native students. Thus, if one of the goals of such instruction is to learn how a genre is taught within a culture, great care should be taken to establish any differences between the way an outsider is taught and the way an insider in the culture is taught.

It should also be remembered that some musical styles may be beyond the competence of the scholar. If it becomes apparent that the learning of a style is causing the community to react negatively in any way, the study should be dropped immediately.

Even in the best of circumstances, care must be taken in selecting a teacher. If the teacher is too reknowned, one runs the risk of finding the level of instruction too high to comprehend easily. Throughout much of the world, the common teaching method is an aural one, not assisted by written materials. The teacher will play, sing, or dance a piece and the student is expected to learn it from the experiencing of the music. Performance is at full speed with complete ornamentation. If this is the case -- and the scholar is not accustomed to learning material in this way -- it may be necessary to record the lesson sessions so that they may be referred to later. It is also not a good idea to study with a teacher who is badly thought of. The danger in this case is that the student will be given incorrect theory or mediocre performance techniques.

In those instances in which practitioners of a genre disagree as to how it should be properly performed, the choosing of a single teacher is perhaps not a good idea. This is also true in situations where factionalism is present. Special care is necessary to maintain rapport on both sides of the question at hand. In these cases, it might be best to study with more than one teacher. If it is necessary, due to the local situation, to choose only one teacher, this should be done with extreme care.

CONCLUSION

In approaching questions of field methodology, it is difficult to remain general. The preparation necessary for field work is different in each case. Each scholar must take his own abilities and maximize them wherever possible, remembering that all ethnomusicologists are limited in some way and must learn to

155

overcome this. In a real sense, each field worker is committed to a transcendence of his/her limitations, so that each new experience may be manifested in new understandings.

Preparation for field work must proceed as thoroughly as possible. It is necessary to read widely, not only about the music of an area, but also about the culture, climate, geography, economics and politics.

There are many types of informants. Each person in another culture will have some information for the scholar which can be valuable. However, informants must be chosen carefully and thoughtfully. In some instances, one will wish to focus on particular groups of people, depending upon the framework of questions which have been set up to form the basis of field ventures. It should be remembered, however, that even liars and failures will provide good information.

The setting up of hypotheses is absolutely vital to field methodology. These hypotheses should not be so seductive that they are not thoroughly checked. It is the responsibility of the field worker to try to tear down those hypotheses which look most attractive.

Finally, great care should be taken in choosing which method of approach is going to be most valuable in a particular situation. Many people have often said that anthropology is only a matter of commonsense. By extension, this might be said of ethnomusicology as well. The prime factors, in any event, are not only commonsense, but thorough preparation, curiosity, good will and flexibility.

Field Techniques

Attention is now turned to the less prosaic areas of field experience. Although field techniques are more mundane than field methods, they are essential and vital.

RECORD-KEEPING

The keeping of records in ethnomusicology presents special problems because of the diversity and complexity of the data. In this section, an attempt is made to indicate which types of record-keeping and retrieval have proved most useful, as well as how strategies differ from one type of investigation to another.

In general, the problem of recording data is directly related to the problem of observation. One needs to remember "what", "when", "where", "who", "how" and "why" (see Human Organization, Fall, 1950 through Fall, 1951).

The "what" of ethnomusicology is the music, dances, instruments played, occasions on which musical performances occur -- the tangible and intangible qualities. These must be approached with tape recordings, photographs, maps and, in some cases, videotape.

The "where" may require simple geographical statements or may involve much more. It has been found that flow charts and time-and-motion study maps are occasionally useful in situations where complex inter-relationships are present.

The question of "when" requires several time dimensions to be considered, such as the amount of time required for a musical situation to begin, the presence of warm-up activity or tuning, and the kinds of time limitations on performers. These may be tracked in ordinary notes.

The "who" of ethnomusicology is similarly managed through note-taking, while the "how" and "why" are often the most time-consuming portions of the questioning procedure.

The basic principles of record-keeping will differ from one methodology to another; however, the purpose of record-keeping is to retain information in a retrievable form. The following comments refer to techniques for recovering information in different

types of situations. The diary or journal form of general recording is preferred, although this particular type makes retrieval difficult unless indexing is done thoroughly. Some researchers use cards -- indexed by topic -- which tend to impair
continuity and cross-checking. However notes are taken, they
must be intelligible and retrievable.

TYPES OF NOTE-TAKING

A major problem is when and where one may take notes or make
recordings. In some societies, investigators are expected to
have notebooks and informants feel cheated if their comments are
not written down. This is the ideal situation, of course; it
gives validity to the investigation in the eyes of all parties.
In some instances, however, it is simply unwise to produce a
notebook or to make a recording.

Photography can be a similar problem, especially in cultures
influenced by Islam, where photographs of the human form are for-
bidden. The question of when one is allowed to make a record
publicly must be sensed in any given case. Etiquette is frequently involved; individuals who may refuse to be recorded in any way
at one stage of etiquette may find it perfectly acceptable at another.

A number of choices for recording information are available.
The authors find a small, bound notebook of approximately 4 by 6
inches to be the handiest method for keeping track of initial
comments. The contents of this notebook are transcribed into a
typed diary-form of record later in the day. A fully equipped
ethnomusicologist looks like a comic figure; pencils, notebooks,
tape recorder hanging from one shoulder, film and camera bag from
the other -- the perfect picture of an over-enthusiastic tourist.
Until someone invents completely miniaturized equipment, there is
probably no solution to the problem of weight, or the ungainliness
of the effect. But it is far better to arrive looking like a cir-
cus troupe than never to take a single note or make a single recording. A small, compact notebook in bound form reduces loss and
weight and even though it will mean a later re-transcription of
the material, it has been found to be the most useful way of approaching the problem.

It is a frequent case that one is simply not able to take
notes during a particular moment of time, even though the information being gathered is very valuable. An effort at total recall is a worthwhile attempt. While no one can remember the absolute contents of conversation for more than a few hours, a handy retreat to the restroom may allow one to jot down outlines of
important information. In such cases, it is absolutely necessary

that full notes be made immediately, for information fades quickly from the mind.

In cases where one is allowed to take notes, but under circumstances which preclude their being particularly good, the development of mnemonic devices of some sort aids in unscrambling a manuscript later. If someone is looking over the scholar's shoulder, for example, the constraint on writing down exactly what one sees or hears may be sufficiently great that he might wish only to draw pictures. Doodling, as every university student knows, can later be unscrambled as a series of statements if mnemonic devices are incorporated in the doodles.

Both authors tend to avoid the use of questionnaires. Since they are created in the absence of information about specific situations, they frequently have little or nothing to do with the actual situation in which one finds one's self. Also, most questionnaires now developed are statistical in nature. Their purpose is to derive norms of behavior. It is honestly believed that while art forms are indeed stylistically stereotypic, the people who perform them are frequently not stylized individuals at all, and it is their free-form approach to life which makes the study of ethnomusicology such a delight. It is repugnant to reduce individuals of this kind to normalized statements.

Thus, one tends to use the more time-consuming devices of checking the comments and behavior of one informant against others, in hopes that both levels of introspection and of expertise in the various creative artists with whom one deals will be revealed. Out of experience, it has been found that taping interviews is not a good idea; they take too long to transcribe afterwards and many a fine comment has been left "in the can" for lack of time.

The ideal situation in note-taking is where one hires an informant to sit and be questioned eight hours a day. In such a situation, the information can be typed directly onto the final copy of notes. Although this has been achieved on occasion, the situation is rare. Most note-taking occurs under the most difficult circumstances and requires some kind of shorthand or elliptical English. The learning of shorthand is often a good idea. McLeod uses condensed forms of English; Herndon uses mentally-learned short statements which can later be unraveled into longer ones.

If one is learning to play an instrument, notes must be correlated to tape recordings -- a most difficult and time-consuming process. Perhaps the best method of approaching this is to use a tape recorder which has a cueing device, indicating on the tape where a particular set of notes belongs.

159

SAFEGUARDING THE MATERIAL

While most scholars make only two copies of notes, wear and tear and the international postal service makes a few extra copies a better idea. Four copies are suggested: one to send away to one's university; a second to store in a local place; a third for use and a fourth to cut up and re-assemble under specific headings. This is the system which has been found most useful by the authors. While the record of the international mail system is not all that bad, one entire set of field notes was lost, and part of one set of taped transcriptions also went astray between Malta and the United States. Four copies in hand is felt safer than two.

CONTENT OF NOTES

All notes must be taken promptly and should indicate context in which data is acquired. Time, source and length of time between receiving information and making the notes -- whether the information was spontaneous or in response to a question -- whether the informant was alone or with others -- displays of feeling and so forth -- are natural components. The reactions and impressions of the scholar are also necessary. The device of the parenthesis is used to inject one's own feelings into the notes, so they may be extracted later if inappropriate. Thus, a set of notes might read:

> Met John at the bar about 8:30. He was with
> three other people: John II, Paul, and a third
> boy I didn't know. They seemed in fine fettle.
> After half an hour or so, they decided to sing.
> As no guitarist seemed to be around, John asked
> if we might borrow the Cardona from the wall.
> Mary said it was all right, and produced another
> guitar from the backroom. John and I played.
> (I felt God-awful and played like a pig. Spoiled
> the whole recording. Grumble, grumble).

Some authors suggest different devices, such as using two pens with different colors of ink, to indicate different things in notes. This will not transfer well to typing and this is why the parenthesis is used to put personal feelings separately. This journal-form must be later systematized by a cross-index. It is a good plan to add questions at the end of each day's notes.

Recordings require some standardized form for indentification and retrieval as well. The exact form of the recording sheet is not rigid. It will vary according to the design and location of the field work and the preferences of the individual. Appended here is as an example only of one possible approach. This sheet is generally a mimeograph made before going to the field; approximately 1,000 copies should be sufficient. Such sheets can be placed in order and kept in snap-back binders. Again, it is recommended that there be four copies.

RECORDING SHEET _____

TAPE:

SONG:

TITLE:

DATE:

PLACE:

PERFORMERS:

INSTRUMENTATION:

DANCERS:

AUDIENCE: Type
            Response

SUB-STYLE:

OCCASION:

REFERS TO FIELD NOTES PP.:

REFERS TO PICTURES #

REFERS TO TRANSLATION #

CONDITIONS OF RECORDING:

        ips
        dynamics
        batteries
        interference
        mike placement
        cut off?
        weather conditions

CROSS REFERENCE TO TAPES:

COMMENTS:

CROSS-INDEXING

161

The index style in any given case will partially arise from the research design. As many devices for re-locating information have been developed as there are persons who are taking notes. It has been found useful to number field notes consecutively and to refer back to previous comments, whenever possible, directly in the notes. Retrieving information on individual performers from recording sheets is relatively easy, provided the performers' names are given in each case. Style indexes, performer indexes and text subject indexes have proved a useful addition to the recording sheets.

It is helpful to develop a cross-index system for photographs, to locate negatives in respect to prints, to identify personnel, photographs of similar situations, activities, or places. The possible types of index are obviously endless; the crucial index is in reference to the general notes which bulk so large in importance.

Typical sub-headings for indexes are musical terms, characteristics of singers, learning situations -- any subject specific to the research design involved. The vital thing to remember is simply that indexes of several different kinds will be needed, or the notes will remain an unfathomable area.

THE PROBLEM OF ETICS AND EMICS

While field information comes in a straight line sequence, the depth of complexity is often expressed in terms of etic and emic information. These two terms, taken originally from linguistics, refer to the distinction between highly specific instances and the conclusions from similar instances, be they made by the individuals themselves or by the scholars studying the situations.

A set of musical genres is clearly an emic description. An individual variant within a sub-type is an etic item. In addition to the folk etic and emic, a scholarly emic (one is almost tempted to call it a scholeme) will undoubtedly develop. At this point in description, this is mentioned in order to caution the investigator that all information will not be on the same intellectual level, and that devices should be invented to locate the intellectual level of information available.

The most crucial distinction is that between assumptions made by artists within the system and assumptions made by the persons studying the system. In fact, any given individual within a musical system may know only part of the facts desired. His/her information must then be fitted into a framework, whether it is a superimposition by the scholar or a local cognitive map. In the field investigation, one is constantly bouncing back and forth from one level to another. It is a Herculean task to assess where one is until the entire system is well known.

Because it is difficult to know where one is in the mosaic of information, the authors suggest that continual re-assessment of information is necessary. A "Friday Meeting" is useful in group study. Even if an individual is alone in the field, information should be re-assessed at least once a week. An evaluation of the type and quality of present information, noting whether it is idiosyncratic or generally accepted, is a good idea.

The inclusion in the notes of new questions which should be asked during the following week, in order to prove or disprove hypotheses placed upon data, is exceedingly useful. The journal type of note-taking allows this assessment procedure more easily than others. It is much more difficult to assess one's present position from a series of already-indexed cards which do not indicate time sequences.

SELECTING A TAPE RECORDER

Before beginning field work, the scholar will have to select tape recording equipment. The perils of choosing the proper tape recorder for a particular field situation represents a monograph in itself. There is such a proliferation of makes and models that a student doing his/her first field research may feel overwhelmed.

A primary concern for any field investigation is whether a tape recorder bought and paid for in one country will work under varying local conditions. Electrical current differs widely in several characteristics from one country to another. In America, current is 110-125 volts, alternating current at 60 cycles per second. In Europe, current is either 110 or 220, alternating current or direct current at 50 cycles per second. If it is possible to use electricity, it is frequently necessary to have a transformer, or a machine with a built-in AC/DC switch and 50/60 cycle converter.

In underdeveloped countries in Africa and Asia, the situation of electrical current may be highly variable. Beyond the limits of major population centers, electricity may not be available at all. For this reason, machines with optional battery-operation are recommended. They are useful everywhere. Most models contain adaptors for different currents, or general purpose transformers can be bought for them.

Many battery-operated machines are either full track or two-track and are monophonic. Many persons now prefer to record di-

rectly in stereophonic sound, but the choice among stereophonic
battery-operated tape recorders is somewhat limited and carries
the additional caveat that the scholar may inadvertantly alter
the recording levels to accommodate to Western models.

Another major problem with all recording devices is weight.
Tape recorders which operate on current are usually large and
bulky. Unless the investigator is sure that he/she will always
be in the same place, immobile, and knows precisely what the current requirements are locally, it is suggested that sacrifice of
the sophistication of extensive sound mixing or 8, 16, 32, or 64-
track machines be made for the lightness and convenience of battery-operated models.

Since the aim of taking a tape recorder into the field is to
make high-quality recordings, the use of battery-operated machinery immediately creates problems of price. In one opinion, the
medium-priced battery-operated machines available at present,
such as Sony and Uher, are not of sufficient quality for the making of commercial recordings. The only tape recorder recommended
by the authors is the Kudelski Nagra. Unfortunately, this is an
expensive tape recorder. However, it is felt that it is well
worth its price. Nagra comes in a number of models, each very
light, all designed to accommodate to all varieties of current
and all types of tape. Stereophonic models are also available.
Given all the factors which can be involved in the purchase of a
tape recorder, Nagra is the only machine which will fit all professional requirements, including the production of commercial
quality in recordings.

Before buying a tape recorder, it is advisable to know something about how these machines operate. A working knowledge of
the technical aspects of specifications and performance is useful in enabling one to choose the right machine for field purposes.

A tape recording involves the magnetic storage of electrical
impulses. The electronic and the mechanical stages in this process combine to determine the quality of the resulting recording.
The physical property known as electromagnetism is the basis of
the recording process. Every wire which carries an electrical
current is surrounded by a small magnetic field which has the
properties of a magnet. This magnetic field can be easily intensified by winding a current-carrying wire into a coil and placing
an iron core in the center. The strength of the magnetic field
varies with the intensity of the current flowing through the wire.

Magnetism will remain in a magnetic substance by induction,
which is the means by which tape recordings are made. Fluctuat-
ing intensity of sounds are converted into electrical currents of
sounds flowing through a coil known as the recording head. A
ribbon of plastic, coated with iron oxide, passes over the re-

cording head and is magnetized. The intensity of the magnetism is determined by the changes in the electronic signal.

The reverse principle applies to the reproduction. As a coil of wire generates its own magnetic field, a magnetic field which passes near a coil will induce an electric current in it. The magnetized tape can be run over a head which is also a coil, and thereby re-induce in that coil the same currents which made the recording in the first place. The current is then reconverted into sound impulses in order to hear the recording.

The prospective user of a tape recorder should be able to understand the terms by which a manufacturer describes a given machine. The quality is reflected in the specifications provided, and the proper interpretation of these will enable one to fit a recorder to his needs. Some of the figures in a "spec sheet" refer to the electronic and others to the mechanical performance of a recorder. At present, there is no industry-wide standard for these figures. Different testing procedures and standards result in confusing claims which must often be unraveled before an accurate comparison from brand to brand can be made.

ACOUSTICAL RESPONSE. A machine with fine electronic properties may produce recordings of low acoustic quality because of factors outside the recording cycle. Recording begins with the amplifier, which provides the proper electrical level to the recording head, and also makes changes in the signal which overcome certain limitations of the actual recording process. This change, called equalization, is different for each recording speed. In the playback stage, provision is made for the restoration of the signal to its original form. The quality of the recording is determined by the fidelity of the recorder to the electrical analogue of the sound impulse and has several standard measurements. They are described below.

DECIBEL LEVEL. Within the frequency range of the normal ear (20-20,000 cycles), measurement of sound intensity uses the measurement unit called "decibel". The response of the ear is non-linear, and the decibel is a logarithmic unit expressing varying sound intensities on a linear scale. The decibel is not a fixed unit; it is an indication of ratios between sound levels. A change of one decibel can barely be perceived. Three decibel produces a definite difference in volume to the normal ear. Conversation in a crowded room is about 40 decibels; a symphony orchestra is around 70.

If a reference level is set, the decibel represents a specific scale of values. This is how frequency response is measured. Some center frequency is taken, usually 1,000 cycles; its volume level is assigned the value of zero db. The relative response of a recorder along the frequency spectrum is then expressed in

165

terms of deviation. A deviation of minus one db is not percept-
ible; minus three db is noticed. A figure such as 50-15,000 (minus two db) gives the boundaries of frequency response for any
given machine.

While sounds may be recorded above and below this level,
they will be softer than is true of the rest of the frequency
range. It is also important that a smooth frequency response occurs all along the range. A tape recorder with a flat response
between 50 and 15,000 cycles is very good, indeed.

Depending on what is recorded, different frequency ranges
are required. Perfect fidelity for speech requires 100 to 8,000
cycles. Because of the presence of high overtones, music requires at least 40 to 15,000 cycles. A restricted frequency response reduces the brilliance of a recording. Lack of lows
causes a thin sound; lack of highs causes distortion of timbre
and muddiness. It should be remembered that frequency response
is only one property to be considered. Distortions may be con-
tributed by other elements in the recording process.

ADDED DISTORTION. A reproduced sound is distorted if additional
components not present in the original are discernible. These
components have two forms -- harmonic and non-harmonic. Harmonic distortion is the generation of new tones in an electronic
circuit in addition to those recorded. This is difficult to mea-
sure, since elements of harmonic distortion blend with harmonics
already present on the tape. Distortion at frequencies which are
not multiples of frequencies already present can easily be heard
and soon become objectionable. Another type of harmonic distortion (often called inter-modulation distortion) is the result of
the presence of combination tones.

Distortion is measured as a percentage of spurious signals
contained in the total. It is difficult to specify a figure
which represents an acceptable level of distortion, because of
the wide range of testing procedures and standards in the industry; however, for a machine to be classed as having high fidelity, the distortion ratio should be below 2%. As the volume level of recorded sound increases, so does distortion. This figure
represents acceptable distortion at maximum recording levels.

Noise, another added complement, usually takes the form of
a low hum or a high hiss. A machine should not record a sound
lower than the level of the inherent noise of the circuit. This
point is usually assigned a minimum value of zero db. The loudest signal permissible before objectionable distortion occurs can
then be expressed in relation to this point. The ratio between
these two figures is called the signal-to-noise ratio. In decibels, the greater the signal-to-noise ratio, the better the machine. Following is a list of representative ratios:

166

```
35-50 db:   home tape recorders
45-60 db:   professional tape recorders
65-70 db:   laboratory conditions
```

MECHANICAL SPECIFICATIONS. In a good recorder, the electronic
elements must meet certain standards, but there must also be re-
liable performance from the mechanical sections. The recording
is created by moving tape evenly across the record head because
any imperfection in speed or evenness will mar the finished product. Small regular or irregular variations will cause fluctuations in pitch known as "wow" and "flutter".

Slow variations are called "wow"' if the variations in pitch
are too fast to discern the individual fluctuations, this sensation is called "flutter" which is expressed in percent. The ear
varies its sensitivity to "wow" and "flutter", and evaluation of
its effect is still under study; standards for this measurement
are therefore unstable. Some values which will be of help are:

```
.5% poor home machine
.3% good quality home machine
.1% professional quality
```

Overall speed accuracy is also an important quality. Several standard speeds are in use today, expressed in inches per second (ips). Tape speed determines the frequency response; for a
given tape speed, quality is determined by factors most easily
measured by cost. In other words, tape speed is related to frequency response and frequency response is related to cost. Technical strides made recently have extended the response available
from the slower speeds; however, at the present time, 7 1/2 ips
on a good quality machine will deliver 40-14,000 cycles per second (cps), while 15 ips should deliver from 30-15,000 cps. Refinements in head design and electronics have enabled the best
machines at 7 1/2 to approach the performance of 15 ips.

Type of recording also influences response. A full-track
tape delivers a better recording than a dual-track; the dual-
track tape has a signal-to-noise ratio of about 3 db lower than a
full-track recording. A four-track recording is accompanied by
additional losses in the signal-to-noise ratio, and in addition,
four-track tape increases the friction and wearing on the head.
The physical shape of the recording head has a great deal to do
with quality because a four-track head wears out more quickly
than a full-track.

While the electronic requirements of recorders are almost
the same, the physical set-up may differ from one machine to another. Most recorders have a head which produces a signal to e-
rase any previous recordings on the tape. Some machines use the
same head for playback and recording, with automatic switching
for each mode. Better machines include additional heads and cir-

cuits to provide the sound reproduction mode. With a machine containing separate recording and playback heads, the recorded signal can be monitored immediately after recording which gives the operator a chance to check the quality, directly. Separate recording and reproduction heads are considered to be an absolute necessity in the field.

SELECTING MICROPHONES

While the choice of a microphone is crucial, the dazzling display of various microphones is even more difficult to unravel than that of tape recorders. While the price of a microphone is a good indication of quality, it is not the only consideration. A good indication of quality is the maxim that when buying a low or medium priced recorder, one should pay 40% of the cost of the machine for the microphone.

Microphones come in three pick-up patterns: uni-directional, bi-directional and omni-directional. Uni-directional microphones are sensitive to sounds from only one direction. Bi-directional microphones pick up sounds from opposite directions and discriminate against sounds on the sides, while omni-directional microphones are equally sensitive to sounds from all sources. In making field recordings, uni-directional microphones have been found to be the most useful, since the major problem in non-studio recording situations is extraneous noise and echo. Uni-directional microphones are also easier to use, since the center of the sound can be tested before the recording is made.

Microphones are built in one of two modes as far as the quality of _impedence_ is concerned. Whenever electronic instruments must be linked together, the impedence between the two must be equal and must be at the same electrical level. This is also true of microphones where the impedence is either high or low. In general, a low impedence occurs between 4-500 ohms, while high impedence is generally above 10,000 ohms. Most signal sources are of high impedence, while only microphones are either high or low. Tape recorders used by amateurs have a high impedence input and a rather low sensitivity, thus matching most inexpensive microphones.

Impedence is an important quality for a field tape recorder because a high impedence microphone cannot be used with a connecting cable of more than 20 feet in length, without substantial signal loss. A low impedence microphone can have as much as 100 feet or more of cable without signal loss. This can become extremely crucial if the ethnomusicologist is not allowed to move about during a ceremony. Long cables also become crucial in recording staged performances where microphones must be dropped from overhead booms.

Four major types of microphones are manufactured: the Piezo-electric, Dynamic, Ribbon and Condenser types. They range in price in the order listed, with the Piezo-electric being the least costly. Aside from the first type, the other three are well produced in either high or low impedence, but only the Condenser microphone is available in any pick-up direction with the significant quality of sturdiness.

Piezo-electric microphones are fragile and subject to humidity. Ribbon microphones are also somewhat fragile. Both Dynamic and Condenser microphones are sturdy, but humidity is a problem with some Condenser types. On the whole, even though there is a wide range in price, Condenser microphones of low impedence which are uni-directional are recommended. Of these, the authors prefer the Beyer microphones because each microphone carries a test sheet of its own, indicating the specifications for that particular microphone rather than the model. Dynamic microphones have the most moderate output and are of good quality; ranging widely in price and again, the Beyer is recommended.

The obvious problem here is that the microphone must match the tape recorder. A low impedence microphone will match a high impedence input on the tape recorder only if a transformer is added. It is therefore wise to check the impedence of both microphone and recorder before making a selection.

Microphones, then, are fit for a number of uses, and, like tape recorders, they have acoustic properties which can be measured. A good microphone is capable of responding to a wide dynamic range. It has a wide, flat frequency response; responds easily to sounds of short duration; has low distortion and is rugged.

Since recordings will only be as good as the tape recorder and microphone can make them, it is wise to prepare one's self for emergencies, although such preparation is expensive. If the ethnomusicologist is planning to work in an isolated area, it is suggested that he/she carry a back-up machine and microphone.

SELECTING EARPHONES

The purchase of earphones is the most personal part of machine selection, with comfort and proposed usage tending to dictate choice more than quality. In general, earphones can range between $10.00 and $90.00 and carry no specifications. This is so because the shape of the ear of an individual determines how well any given earphone may operate.

There are basic styles of earphones, each with its advantages and disadvantages. The teardrop shapes are placed lightly into the ear but do not cover it completely. For long wear, they have the advantage of lightness, with the disadvantages that less bass is heard. The cup style seals off the entire ear, covering it entirely with a rubber or foam cap. These have the advantage of better transmission of bass and the disadvantage of being heavy to wear. The crucial factors are: perception of bass, comfort and lack of external noise.

For use in recording with machines which allow audition of the actual recorded sound rather than the external, cup style earphones are essential. Internal circuitry in such machines causes the sound recorded to be heard a fraction of a second after the actual sound. Unless outside sounds are damped, the two sounds will appear to echo and cause extreme discomfort. Cup style earphones are also more practical for transcription and analysis because of the reduction of outside noise.

Sturdiness is a considerable problem, since those manufacturers who do repair their product ask that it be returned to the manufacturer. The best advice is to know the serviceman or salesman and be assured about sturdiness and repair guarantees. Quality of sound can only be determined by trying out various earphones. For those planning to work in hot climates, it is a good idea to buy an extra set of foam or rubber caps because they tend to deteriorate rapidly in heat.

SELECTING TAPE

In a way, tape selection dictates the machine selection. At present, tape for cassette recorders is getting better and better, but the best high-quality tape is still only available for reel-to-reel recorders. On the whole, the recorder market has broken into two components, with higher quality recorders and tapes being available in reel-to-reel. The allure of more portable cassette machines is undeniable, but at present, studio-quality field recordings are still only possible on reel-to-reel machines.

For this reason, cassette recorders are not recommended because they are fragile; difficult to repair; use tape which often must be returned to the manufacturer for simple operations such as splicing.

Tape is essentially made of two components, the backing and the coating. The older backings -- acetate or mylar -- neither of which material aged well, represented a different problem under stress. Mylar tended to stretch, while acetate snapped. The newer polyester backing has been in use for several years and thus far, no major problems seem to have developed. Aging does not seem to be a factor and print-through is not as serious -- for,

170

when tape is stored for any length of time, the magnetic signal impressed on it may imprint itself by induction onto the adjacent layers.

Better-quality tape has a back-coating on the backing, which gives it a rough feeling unlike the slickness of earlier types. This coating has been applied to allow smoother rewinding; a side-effect has been the reduction of print-through. In previous years, the slickness of the backing caused some severe problems in tapes which had been re-wound. Any tape recorder has less speed control on rewind or fast forward than on regular play or record; as a result, the lack of friction on earlier tapes caused re-wound tapes to have an uneven layering. If stored in this condition, they tended to develop transverse creases which often pulled entire reels out of shape.

One colleague had a set of tapes which were triangular rather than round, and he could not flatten the tape by running it. While the new back-coating claims to solve this problem, it is still recommended that tapes be stored backwards, since the speed controls of the forward sequence layer the tape most evenly on the reel.

The coating of a tape can vary from one manufacturer to another, but iron oxide is standard on the better quality tape. Experimental coatings in cassette tapes may change this; at present, however, reel tape quality is determined mainly by the technology of applying the oxide. The more evenly the molecules are distributed on the tape, the better the sound will be.

The best tapes are identified by the generalization "low-noise", which is an indicator that the manufacturer's best technology has been applied. Budget tape is still made, even for reel-to-reel recorders which differs from low-noise tape in the less regular distribution of molecules in the oxide coating. One side effect of the use of budget tape is that it wears the heads of the recorder more quickly than does better quality tape.

Reel tape comes in several sizes: 3-inch, 5-inch and 7-inch are standard for portable models. Each recorder is adapted for a particular size; the use of other sizes may cause problems in braking, rewind and fast forward modes. Use of 7-inch tapes on a model designed for 5-inch reels causes wear on pressure pads and the rewind motor. It is best to use the size for which the machine is designed.

Recording tapes are available in several thicknesses; the commonest are .5 mil, 1 mil and 1.5 mil. By reducing the thickness of the backing, the length of tape on a standard size reel can be increased. Depending on the speed of recording, a 5-inch tape can be extended 15 to 30 minutes from the 1.5 mil standard; but the use of any other than 1.5 mil tape is not recommended because of print-through. Print-through -- sometimes called pre-

171

and post-echo -- can ruin a recording, particularly if the highs are loud. For this reason, the use of the thickest possible tape is recommended for field recordings because tapes will probably be "stored" for significant lengths of time in the field as well as in the archive.

Low-noise tape with back-coating is somewhat safer than budget tape as far as print-through is concerned. Manufacturers now believe that 1 mil tape is safe from this problem. Since the use of back-coating is fairly new, the authors prefer to wait until various archives report their experiences with it. This frequently produces another kind of problem for the researcher in that he/she must carry more tape into the field. A similar maxim to that used by photographers is suggested: Waste tape, not time. Just as a photographer may take hundreds of pictures to achieve the one he wants, a professional ethnomusicologist does everything he/she can to preserve the precious materials obtained, as well as preserve one's limited time. Print-through can occur at once where dynamics are extreme and, if a recording is spoiled by this, requiring re-recording, the time and effort may be too great and the music lost.

This produces yet another problem: the use of 1.5 mil tape usually means that the tape will be shorter than the musical performance. This is best solved by the use of two machines and run-on recordings -- starting up the second recorder before the first tape actually finishes.

TESTING LOW-PRICED GOODS

The major compromise between high- and low-priced materials lies in the way in which the specifications of machinery and tape are handled by the manufacturers in question. With high-priced professional equipment, there is no standard specifications for a model; rather, each instrument within the model type carries its own specifications. Low-priced goods, on the other hand, have specifications by model rather than by individual instrument. This means that there will be a distinct possibility that the particular instrument one is trying to purchase will have little or no relationship to the specifications for the model as a whole. In such cases, the individual machinery and tape should be tested.

Such tests are not complex. In buying a machine, for instance, one is usually allowed to take the machine to a tape recorder repairman, university laboratory, or electronic music composer in order to determine the particular specifications of the instrument in question. While it is not possible to test every reel of tape, one may learn the specifications of a batch of tape in the same way.

Whenever specifications are given for the model rather than the individual machine, the buyer is in the same position as buying a car -- judging its miles-per-gallon consumption by EPA standards. Let the buyer beware.

RECORDING TECHNIQUES AND STRATEGIES

The individual situation will dictate how particular recordings must be managed. Only general advice can be given here, with some specific examples of the way of using tape recorders which have proved useful. Since the ethnomusicologist is in the business of studying music, the selection of good equipment and the use of back-up equipment may be vital. Just as important is that the operator of the equipment know as much as possible about how tape recorders work, how a particular machine operates and what difficulties may be encountered.

The Nagra, for instance, is an almost perfect machine in many respects; however, it lacks one feature found on less expensive machines. The record cycle has no lock and it is possible to accidentally record over a tape one is trying to play. Each machine has its own idiosyncrasies of this kind. The only solution is to be aware of the potential dangers and to train one's self into a mode of operation which will avoid them.

It is suggested that tape and all equipment be bought before going into the field. This suggestion is predicated on the assumption that selection will be severely reduced elsewhere, particularly with regard to the testing of tape. This produces a problem in transport, however. Tapes are designed to accept magnetism from any source, and may pick up residual noise during shipment which will later be impressed directly onto the heads of the machine. The best solution to this problem is to wrap tapes in aluminum foil for shipment, since magnetism does not penetrate aluminum. During an extended period of study, a suggestion is to leave unused tapes wrapped in aluminum foil if one plans to work in an area which is not near a major industrial city.

Tape is bulky; this raises the question of how much tape should be needed. One rule of thumb, here, is to take four times as much tape as it is believed will be needed. This rule has generally worked well -- in Madagascar, McLeod used three times as much tape as was anticipated; in Malta, almost four times as much tape was used as had been planned.

It is wise to select the preferred type of leader tape in a large city where choice is available. Some recording tapes come

173

with leader tape already attached. One brand offers the advantage of a green leader tape at the beginning and red at the end, so that it is easy to see whether a tape has been re-wound or not.

The authors prefer to attach their own leader tape, using white tape for the beginning and another color for the end because it is easy for a tape to get out of its box. With white leader tape, one can write the tape number directly on the tape with a grease pencil.

Tape sheets should probably be made up before going into the field because reproduction facilities and costs vary considerably throughout the world.

Each tape box should be labeled. There are as many systems for this process as there are ethnomusicologists. Some tend to number boxes in Roman numerals, with an additional symbol to indicate in which field of study each belongs. This becomes essential only if one plans to do work in more than one country or area. Additional information may be included such as general type of recording, village, date, type of ensemble, etc.

Since the question of tape size of recording samples from different communities has been raised on a number of occasions (see Merriam, 1964), the question of how many recordings are going to be necessary becomes vital. Again, as a rule of thumb, it is wise to estimate that 50% of all recordings made will be spoiled by circumstances beyond the control of the researcher. Time, airplanes, goat-bleats, crowd noise and high winds all take their toll. While spoilt recordings can be used for something, there are a number of cases in which the recovery of the sound is simply not possible at particular points on the tape. Major problems such as high dynamic distortion are impossible of solution in some cases, even for a Nagra.

In Malta, the authors found a female singer whose voice was so powerful that she simply could not be properly recorded, even in a 40-foot long room. Recurrent pleas for recordings in the open air failed to solve the problem, and even the Automatic Record was unable to accept the overload. Such problems become severe only if one is planning to use the bulk of one's material for commercial purposes.

While studio-like recordings are seldom possible, once rapport has been well established, it is often possible to make an ordinary room similar to a studio for the purpose of special recordings at 15 ips for later release. Construction of studio conditions in the field is a true test of the ability and the imagination of the individual. The authors have had more success in damping empty or nearly empty rooms in order to arrive at a decent echo than in attempting to use rooms that are too well insulated. Blankets are a favorite method of reducing echo.

However one goes about it, the question of how much is enough is not easy to answer. It is sincerely suggested that all individual pieces of music should be re-recorded at least once. In some cases, this will not be possible. The best solution is to have the same pieces recorded several times by individual singers, and then to have several recordings of the same piece by different performers. Singular examples have a habit of being atypical. The best rule is that one will never get it all; depending on the richness of the musical tradition with which one is working, the problems may be more or less severe.

Run-on recordings have been mentioned before. In many parts of the world, music is an endurance contest for the performers wherein the length of a performance is as valuable as the content. Because of the tendency of Western folk music to be strophic, many scholars make the automatic assumption that a "verse" of a song is a sufficient sample. Close study of long recordings of music which is not improvised have clearly shown that even where a verse structure is present, large form is indicated by variance in verse structure at significant points in the piece. This is particularly true of introductory passages and cadential passages, although it may also be found at points of structural significance within a piece.

The seeming litany of east Africa, for instance, actually has a large form based on internal variance. It is for this reason that it is recommended that entire recordings be made, no matter what length they may be.

In Malta, the height of the musical year -- Mnarja -- has as one of its features an endurance contest for singers. On one occasion, singing of the same song lasted from 6:00 at night until 10:30 the following morning. Among the Bara of Madagascar, some ritual songs cannot be recorded in their entirety since they run for as long as the performer can continue to hold his instrument. This is particularly true of the songs of the bilo, the music performed for persons possessed by evil spirits. In view of the differential length of "pieces" throughout the world, run-on recordings may be essential.

The quality of a recording often depends upon microphone placement. In many situations, it is impossible to place the microphone before the performance begins due to local conditions not under the control of the researcher. Where it is allowed, a rule of thumb relates to the use of a uni-directional microphone, often hand-held, with the auxiliary use of a test record circuit.

Before a recording is made, test sounds can be checked with various microphone placements by wearing earphones and walking the microphone, machine, and reseacher into what seems to be the "center of the sound". This is not necessarily a very scientific way of stating it; however, the practice in making recordings will indicate that any musical person can locate the proper place from

175

which to make a recording. This implies a mobile investigator with a mobile tape recorder.

Some of the situations in which recordings have to be made are somewhat ludicrous. At one point, McLeod found herself standing on top of a grand piano, holding a microphone directly over the head of a singer in order to catch the 1/2 second echo from the back of the room. Among the Betsileo, the best recordings for study purposes had to be made by placing the microphone inside the softest instrument of an ensemble. These examples may indicate that the rules for making a tape recording are mobility, flexibility of thought and inventiveness. The basic assumption behind this is that somewhere in the air is one place where all the sounds come together best.

A major problem in ensembles is that of distortion from instruments whose dynamic range is much greater than machinery can accommodate. One solution to this is the wind screen, a device made to fit over the microphone to reduce wind noise. Wind screens are made of non-flexible styrofoam bubbles. As the bubbles in styrofoam wind screens are erratically placed and their surfaces are round, sounds such as wind noise will be dispersed while persistent sounds, such as pitch, will reach the mircophone. The same principle is to be found in the use of a crumpled handkerchief. While the fibers of a handkerchief are generally fairly straight, once the flexible surface is crumpled, it, too, represents an erratic surface. The use of wind cones for the dispersion of casual noise is not recommended because they are of a uniform thickness.

Noise can be slight or great. Small casual noise, such as the buzzing of an instrument placed on a table, does not require the thickness of irregular surface represented by a wind cone. The use of such a device would actually cut down on the fidelity of the recording. Therefore, preference is to use that kind of flexible styrofoam cloth used in packing. This cloth, usually about 1/8 inch thick, can be layered onto a microphone in different thicknesses and held in place with a rubber band. For tiny casual noises, one thickness is usually sufficient. The flexibility of this material as a means of reducing distortion makes it preferable to a wind cone, even though the wind cone is easier to slip on and off the microphone. Flexible styrofoam will not work well in a high wind, however; unfortunately, no wind cone seems to solve this problem, either.

Recording techniques, then, basically require a knowledge of one's own limitations as a recording technician, combined with flexibility, inventiveness and mobility. The problems of sampling almost require multiple recordings of the same phenomena. Selection of one performer, one style, one instrument over another are areas in which one can bias his sample. The best advice is: know your machine and its limitations; know yourself and your limitations; then operate as well as possible within these limitations by knowing as much as possible about the art of recording music.

Every recording is a frozen example of a span of time and space. As such, it is the combination of the sounds of that time and space -- the web of technology and ability in which it is caught. The best recording is made when the technician is comfortable with the technology but not enamoured of it.

PRESERVATION OF MATERIALS

Since recording tape is subject to magnetism, the preservation of recorded tapes in or out of the field is mainly concerned with the protection of the integrity of the recorded sounds. Stray magnetism in the air from such sources as motors with magnetos, magnetized iron, belt buckles, certain electronic watches, car generators and so forth, has a range of only three feet in open air. It is easy enough to avoid most magnetic sources by the simple process of placing tape at the requisite 3-foot distance from them.

Other problems of tape storage are less severe. Protection against fire, excessive humidity, excessive dryness, flood and dust are matters of one's innovation. An inexpensive humidity gauge should be kept with the tapes, so that appropriate action can be taken to add or subtract moisture as needed. The use of Navy duffel bags practically eliminates the problem of dust; however, this precaution does not always work. One solution for cases of excessive dust is to shake the tapes, tapping them on the back and sides. Tapes immersed in salt water must be unrolled and dried, then dipped in clear water and dried again.

The commonest problem in tape storage and maintenance is snapping. Swift braking systems can snap most tapes; human error is always a possibility as well. Splicers and splicing tape should be carried at all times whether a commercial splicer or the preferred anti-magnetic scissors.

If it is necessary to listen to particular tapes on numerous occasions in the field, it is wise to make work-copies. Originals should be stored backwards and not used regularly until they are copied in the laboratory. Since, from time to time, it is a good idea to attempt analysis in the field in order to determine the depths of problems involved, work tapes in the field are a necessity. The presence of a back-up recording machine makes this possible. Records of local manufacture should also be put on tape immediately before their surface is marred by repeated playing. On return from the field, of course, duplicates should be made of all originals.

CONCLUSION

The major techniques which have been considered here are of two varieties: first, the sheer weight of problems concerning record keeping and preservation; second, a few comments on the nature of content. In both cases, the worth of information collected is only as good as its retrievability and quality. The suggestions made are limited by the authors' own research interests, as well as exigency.

While there is simply no way to prepare one's self for the situations of field research, a thoughtful approach to the problems before leaving; the consideration of the relationships between the methodological design; the expected results will undoubtedly end in an accommodation of various problems. As Julitte Alvin Robson, the famous 'cello teacher, once remarked, "Technique and interpretation are the same thing". Techniques are merely a means to an end; therefore, it is the end that should define the means.

THOUGHTS AND PROSPECTS

Throughout the planning, writing and reading of this book, there are several underlying assumptions, questions and implications lying unanswered, like threads waiting to be gathered together into a tapestry.

Perhaps the most important of these is a question which can really never be answered -- why do people make music? If we do not make our definition of music too narrow, it soon becomes apparent that all human groups have something which might be called music. In some cases, this music is functionally for the same purpose, cross-culturally. In other cases, music is found to serve unique structural purposes for a given group.

Whatever the case, the extremely wide distribution of musical phenomena throughout the world has led many people to muse, to ponder, and to begin to investigate for themselves this elusive, complex and diverse human activity.

Subjectively, it is probable that as long as there have been aware human beings acting, behaving, thinking and living in groups, there have probably been those among them who mused, reflected, or wondered why people were engaged in particular activities or beliefs.

Objectively, the appearance of specialists who attempted to systematize, to compare cross-culturally the wide range of human activity called music is a fairly recent phenomenon.

Yet, the observations, examinations and speculations concerning the question, "why do people make music?" must remain elusive, for this is a question which cannot be directly approached. Rather, it must be approached indirectly. Thus, we find ourselves asking not "why", but "how do people make music?" How do they think about it -- classify it -- theorize about it? How does the participation in, or listening to, music affect the physiology? How does music relate to narrative, myths, belief systems, or basic values?

Through this kind of questioning, and through meticulous and systematic ethnographic descriptions of musical systems, it is thought possible to accumulate a data bank large enough to allow more objective approaches to the underlying question of "why do people make music?"

Another underlying question -- although probably not of the same magnitude as the first -- is the question, "why do people

179

study ethnic musics?" That is, why do people worry about, think about, probe into why people make music? What kind of people are they -- where do they come from -- what is their background -- and, what is their intention?

Ethnomusicology, the umbrella under which those who study ethnic musics work, is itself very unclear and ephemeral. There is no agreement among those calling themselves an ethnomusicologist as to whether ethnomusicology is a discipline, a field of study, or simply a helpful adjunct to other fields.

The training of ethnomusicologists has been, and continues to be, diverse. Most of the scholars currently operating in the field of ethnomusicology come from many different backgrounds and few people hold advanced degrees specifically in ethnic music. Of those who do, their training, point of view, and self-conceptualization ranges over a vast territory, indeed. Perhaps the only common ground for those found under the umbrella of ethnomusicology is a certain amount of curiosity about music other than their own, a tendency toward involvement in active participation in some kind of music, itchy feet, and the tendency to rebel against established norms and disciplines.

There are those who devote a lifetime, both professionally and personally, to the exclusive study of music. There are others whose profession and employment lies elsewhere, who may be equally devoted to specific aspects of the study of ethnic music. And there are those who have only a passing interest in ethnomusicology, yet nevertheless manage to provide valuable insights to the pool of knowledge in this area.

Perhaps the best answer to the question, "why do people study ethnic music?" is a very simple one -- because they want to. In some instances, the reason is that they must, because of some compelling force, study musics other than their own. For others, the level of involvement may be transitory, minimal, or highly specific.

In the final analysis, though, the answer to this question really does not matter. What _does_ matter is that this is an area open to all comers, a realm whose parameters are as yet uncharted, whose questions are as yet little understood, and whose promise for the understanding of human behavior is great.

This very openness, not only of the area of ethnomusicology, but also of its practitioners, explains better than anything else the reasons that an introductory text maintain a professional level, without the expectation that the reader will necessarily devote full time and energy to the pursuit of ethnic music in any way. Rather, this is an area in which everyone can potentially make contributions. It is hoped that through an understanding of the rigorous approaches to ethnic music, former excesses of both zeal and ethnocentrism can be avoided.

Yet another underlying assumption regarding this book and the field of ethnomusicology is the recognition of, and salute to, the fact that music is performed. Whether a particular human group has aural music orally transmitted or aural music transmitted in written form, all music is performed. Thus, the areas of kinesics, performance and context play an extremely important role in the apprehension of musical phenomena and thinking about music. That is, it is human beings who make music, think about it, hear it and learn it. It is also human beings who study music. We are dealing with a sound process which takes place in time, in space and in consciousness.

In many ways, this recognition of the importance of the performance of music represents a serious departure from trends of thought within Western musical scholarly circles. There, the tendency has been to treat music as a thing instead of a process, resulting in different kinds of questions and assumptions regarding the preservation of materials, and the discussion of their implications. With ethnomusicology comes the recognition and salute to music as a process -- an activity of human beings.

As an activity of human beings, music is an integral part of culture. It has ties with other aspects of human behavior -- particularly religion. In addition, the economics, the politics and other areas of human organization and activity are also intimately involved with musical activity. As a result, any study of music in an ethnomusicological sense means that music must be simply a point of departure and not an end in itself.

It is likely that the questions which are arousing interest, discussion and participation at one point in time will be replaced by totally different questions at another point in time. It is also likely that approaches to the study of music will change, particularly as technology makes available more and more sophisticated and lighter equipment. It is possible that even the presentation of understanding regarding music, musicians, and musical systems will change through time.

Yet, music remains. A specific musical system or style changes through time, adapts, alters itself to changing circumstances. Thought forms surrounding it may also change. Yet, music as a human creation, a human expression, and a human activity will probably endure. Also, it will probably endure as an enigmatic distant beacon, drawing and driving ethnomusicologists (and others interested in its study) ever forward into its beckoning flame.

The pursuit of music is a pleasurable, challenging and exciting activity. The questions it raises are difficult and momentarily impossible to answer. Yet the pursuit of answers to those questions can be a joyful one. It is our hope that this book will have transmitted at least some of the excitement, some of the questions, some of the rewards of this particular pursuit.

Our intent has been frankly seductive. The challenges in the pursuit of music and musical systems are great; the questions are transcendental; the rewards are elusive. But the final prospects of ethnomusicology rests not with the current practitioners, but the future ones. We have done our best; we are doing our best; we will continue doing our best.

Will you follow us and do better?

GLOSSARY

Acculturation - modification of the ways of life of one culture through contact <u>with</u>, or domination <u>by</u>, another culture.

<u>Anga</u> - special feast occasion in Tikopia.

Aural - information perceived by the ear.

Base line - a point of reference for measurement of alteration or change in any system.

<u>Bilo</u> - a variety of possession in Madagascar in which an individual is either made ill by evil spirits, or is forced to dance by them.

<u>Bormliza</u> - Maltese short verses, sung in semi-impromptu style.

Canalization - cultural process by which general needs (e.g. for liquid) become specific preferences (e.g. for coffee).

Caveat - a warning to beware.

Cognition - the mental process or faculty by which and through which knowledge is acquired, processed, stored, or disseminated.

Context - environment or overall situation in which an event takes place.

<u>Czimbalom</u> - struck zither.

<u>Dilettant</u> - Maltese word describing both those who perform and those who love to listen to music.

Enculturation - all forms of learning and/or acquisition of awareness of musical behavior and comprehension.

Ethnocentric - the view that one's own way of life or system of thought is best, to the extent of precluding understanding of different approaches or points of view.

Ethnography - the systematic description of ways of life, customs, or world views of human groups.

Ethnologitis - depression, dejection, or irritability caused by the strain of psychological accommodation due to living in a culture other than one's own.

Ethnology - the formal or scientific study of ways of life, customs, or world views of human groups.

183

Ethnomusicology - the study of the music either past or present, of all who participate in music as creators, as performers, or listeners of sound patterns; taking into account all factors which lead to a better understanding of this particular type of creative human behavior.

Fatt - long ballad-like, factual songs from Malta.

Feasinga - larger, daytime dance festivals given by chiefs in Tikopia.

Feuku - derisive sexual songs from Tikopia.

Fundamental - the lowest pitch or sound; also, the first harmonic.

Genre - a distinctive class, type or category of items.

Haka - Maori war dance which is shouted rhythmically.

Hira-gasy - a staged presentation of long moral stories sung by eight singers and accompanied by a small orchestra in Madagascar.

Kitteri-bis - Maltese solo guitar style.

Liturgy - the authorized, officially approved service of Christian churches, particularly the Roman Catholic Church.

Mako - Tikopian word for dance.

Manitou - spirit being, particularly in North American Indian groups.

Matavaka - canoe-bow dance done by young people in Tikopia.

Melisma - the singing of a single syllable of text to multiple pitches; as opposed to syllabic style, in which a syllable of text is sung to a single pitch.

Melograph - complex mechanical aid to transcription developed at the instigation of Charles Seeger, which will display a number of characteristics of a monophonic piece of music.

Mgodo - Chopi performance events which allow for direct insults and/or comments on the behavior of members of the community.

Mnemonic device - any device or cue designed or intended to assist or aid recall of larger bits of information.

Notation - the conventions and methods used for putting music into written form.

Nupika - Kutenai spirit beings who may bestow good luck.

Occasion, musical - the point of time-space focus encompassing the perception, performance or creation of music.

Oral - spoken, rather than written.

Overtones - musical instruments do not produce pure tones, consisting of a single frequency, but composite tones, consisting of many pure tones, produced simultaneously. The lowest and loudest of these is the fundamental which is colored by a selection of harmonics above it.

Pitch - the location of a musical sound within a culturally-determined sound system; a measurable number of vibrations per second (frequency) of a sound.

Purotu - expert composer in Tikopia.

Raga - traditional Indian melodic pitch and tonal systems used to delimit essential features of improvised musical performances.

Repertoire - the stock of songs, etc., that a person or group know(s) or is prepared to perform.

Rija - a variety of minstrelsy found in Madagascar.

Salegy - trance-related case-zither in Madagascar.

Serata - any paid performance in Malta which is not for broadcast purposes.

Sfida - challenge between two Maltese musicians.

Strophe - a single unit of music within a strophic piece.

Strophic - a song in which all stanzas of the text are performed to the same music.

Tauangutu - derisive sexual songs from Tikopia.

Teghla - final, falling phrase in improvised Maltese guitar music.

Tessitura - the general position of a vocal part, whether high or low in average pitch.

Timbre - tone color; the quality of a pitch as produced on a specific instrument or combination of instruments, as distinct from the quality of the same pitch if played on a different instrument.

Transcription - the process of converting performed music, usually recorded on tape or records, into one of the conventional written notation systems.

Triad - in Western music, one of several conventional arrangements of three pitches sounding together.

Valiha - tube zither found in Madagascar.

Vendetta - that condition in which an argument leads to total lack of social contact except for violence.

Xalata - Maltese musical occasion for the singing of folksongs on a combined picnic and ride, often in a bus or cart.

INDEX

Bibliography

Abrahams, Roger
    1976 "The Theoretical Boundaries Of Performance" in
    Proceedings Of A Symposium On Form In Performance,
    Hard-Core Ethnography, Marcia Herndon and Roger
    Brunyate, eds., Austin Texas:Office Of the College
    Of Fine Arts, The University Of Texas

Ames, David W.
    1973 "Igbo And Hausa Musicians: A Comparative Examina-
    tion", Ethnomusicology 17(2):250-78

Anonymous
    1950-51 "Observation I-V", editorials, Field Methods And
    Techniques Section, Human Organization, Fall,
    1950, through Fall, 1951

Anonymous
    1954 Notes And Queries On Anthropology. British
    Association For the Advancement Of Science.
    London:Routledge And Kegan Paul

Apel, Willi, ed.
    1969 Harvard Dictionary Of Music. Cambridge:Harvard
    University Press. (1944, first edition)

Bailey, F.G.
    1963 Politics And Social Change. Berkeley:University
    Of California Press

    1969 Strategems And Spoils: A Social Anthropology Of
    Politics. New York:Schocken Books

Bauman, Richard & Joel Sherzer, eds.
    1974 Explorations In the Ethnography Of Speaking.
    New York:Cambridge University Press

Bauman, Richard
    1976 "The Theoretical Boundaries Of Performance" in
    Proceedings Of A Symposium On Form In Performance,
    Hard-Core Ethnography, Marcia Herndon and Roger
    Brunyate, eds. Austin, Texas:Office Of the Col-
    lege Of Fine Arts, The University Of Texas

Berger, Peter & Thomas Luckmann
    1966 The Social Construction Of Reality. Garden City,
    N.Y.:Doubleday

Bingham, W.V.
    1914 "Five Years Of Progress In Comparative Musical Science".
    Psychological Bulletin 11:421-33

Boissevain, Jeremy F.
    1965 Saints And Fireworks: Religion And Politics In Rural
        Malta. (London School Of Economics Monographs On Social
        Anthropology 30) London:The Athlone Press

    1969 Hal-Farruġ: A Village In Malta. (Case Studies In Cul-
        tural Anthropology, George and Louise Spindler, eds.)
        New York:Holt, Rinehart and Winston

Bowen, Elenore Smith (Laura Bohannan)
    1964 Return To Laughter. Garden City, N.Y.:Doubleday

Bullough, Edward
    1912 "Psychical Distance As A Factor In Art And An Aesthetic
        Principle". British Journal Of Psychology 5:87-98

Cachia, Pierre
    1973 "A 19th Century Arab's Observation On European Music",
        Ethnomusicology 17(1):41-51

Chase, Gilbert
    1958 "A Dialectical Approach To Music History". Ethnomusicol-
        ogy 2:1-9

Clark, Terry N.
    1968 Community Structure And Decision-Making: Comparative
        Analyses. San Francisco:Chandler Publishing Co.

Critchley, Macdonald & R. A. Henson, eds.
    1977 Music And the Brain, Springfield, Illinois:C.C. Thomas

Draper, David
    1976 "Mardi Gras Indians", in Proceedings Of A Symposium On
        Form In Performance, Hard-Core Ethnography, Marcia
        Herndon and Roger Brunyate, eds., Austin, Texas:Office
        Of the College Of Fine Arts, The University Of Texas

Dudden, Rev. Frederick Homes
    1926 Gregory the Great. London:Longmans, Green & Co. (first
        ed., 1905)

Durbin, Mridula A.
    1971 "Transformational Models Applied To Musical Analysis:
        Theoretical Possibilities", Ethnomusicology 15:353-62

England, Nicholas M.
    1964 "Symposium On Transcription And Analysis: A Hukwe Song
        With Musical Bow", Ethnomusicology 8(3):223-77

Faublee, Jacques
    1954 Les espirits de la vie a Madagascar. Paris:Presses
        universitaires de France

Firth, Sir Raymond
    1939 Primitive Polynesian Economy. London:George Routledge
        & Sons, Ltd.

    1952 Field Notes Taken On the Island Of Tikopia. Unpub. By
        permission of Sir Raymond Firth

Fogelson, Raymond
    1971 "The Cherokee Ballgame Cycle: An Ethnographer's View",
        Ethnomusicology 15:3:327-38

Gilman, Benjamin I.
    1909 "The Science Of Exotic Music". Science 30:532-35

Gladwin, Thomas and Seymour Sarason
    1953 Truk: Man In Paradise. Viking Fund Publications, #20.
        New York:Wenner Gren Foundation For Anthropological
        Research

Gluckman, Max
    1963 "Gossip And Scandal: Essays In Honor Of Melville J.
        Herskovits", Current Anthropology 4(3):307-16

    1964 Closed Systems And Open Minds: The Limits Of Naivete
        In Social Anthropology. Chicago:Aldine

    1968 "Psychological, Sociological And Anthropological Expla-
        nations Of Witchcraft And Gossip: A Clarification".
        Man 3(1):20-34

Goodenough, Ward
    1957 "Cultural Anthropology And Linguistics" in Report Of the
        Seventh Annual Roundtable Meeting On Linguistics And
        Language, Paul Garvin, ed. Washington, D.C.:Georgetown
        University Press

Gourlay, Kenneth A.
    1972 "The Practice Of Cueing Among the Karimojon Of North-
        East Uganda", Ethnomusicology 16(2):240-47

Halpern, Ida
    1976 "On the Interpretation Of 'Meaningless-Nonsensical
        Syllables' In the Music Of the Pacific Northwest Indians",
        Ethnomusicology 20(2):253-71

Harris, Zelig
    1951 Structural Linguistics. Chicago:University Of Chicago
        Press

Herndon, Marcia A.
    1971 "The Cherokee Ballgame Cycle: An Ethnomusicologist's
        View", Ethnomusicology 15(3):339-52

1972 "The Use Of Nicknames As Evaluators Of Musical Competence In Malta", Texas Working Papers In Sociolinguis-
tics, #14. Austin:Center For Intercultural Studies In
Folklore And Oral History

1974 "Analysis: The Herding Of Sacred Cows", Ethnomusicology
18:219-62

Herskovits, Melville J.
1937 Life In A Haitian Valley. New York:Alfred A. Knopf

1950 Man And His Works: The Science Of Cultural Anthropology.
New York:Alfred A. Knopf

Hood, Mantle
1957 "Training And Research Methods In Ethnomusicology",
Ethnomusicology Newsletter 11:2-8

1971 The Ethnomusicologist. New York:McGraw-Hill, Inc.

Ilg, B.
1909 Maltesische Volkslieder im Urtext. Leipzig:J.C.
Hinrichs'sche Buchhandlung

Kaeppler, Adrienne
1971 "Aesthetics Of Tongan Dance", Ethnomusicology 15(2):
175-85

Kay, Paul
1970 "Some Theoretical Implications Of Ethnographic Semantics"
in Current Directions In Anthropology, Ann Fischer, ed.
Anthropologist Bulletins Vol. 3, No.3, Part 2

King, Arden Ross
1976 Comments in Proceedings Of A Symposium On Form In Performance, Hard-Core Ethnography. Marcia Herndon and
Roger Brunyate, eds. Austin, Texas:Office Of the Col-
lege Of Fine Arts, The University Of Texas

Kolinski, Mieczyslaw
1957 "Ethnomusicology, Its Problems And Methods", Ethnomusicology Newsletter 10:1-7

Kunst, Jaap
1955 Ethno-Musicology. The Hague:Martinus Nijhoff. (1950,
original title "Musicologica", Amsterdam:Royal Tropical
Institute

Lamphere, Louise
1970 "A New Look At Navajo Witchcraft, Gossip, And Coopera-
tion", paper presented at the 69th meeting of the AAA,
San Diego, California

Linton, Ralph
    1936 The Study Of Man. New York:D. Appleton-Century

Lomax, Alan
    1968 Folk Song Style And Culture: A Staff Report On Canto-
        metrics, Washington, D.C.:American Association For the
        Advancement Of Science, Publication #88

Lowie, Robert H.
    1937 The History Of Ethnological Theory. New York:Holt,
        Rinehart and Winston

McAllester, David P.
    1960 "The Role Of Music In Western Apache Culture", in
        Selected Papers Of the Fifth International Congress Of
        Anthropological And Ethnological Sciences, Anthony F.C.
        Wallace, ed. pp 468-72

McAloon and Mihaly Csikszentmihalyi
    1975 "Chapter 6" in Beyond Boredom And Anxiety, Mihaly
        Csikszentmihalyi, San Francisco:Jossey-Bass

McLeod, Norma
    1964 "The Status Of Musical Specialists In Madagascar",
        Ethnomusicology VIII:3:278-89

    1966 "Some Techniques For the Analysis Of Non-Western Music",
        Unpub. Diss., Northwestern University

    1974 "Ethnomusicological Research And Anthropology", Annual
        Review Of Anthropology, B. Siegel, ed. Stanford:
        Stanford University Press, 3:99-115

Malinowski, Bronislaw
    1948 "How An Anthropologist Works In the Field", in Personal
        Character And Cultural Milieu, D.G. Hoving, ed.
        Syracuse:Syracuse University Press, 452-75

Mead, Margaret
    1952 "The Training Of Historical Ethnologists In America",
        American Anthropologist 54:343-46

Merriam, Alan P.
    1960 "Ethnomusicology: Discussion And Definition Of the Field",
        Ethnomusicology 4:107-14

    1964 The Anthropology Of Music. Evanston:Northwestern Uni-
        versity Press

Murdoch, George Peter
    1949 Social Structures. New York:The MacMillan Company

Nadel, S.F.
    1952 "Witchcraft In Four African Societies: An Essay In
         Comparison", American Anthropologist LIV (1952):18-79

Needham, Rodney
    1972 "Percussion And Transition" in Reader In Comparative
         Religion, W. A. Lessa and Evon Z. Vogt, eds. New York:
         Harper & Row

Nettl, Bruno
    1956 Music In Primitive Culture. Cambridge:Harvard Univer-
         sity Press

    1964 Theory And Method In Ethnomusicology.New York:The Free
         Press Of Glencoe

Osgood, Cornelius
    1951 The Koreans And Their Culture. Yale Publications In
         Anthropology. New York:The Roland Press

Paul, Benjamin D.
    1953 "Interview Techniques And Field Relationships" in
         Anthropology Today, A.L. Kroeber, ed. Chicago:Univer-
         sity Of Chicago Press:476-87

Popper, Sir Karl R.
    1968 The Logic Of Scientific Discovery (3rd ed., revised)
         London:Hutchinson (1965, 1959)

Rhodes, Willard
    1956 "On the Subject Of Ethnomusicology", Ethnomusicology
         Newsletter 7:1-9

Sachs, Curt
    1959 Vergleichende Musikwissenschaft; Musik der Fremdkulturen,
         2nd edition. Heidelberg:Quelle and Meyer

    1962 The Wellsprings Of Music. The Hague:Martinus Nijhoff

    1977 The Wellsprings Of Music, Jaap Kunst, ed. New York:
         DaCapo Press (reprint of 1962 ed. The Hague:Martinus
         Nijhoff)

Sahlins, Marshall D.
    1961 "The Segmentary Lineage: An Organization Of Predatory
         Expansion", American Anthropologist 63:322-45

Saussure, Ferdinand de
    1908 Melanges de linguistique, Paris:La societe de linguis-
         tique. Collection linguistique #2

　　　1916 Cours de linguistique generale, Charles Bally and Albert
　　　　　　Sechehage, eds. Paris:Payot (tr. by Wade Baskin. London:
　　　　　　P. Owen, 1959, 1964)

Schneider, Marius
　　　1957 "Primitive Music", in Ancient And Oriental Music, Egon
　　　　　　Wellesz, ed. London:Oxford University Press, pp 1-82

Seeger, Charles
　　　1960 "On the Moods Of A Music-Logic", Journal Of the American
　　　　　　Musicological Society 13:1-3:224-61

Singer, Milton B.
　　　1955 "The Cultural Pattern Of India", The Far Eastern Quarter-
　　　　　　ly, XV:23-36

Slonimsky, Nicolas
　　　1965 Lexicon Of Musical Invective. New York:Coleman-Ross
　　　　　　Company, Inc.

Smith, M.G.
　　　1956 "Segmentary Lineage Systems", Journal Of the Royal
　　　　　　Anthropological Institute, 86(2):39-80

Speck, Frank
　　　1909 Ethnology Of the Yuchi Indians. Philadelphia:The
　　　　　　University Museum

　　　1911 Ceremonial Songs Of the Creek And Yuchi Indians.
　　　　　　Philadelphia:University Museum

Sturtevant, William C.
　　　1964 "Studies In Ethnoscience" in Transcultural Studies In
　　　　　　Cognition, A.K. and R. G. D'Andrade, eds.   American
　　　　　　Anthropologist Vol. 66, Part 2, #3

Tracey, Hugh
　　　1948 Chopi Musicians: Their Music, Poetry, And Instruments.
　　　　　　London:International African Institute (Re-Issued 1970)

Turner, Victor
　　　1967 The Forest Of Symbols. Ithaca, N.Y.:Cornell University
　　　　　　Press

　　　1969 The Ritual Process: Structure And Anti-Structure.
　　　　　　Chicago:Aldine

Wang, Betty
　　　1965 "Folksongs As Regulators Of Politics" in The Study Of
　　　　　　Folklore, Alan Dundes, ed. Englewood Cliffs:Prentice-
　　　　　　Hall, Inc.

Werner, Oswald and Jo Ann Fenton
    1971 "Method And Theory In Ethnoscience Or Ethno-epistemology"
    in A Handbook Of Method In Cultural Anthropology, R.
    Naroll and R. Cohen, eds. Garden City:Natural History
    Press